SUCCESSFUL GARDENING

A–Z of DECIDUOUS
TREES & SHRUBS

Staff for Successful Gardening (U.S.A.)
Editor: Carolyn Chubet

Contributors
Editor: Thomas Christopher
Art Editor: Richard Boddy
Editorial Assistant: Troy Dreier
Consulting Editor: Lizzie Boyd (U.K.)
Consultant: Dora Galitzki
Copy Editor: Sue Heinemann
Art Assistant: Antonio Mora

READER'S DIGEST GENERAL BOOKS
Editor in Chief: John A. Pope, Jr.
Managing Editor: Jane Polley
Executive Editor: Susan J. Wernert
Art Director: David Trooper
Group Editors: Will Bradbury, Sally French,
Norman B. Mack, Kaari Ward
Group Art Editors: Evelyn Bauer, Robert M. Grant, Joel Musler
Chief of Research: Laurel A. Gilbride
Copy Chief: Edward W. Atkinson
Picture Editor: Richard Pasqual
Head Librarian: Jo Manning

The credits and acknowledgments that appear on page 176
are hereby made a part of this copyright page.

Originally published in partwork form.
Copyright © 1990 Eaglemoss Publications Ltd.

Based on the edition copyright © 1993
The Reader's Digest Association Limited.

Library of Congress Cataloging in Publication Data

A-Z of deciduous trees & shrubs.
        p.   cm. — (Successful gardening)
    ISBN 0-89577-615-4
    1. Ornamental trees—Encyclopedias.   2. Ornamental shrubs—
Encyclopedias.   I. Reader's Digest Association.   II. Title: A–Z of
deciduous trees and shrubs.   III. Series
SB435.A2   1994
635.9'76—dc20   94-13100

Printed in the United States of America

Opposite: A paperbark maple *(Acer griseum)* is the stunning
focal point in a mixed border of shrubs and perennials.

Overleaf: The hybrid tea rose 'Fragrant Dream' bears well-
shaped, golden-apricot blooms throughout summer.

Pages 6-7: The bare branches of dormant trees and shrubs
are etched with frost in this attractive winter scene.

THE READER'S DIGEST ASSOCIATION, INC.
Pleasantville, New York / Montreal

SUCCESSFUL GARDENING

A–Z of DECIDUOUS
TREES & SHRUBS

CONTENTS

Special Features

Trees in the garden   10-13
Versatile shrubs   66-69

A–Z of Deciduous Trees

Acer – Alnus   14-17
Betula – Crataegus   18-25
Davidia – Gleditsia   26-30
Halesia – Koelreuteria   30-32
Laburnum – Liriodendron   32-36
Magnolia – Morus   36-41
Nothofagus – Ostrya   42-44
Parrotia – Pyrus   45-51
Quercus – Robinia   51-54
Salix – Styrax   55-59
Taxodium – Ulmus   60-63

A–Z of Deciduous Shrubs

Abelia – Buddleia   70-76
Callicarpa – Cytisus   77-93
Daphne – Exochorda   93-97
Forsythia – Genista   98-100
Hamamelis – Kolkwitzia   101-107
Lavatera – Menziesia   108-112
Paeonia – Punica   113-124
Rhamnus – Rubus   124-130
Salix – Tamarix   131-138
Vaccinium – Vitis   139-142
Weigela – Wisteria   142-145

A–Z of Roses

Climbing roses   148-152
Floribunda roses   153-155
Hybrid tea roses   156-159
Miniature roses   160-161
Modern shrub roses   162-165
Old garden roses   166-170
Polyantha and rambler roses 171-173
Species roses   174-175

Scarlet oak True to its name, the scarlet oak *(Quercus coccinea)* is a dazzling sight in fall.

A–Z of Deciduous Trees

Trees play an essential part in the earth's ecological balance as they transform carbon dioxide into vital oxygen, temper the effects of the sun and wind, and prevent soil erosion. They sustain and shelter wildlife, and in a domestic setting they frame and define the style of a house and its garden. Trees add depth, scale, color, texture, and vertical interest; they also blot out eyesores and offer privacy and protection.

The great oaks, ashes, and sycamores found in forests and parklands are too large for the average garden, but there are plenty of dwarf cultivars and other small decorative trees from which to choose. Popular selections include maples, with their striking fall foliage colors, elegant birches, summer-flowering dogwoods, ornamental hawthorns, and magnificent magnolias. Crab apples combine some of the best features of all ornamental trees — manageable size, spectacular blooms, fall foliage colors, and attractive fruits.

Before choosing a tree, take into account its height and spread when fully grown, its growth rate, and the density of the shade it casts. Consider how it will look with surrounding plants, and the type of soil and conditions it needs in order to thrive for decades to come. A site can radically affect a tree's eventual shape — in a windswept spot a tree will seem to lean with the prevailing wind, so support with strong stakes is essential during the formative years. A tree denied adequate space and light will grow excessively tall, with a sparse crown of branches. It is also tempting to plant trees close together for quick effect, but they need ample space in which to spread and develop their true beauty.

TREES IN THE GARDEN

**Trees respond to each new season with
a display of blossoms, foliage, fruits, or bark, delighting
the eye and bringing life to the garden.**

The impact of trees in a garden exceeds that of any other plant group. Trees set the scene and add variety with the changes they bring in different seasons.

Spring arrives in a burst of joyful color from bulbs and early-flowering plants, but it is the explosion of bloom from ornamental cherries, crab apples, and magnolias that announces the season's real arrival. Later come the golden laburnums and the pink and white blossoms of redbuds *(Cercis)* and dogwoods.

An infinite variety of foliage is displayed in early summer — the shimmering silver of ornamental pears, the elegant leaf fronds of honey locusts, the coppery tones of weeping beeches, and the gold of *Robinia pseudoacacia* 'Frisia.' The leaf canopy created by such trees as catalpas and mulberries offers shade from the hot sun, while stewartias stand draped with white flowers.

Fall brings forth a wonderful blaze of color, ranging from the brilliant leaves of maples, sweet gums, nyssas, oaks, parrotias, and hornbeams to the bunches of colorful fruits on crab apples, mountain ashes, and wingnuts.

In winter, trees divert attention from the bleakness of the rest of the garden. They display a graceful tracery or contorted spirals of naked branches. The gleaming white trunks of birches, the glowing red bark of ornamental cherries, and the violet-black of willow stems add dramatic touches of color.

▼ Chinese witch hazel Blooming even before winter's end, the Chinese witch hazel *(Hamamelis mollis)* takes advantage of any thaw to clothe its naked branches with sweetly scented spidery flower clusters of gold touched with red.

▲ Japanese pagoda tree The stiff, weeping branches of the Japanese pagoda tree *(Sophora japonica* 'Pendula') are etched with frost in this still winter garden. Apparently lifeless, this fine mature specimen tree will awaken from its slumber to drape itself with long sprays of creamy pealike flowers in summertime.

◄ Scarlet willow Radiant in winter sunshine, the scarlet willow *(Salix alba* 'Britzensis') glows in contrast to the frosty ground. Related to the common white willow that inhabits wetlands, ornamental cultivars of this graceful tree need severe pruning every other year in early spring in order to retain the brilliant color of their young shoots' bark. Set them well away from house foundations and drainage systems, as their roots run deep and wide in search of water.

▲ **Silver pear** By late spring the ornamental pear (*Pyrus salicifolia* 'Pendula') has unfolded its willowlike silver-gray foliage, which ripples like a waterfall from the weeping branches over an underplanting of white tulips. The clusters of small cream-white flowers, still in bud here, develop into tiny inedible pears by early fall. This sturdy, cold-hardy tree thrives in all types of good soil and on all kinds of sites.

◄ **Pink blossoms** A shrub border acquires bright color from a mature cherry tree in a neighboring garden. Smothered in pale pink blossoms in midspring, the ornamental cherry tree will later shield the purple and variegated shrubby maples from the effects of the hot summer sun.

11

▲ **Golden summer** The Indian bean tree (*Catalpa bignonioides*) is a magnificent shade tree, with huge heart-shaped leaves. It is particularly striking in the golden form 'Aurea,' seen here in a pleasing association with a clipped, pyramid-shaped soft yellow *Juniperus chinensis*. Mature catalpas bear large clusters of white-and-yellow foxglovelike flowers in late spring or early summer.

▶ **Distant vista** A mixed border brimming with roses, flowering shrubs, tall foxgloves, and billowing lady's-mantle is eclipsed by a purple-leaved cherry plum (*Prunus cerasifera* 'Nigra'). Flowering profusely with pink blossoms in early spring, the tree retains its purple-black color until leaf fall.

▲ **Fall harvest** The English hawthorn (*Crataegus monogyna*) is one of the most accommodating garden trees. Easily adaptable to either the polluted air of urban gardens or windswept coasts, its sweetly scented white blossoms delight the eye in late spring. It makes an impenetrable hedge, and in fall the foliage echoes the color of the long-lasting orange-red berries.

◄ **Form and foliage** The maples (*Acer*) display enormous differences in growth habit, leaf shapes, and colors. Highly ornamental, maples range from wide-spreading trees to slender columns and low shrubs; they are all magnificently colored in fall.

▼ **Color contrast** Among the birches, the Himalayan species, *Betula utilis jacquemontii*, is very striking. Its white trunk and branches look dazzling set against crimson-scarlet Japanese maples (*Acer palmatum* 'Atropurpureum').

Acer
maple

Acer pseudoplatanus 'Brilliantissimum,' spring

Acer platanoides 'Columnare,' fall

Acer circinatum, fall

❏ Height at 25 years 8-35 ft (2.4-10.5 m); when mature, up to 70 ft (21 m)
❏ Spread 8-30 ft (2.4-9 m) or more
❏ Adaptable to wide range of soils
❏ Deciduous broadleaf
❏ Hardy zones 3-9
❏ Features: bright summer and fall foliage; attractive bark

Beautiful in summer, with its full, usually rounded top, the maple is even more outstanding in fall, when its palmate foliage turns orange, red, and yellow. Some species also have striped or peeling bark.

The leaves have three, five, seven, nine, or more lobes and are typically pale, mid-, or bright green in summer; new growth may be tinted red. The genus has many tall, spreading species, as well as many medium and small ones. For shrubby maples, see page 70.

Popular species
Acer capillipes, about 35 ft (10.5 m) high and wide, is an upright tree with greenish, white-striped bark. The narrow three-lobed leaves are tinted red when they open, later turning midgreen and then crimson in fall. The winged seeds hang in long clusters.

Acer cappadocicum, a fast-growing spreading tree, 30 ft (9 m) high and 15 ft (4.5 m) wide has glossy dark green, five- or seven-lobed leaves, which turn a rich yellow in fall. Cultivars include 'Aureum' (young leaves open yellow, then turn green, and finally yellow again in fall) and 'Rubrum' (young leaves deep red).

Acer circinatum (vine maple) grows as a small multistemmed tree that is up to 10-20 ft (3-6 m) high and wide. The branches twist and spread to form a rounded head, and the seven- or nine-lobed, almost circular, midgreen leaves are red and orange in fall. Clusters of white and red-purple flowers appear in midspring. The species tolerates dry soil and a shady site, but is best adapted to its native Pacific Northwest.

Acer davidii, a variable tree, but typically small, to 20 ft (6 m) high and 10 ft (3 m) wide, has greenish-gray, white-striped bark, particularly if it is grown in partial shade. The dark green, undivided, red-stalked leaves are tinged red-bronze when young, and yellow, red, and purple in fall.

Acer griseum (paperbark maple), 20-30 ft (6-9 m) high, spreading half to equal its height, is a slow-growing tree. The toothed, three-lobed midgreen leaves turn red and orange in fall. The bark peels to reveal orange-brown patches.

Acer negundo (box elder) grows rapidly 30-50 ft (9-15 m) high, with an equal or greater spread. Its pale green to midgreen leaves have three- or five-toothed leaflets. Cultivars include 'Elegans' (bold yellow leaf margins) and 'Variegatum' (white margins).

Acer pensylvanicum (snake-bark

Acer griseum, bark

maple) grows rapidly to 20 ft
(6 m) high and 10 ft (3 m) wide.
It is an upright tree, with the
young green bark striped white.
The leaves, which are pale green
to midgreen with three pointed
lobes, are tinged pink when
young and turn yellow in fall.
The tree dislikes alkaline soils,
heat, and drought; it prefers well-
drained, shady sites.

Acer platanoides (Norway maple), 40-50 ft (12-15 m) high with
a spread two-thirds or equal to its
height, has a dense, rounded
head and bright green five-lobed
leaves that turn yellow in fall.
Cultivars are 'Columnare' (columnar shape), 'Crimson King'
(purple-crimson leaves), 'Drummondii' (broad white leaf margins), 'Globosum' (to 20 ft/6 m
high; dense mop-head shape),
'Schwedleri' (young leaves crimson, turning green), and 'Sum-
mershade' (fast-growing and heat
resistant; little fall color).

Acer pseudoplatanus (sycamore
maple), typically 40-60 ft (12-18 m)
high with a spread two-thirds or
equal to its height, tolerates polluted air and seaside conditions.
Thriving on exposed sites and alkaline or acid soil as far north as
zone 5, it does not flourish south
of zone 7. The deep green toothed
leaves have five lobes. Cultivars
include 'Atropurpureum' (leaves
purple underneath); 'Brilliantissimum' (to 15 ft/4.5 m high;
leaves pink, turning yellow, then
green), 'Erectum' ('Fastigiatum';
narrow, upright), 'Leopoldii'
(leaves yellow-pink, then green
marked with yellow and pink),
and 'Worleei' (leaves yellow, then
green).

Acer rubrum (red maple), 40-60 ft

Acer negundo 'Variegatum,' fruits

(12-18 m) high with a spread
equal to or somewhat less than
the height, is an adaptable tree
that flourishes in zones 3-9. In its
dense, round head of foliage, it
bears three- or five-lobed dark
green leaves that are blue-white
underneath and turn red and yellow in fall. It does best in acid
soils. Cultivars are 'Bowhall'
(narrow pyramidal shape; rich
fall color), 'Columnare' (columnar shape), and 'Schlesingeri'
(striking rich scarlet fall color).

Acer saccharinum (silver maple),
syn. *A. dasycarpum,* grows rapidly to 50-70 ft (15-21 m) high with
a spread equal to two-thirds its
height. The drooping branches
bear deeply lobed leaves, bright
green above and silvery white beneath, with yellow fall tints. Cultivars are 'Pyramidale' (broadly
columnar habit), and 'Wieri'
(deeply cut toothed leaves).

Cultivation

Plant in midfall or early spring in
well-drained but moist soil in sun
or partial shade; as a rule, maples
tend to prefer a lightly acid pH,

though several species (such as
A. negundo or *pseudoplatanus*)
tolerate alkaline soils, too.

Pruning Prune reverted all-
green shoots from *A. negundo*
'Variegatum' and *A. platanoides*
'Drummondii' to maintain varie-
gations. Prune *A. platanoides*
'Schwedleri' every other fall for
the best leaf color. Other species
and cultivars need only routine
attention for removal of dead,
damaged, or crossing branches.

Pests/diseases Anthracnose
causes spotting and leaf drop in
rainy seasons. Aphids can cause
sticky and sooty foliage. Coral spot
can cause dieback. Gall mites
may cause galls on the leaves of
maples. Scorching may turn leaf
edges brown. They then shrivel.
Tar spot shows as large black
spots with yellow edges. Verticillium wilt causes sudden wilting
of leaves and dieback of shoots.
Internally affected shoots are
brown or green-brown.

Ailanthus
tree-of-heaven

Ailanthus altissima, summer fruits

Ailanthus altissima

❑ Height at 25 years 30-45 ft (9-13.5 m);
when mature, 65 ft (20 m) or more
❑ Spread 15-30 ft (4.5-9 m)
❑ Any garden soil
❑ Deciduous broadleaf
❑ Hardy zones 5-8
❑ Features: fruits (female tree only)

An excellent tree for urban areas, the fast-growing tree-of-heaven (*Ailanthus altissima,* syn. *A. glandulosa*) tolerates a high degree of air pollution, thrives in any kind of soil, and resists attacks by most pests and diseases. The huge compound leaves of this wide-spreading tree are ash-like, up to 3 ft (90 cm) long and divided into numerous leaflets. These leaflets are bronzy red when they unfurl in the spring, but quickly turn to a rich dark green. The leaves are borne in heavy bunches at the end of short twigs and create a changing pattern of filtered sun and shade.

Originally from northern China, tree-of-heaven is unisexual, being either male or female. Both types bear insignificant yellow-green flowers in summer, which on female trees are followed by large, drooping clusters of attractive reddish-brown winged seeds known as samaras. These are scattered over a wide area but will develop into seedlings only if they have been pollinated by a male tree. Male flowers have an unpleasant scent.

One drawback of this easily grown urban shade tree is its tendency to produce underground suckering shoots, which may pop up at considerable distances from the parent. Because it seeds itself so freely, the ailanthus may become an invasive weed in a suburban yard; in addition, the soft, brittle branches break easily during ice storms.

Cultivation
Plant in midfall or early spring to midspring in any kind of garden soil, in sun or light shade. To protect limbs from breakage, avoid sites that are exposed to strong winds. Stake young trees until established.

Pruning Cut back hard in spring to control growth; young trees can be pollarded annually and grown as multistemmed shrubs. Dig up and remove the suckers when they sprout from the roots; destroy the suckers or use them for propagation purposes.

Pests/diseases Generally trouble free.

ALDER — see *Alnus*
ALMOND, ORNAMENTAL — see *Prunus*

Alnus
alder

Alnus glutinosa, catkins

❏ Height at 25 years 30-40 ft (9-12 m);
  when mature, 60 ft (18 m) or more
❏ Spread 15-40 ft (4.5-12 m)
❏ Prefers moist to wet, acid soil; some
  species tolerate alkaline, dry soil
❏ Deciduous broadleaf
❏ Hardy zones 2-9
❏ Features: catkins; cones

Alder, either conical- or pyramid-shaped, bears yellow to orange catkins on leafless branches in early spring. The shorter female catkins appear alongside the male catkins, later developing into dark brown or blackish woody cones. After the winged seeds disperse, the spent cones may remain on the branches for a year.

While alder is happiest in wet soils, most alders will perform on dry sites as well and are very tolerant of nutrient-poor soils.

Popular species

Alnus cordata (Italian alder), up to 30-50 ft (9-15 m) high and 15-30 ft (4.5-9 m) wide, is a fast-growing conical-shaped species. The glossy midgreen leaves are heart-shaped and the catkins are 1¼ in (3 cm) long. Hardy to zone 6, this tree tolerates alkaline and dry soils.

Alnus glutinosa (European or

Alnus cordata

black alder) is a conical tree growing to 40-60 ft (12-18 m) with a spread of 20-40 ft (6-12 m). Hardy to zone 3, it has deep green leaves and sticky young growth. Yellow catkins appear in early spring. It does not adapt well to southern heat. Cultivars include 'Laciniata' (deeply cut and lobed leaves).

Alnus incana (gray or white alder) is a tree or large shrub up to 40-60 ft (12-18 m) high and 20-30 ft (6-9 m) wide. Hardy to zone 2, its pale green oval leaves are gray beneath soft gray young growth; it bears profuse catkins. Cultivars are 'Laciniata' (leaves cut into 6 to 8 pairs of lobes), and 'Pendula' (weeping habit).

Alnus rubra (Oregon or red alder) is a fast-growing species that is hardy to zone 6. Up to 40 ft

(12 m) high and 15 ft (4.5 m) wide, its drooping branches form a pyramid shape. The leaves and male catkins are 6 in (15 cm) long.

Alnus serrulata (hazel or tag alder) is a multistemmed tree or large shrub, growing 15-25 ft (4.5-7.5 m) high, south to zone 9.

Cultivation
Plant in moist to wet soil in mid-fall or early spring in sun or partial shade.
Pruning Remove dead, damaged or crossing branches in winter or early spring.
Pests/diseases Trouble free.

ASH — see *Fraxinus*
ASPEN — see *Populus*
BEECH — see *Fagus*

17

Betula
birch

Betula papyrifera (white birch)

Betula albo-sinensis septentrionalis, bark

- ❏ Height at 25 years 25-36 ft (7.5-11 m)
- ❏ Spread 10-60 ft (3-18 m)
- ❏ Loamy soil
- ❏ Deciduous broadleaf
- ❏ Hardy zones 2-9
- ❏ Features: bark; catkins; graceful habit

The airy, small-leaved birch, with its slender trunk and branches, is a graceful ornament to any garden. Favorite specimen trees, birches are renowned for their peeling silvery white bark; some species have gray, glossy black, or orange-brown bark. Birches' midgreen toothed leaves, which cast little shade, unfurl in midspring and are broadly ovate, though they may have an oval or diamond shape. They turn yellow in fall.

The upright, greenish female catkins appear with the leaves, later turn into club-shaped cones, which scatter their seeds in fall. The pendent, 2 in (5 cm) long, reddish brown male catkins appear in midspring to late spring.

Birches are a shallow-rooted, short-lived tree, rarely lasting for more than 80 years, and often no more than 20 to 30 years in cultivation. They grow well in most soils, except shallow alkaline soil.

Popular species

Betula albo-sinensis septentrionalis, up to 25 ft (7.5 m) high and 10 ft (3 m) wide, is hardy to zone 6. It has orange-brown to orange-red bark with a grayish bloom. The oval midgreen leaves are covered in short silky hairs.

Betula ermanii, from northeast Asia, is up to 30 ft (9 m) high and 15 ft (4.5 m) wide. It has peeling bark of cream-pink and orange-brown branches. The ovate midgreen leaves can grow up to 3 in (7.5 cm) long. Hardy to zone 6, this species starts growth early in the year and may suffer frost damage in northern gardens.

Betula lenta (sweet birch) reaches a height of 40-55 ft (12-16.5 m) in cultivation, with a spread of 35-45 ft (10.5-13.5 m). Thriving also in rich, moist but well-drained, slightly acid soils, it adapts well to rocky, drier sites, too. Hardy from zone 3 to the uplands of Georgia and Alabama, it remains attractive throughout the year because of the glossy reddish-brown to black bark of its younger trunks and branches.

Betula nigra (black, red, or river birch), from the central and eastern US, grows 40-70 ft (12-21 m) high and 40-60 ft (12-18 m) wide. The diamond-shaped soft green leaves are white underneath; the peeling bark is pinkish orange. Hardy from zones 5-9, this species thrives in damp soils.

Betula papyrifera (canoe, paper,

Betula ermanii

Betula nigra

or white birch) grows up to 50-70 ft (15-21 m) high with a spread equal to half to two-thirds its height. While it will grow as far south as zone 7, it performs best and lives longest in the colder regions and is hardy to zone 2. Its famous peeling white bark adorns a pyramidal tree that may be grown as a single- or multi-stemmed tree. Paper birch is very striking in wintertime amid evergreens; the triangular midgreen

leaves will turn yellow in the fall. *Betula pendula* (European white birch), an exotic species, has silvery bark which becomes rough and blackened at the base of older trees. There are many excellent cultivars, but because these trees are very susceptible to an often fatal pest, the bronze birch borer, they are not often grown in the US. It is hardy in zones 2-6. *Betula utilis* (Himalayan birch), up to 25 ft (7.5 m) high and 15 ft

(4.5 m) wide, is a native of the Himalayas and has peeling reddish-brown bark and oval leaves 2-3½ in (5-9 cm) long. *B.u. jacquemontii* has bright white branches and peeling white bark. It is hardy in zones 6-7.

Cultivation
Plant in midfall or early spring in loamy soil. Do not plant birch close to borders or fences, as it has wide-spreading surface roots.
Pruning No special needs.
Pests/diseases Aphids, caterpillars, and leaf gall aphids attack foliage. Birch leaf miners cause browning of leaves in late spring or early summer. Bracket fungi may enter dead wood, causing rotting of heartwood. Bronze birch borers tunnel into the bark, usually killing trees if not treated. Leaf rust shows on the leaves as bright red-yellow spots.

BIRCH — see *Betula*
BIRD CHERRY — see *Prunus*
BLUE BEECH — see *Carpinus caroliniana*
BLACK GUM — see *Nyssa*
BOX ELDER — see *Acer negundo*
BUTTERNUT — see *Juglans*

Betula pendula 'Youngii'

Carpinus
hornbeam

Carpinus betulus, fall foliage

❑ Height at 25 years 10-30 ft (3-9 m);
when mature, 18-60 ft (5.4-18 m)
❑ Spread 12-40 ft (3.6-12 m)
❑ Any soil
❑ Deciduous broadleaf
❑ Hardy zones 3-9
❑ Features: fluted trunk; attractive fruits
and winter leaves

Hornbeams have distinctive gray fluted trunks and round, densely branched heads. Thickly clothed with rough, toothed midgreen leaves that turn yellow, orange, or scarlet in fall, hornbeams are good for hedging since they keep their brown leaves into winter.

Popular species
Carpinus betulus (European horn-

Carpinus betulus 'Fastigiata'

beam), grows 40-60 ft (12-18 m) high with a spread of 30-40 ft (9-12 m) and is hardy in zones 5-7. Used as a specimen or for hedging, young trees are pyramid-shaped; mature ones are rounded. The oval leaves are veined and sharply toothed. They are tinted yellow in fall. Cultivars are 'Columnaris' (10 ft/3 m; slow-growing; dense, columnar) and 'Fastigiata' (slenderly conical when young, rounded when mature).

Carpinus caroliniana (American hornbeam or blue beech) is smaller than its European relative, growing only 20-30 ft (6-9 m) with an equal spread. More cold and heat tolerant than its European relative, it thrives from zone 3 through zone 9, two zones farther north and farther south than *C. betulus*. It is not a good hedging plant. The leaves turn yellow to orange or scarlet in fall.

Carpinus japonica, a slow-growing spreading tree from Japan, is up to 18 ft (5.4 m) high and 12 ft (3.6 m) wide. It has corrugated, oblong midgreen leaves, tinted red in fall. It is hardy to zone 5.

Cultivation
Plant in midfall or early spring in any soil. For hedging, plant *C. betulus* at 15-20 in (38-50 cm) wide intervals. Keep the young plants moist, and mulch annually.

Pruning In midsummer clip young hedges lightly to shape, and cut back established ones fairly hard.

Pests/diseases Generally pest free.

Carya
hickory

Carya illinoensis

❑ Height at 25 years 20-30 ft (6-9 m);
when mature, 50-100 ft (15-30 m)
❑ Spread half to two-thirds of height
❑ Any good garden soil
❑ Deciduous broadleaf
❑ Hardy zones 5-9
❑ Features: good fall color; edible nuts

Hickory trees are famous chiefly for their utility: the toughness of the wood, its excellence as firewood, and the flavor it can impart on ham or bacon. Yet these North American natives also make exceptional shade trees, as rugged as they look. Placed by a patio, a hickory provides a welcome retreat in summertime, and its golden brown fall foliage is very picturesque. The delicious nuts produced by many species are a bonus.

Popular species
Carya glabra (pignut hickory) grows to a height of 50-60 ft (15-18 m) with a spread of 25-35 ft (7.5-10.5 m). The bark is smooth on younger trees, but becomes rough and ridged on older ones. The large, compound feathered leaves are a dark yellowish green in summer and brighten to an outstanding golden color in fall. This tree thrives on rocky, dry sites. It is hardy in zones 5-9.

Carya illinoensis (pecan) is the fastest-growing hickory — it matures to a height of 70-100 ft (21-30 m) with a spread of 40-75 ft (12-22.5 m). The pecan prefers

Carya ovata

deep, moist soils. With its low, spreading branches and superlative nuts, the pecan tree is one of the most rewarding trees of the American South and flourishes well into the central Midwest. It is hardy in zones 6-9.

Carya ovata (shagbark hickory) is instantly identified by its bark, which on mature specimens peels away from the trunk in long, shaggy strips. Rising 60-80 ft (18-24 m) tall with a rounded crown, it turns a rich yellow in fall and produces large harvests of sweet nuts. It is hardy in zones 5-8.

Carya tomentosa, the "mocker-nut" seems to tease the hungry with its fruits, which are hard to extract and exceedingly small. At maturity it makes an exceptionally symmetrical shade tree, 50-60 ft (15-18 m) tall. It is hardy in zones 5-9.

Cultivation
Plant in any open site in midfall or early spring. Since hickories are tap-rooted trees, it is preferable to buy small nursery-grown specimens.
Pruning No special needs.
Pests/diseases Generally pest free. However, hickory bark beetles may bore into small twigs, causing dieback, and hickory gall aphids may cause pea- or grape-sized green galls to form on leaves.

Catalpa
Indian bean tree

Catalpa bignonioides, fruit

❏ Height at 25 years 20-25 ft (6-7.5 m); when mature, 20-60 ft (6-18 m)
❏ Spread 20-40 ft (6-12 m)
❏ Any good, well-drained soil
❏ Deciduous broadleaf
❏ Hardy zones 5-9
❏ Features: handsome foliage; foxglove-like flowers; beanlike seedpods

Even before its showy flowers appear, the southern catalpa makes a fine garden feature with its low canopy of branches, densely covered with large green leaves. The taller northern catalpa is more upright in form, but is equally valuable, furnishing shade on wet or dry sites, in alkaline soils, and thriving in hot, dry conditions.

The white foxglovelike flowers, marked yellow and purple inside, are held in large upright clusters on established trees, followed by clusters of pendent seedpods. The branches are angular and brittle; the leaves are large.

Popular species
Catalpa bignonioides, from the southeastern US, grows up to 30-40 ft (9-12 m) high with an equal spread. Its bright green heart-shaped leaves are 4-8 in (10-20 cm) long, and are borne in whorls. The flowers are white with purple and yellow markings. It is hardy in zones 6-9. The cultivar 'Aurea' has large velvety leaves.
Catalpa × *erubescens,* syn. *C.* ×

Catalpa bigonioides

hybrida, is up to 20 ft (6 m) high and 25 ft (7.5 m) wide. The leaves, up to 1 ft (30 cm) long, are purple when they open (some are whole; some have three lobes). The flowers are similar to the flowers of *C. bignonioides*, but smaller and more profuse. The cultivar 'Purpurea' has dark purple, almost black, young leaves and shoots, later turning dark green.
Catalpa speciosa can grow up to 40-60 ft (12-18 m) tall, spreading 20-40 ft (6-12 m). It is more upright than *C. bignonioides* with leathery heart-shaped leaves up to 1 ft (30 cm) long. The white, purple-marked blooms are larger than those of *C. bignonioides*, but have fewer blooms in each cluster. It is hardy in zones 5-8.

Cultivation
Plant catalpas in midfall or early spring in virtually any garden soil. The trees like a sunny spot.
Pruning Brittle branches are subject to breakage in storms; remove damaged wood promptly.
Pests/diseases Leaf spot fungi cause browning of leaves. Catalpa midges feed on and distort foliage, leaving circular spots of papery tissue on the leaves. Catalpa sphinx moths may strip trees of foliage entirely.

CAUCASIAN WINGNUT — see *Pterocarya*

Cercis
redbud

Cercis siliquastrum

- ❏ Height at 25 years 15-20 ft (4.5-6 m); when mature, up to 30 ft (9 m)
- ❏ Spread 10-35 ft (3-10.5 m)
- ❏ Any good garden soil
- ❏ Deciduous broadleaf
- ❏ Hardy zones 4-9
- ❏ Features: profuse flowers; seedpods; distinctive foliage

Redbud's spreading, rounded top is a spectacular mass of color in early spring to midspring, when hundreds of pink pealike blooms crowd in clusters along the naked branches and even on the trunk. The flowers often appear before the distinctive foliage and are followed later by conspicuous green seedpods. These are tinted red when ripe and remain on the tree until winter. The heart-shaped or rounded leaves are generally bright green or gray-green.

Redbud may be grown as a single-stemmed tree or a multi-stemmed shrub; it is also decorative when trained against a wall as an espalier.

Popular species
Cercis canadensis (eastern redbud) is a native of eastern North America that ranges naturally from zones 4-9. Up to 30 ft (9 m) high and 35 ft (10.5 m) wide, it has a broad, rounded head with bright green heart-shaped leaves and pale rose-pink flowers in early spring to midspring. The foliage has golden tints in fall. It flowers most freely in sunny sites, but performs well in lightly shaded ones, too. Cultivars include 'Forest Pansy' (pink flowers; reddish-purple foliage) and 'Royal White' (large white flowers).

Cercis canadensis 'Forest Pansy'

Cercis occidentalis is a small tree or large shrub up to 15 ft (4.5 m) high and 10 ft (3 m) wide from the western section of the US. The heart-shaped leathery leaves are bright green and rounded, and the short-stalked rose-colored flowers are borne in clusters. Hardy from zones 7-9, this species tolerates drought.

Cercis racemosa, from China, grows 20 ft (6 m) or more in height and spread, with ovate leaves that are bright green above and downy underneath. Drooping, 4 in (10 cm) long clusters of rose-pink pea-shaped flowers are borne in profusion in late spring on trees that are more than 8 years old. They are followed by attractive seedpods up to 5 in (12.5 cm) long. *C. racemosa* is hardy to zone 7.

Cercis reniformis (Texas redbud) is of shrubby habit, with glossy green blunt-tipped leaves. The cultivar 'Oklahoma' bears wine-red blossoms.

Cercis siliquastrum (Judas tree), from the eastern Mediterranean, is up to 25 ft (7.5 m) high and 20 ft (6 m) wide. This wide-spreading, flat-topped tree or shrub has rounded gray-green leaves. Hardy to zone 6, this redbud bears clusters of rich rose-purple flowers in groups of four to six while the branches are still leafless in midspring. The flowers are followed by flat green seedpods up to 4 in (10 cm) long. These are tinted red when ripe in late summer. This

Cercis occidentalis

species, according to legend, was the tree on which Judas hanged himself — hence its common name. It is hardy to zone 6. A cultivar is 'Alba' (white flowers; pale green foliage).

Cultivation
Redbud thrives in any good garden soil in full sun. Large trees resent root disturbance, so plant only young balled-and-burlapped or (better yet) container-grown specimens, ideally in midfall or early spring. Redbud is not recommended for gardens that have heavy clay soil.

Pruning No special treatment is required, but wall-trained specimens can be cut back for shaping after they flower.

Pests/diseases Cankers, which begin as small sunken areas of blackened, cracked bark, may spread to girdle and kill whole tree stems. Wilting foliage may be a symptom of verticillium. Caterpillars, leafhoppers, scale insects, and treehoppers are also known to infest redbuds.

CHERRY, CORNELIAN —
see *Cornus*
CHERRY, ORNAMENTAL —
see *Prunus*
COCKSPUR THORN —
see *Crataegus*

Cornus
dogwood

Cornus kousa chinensis

Cornus nuttalli, flowers

Cornus kousa, fruit

❏ Height at 25 years 10-20 ft (3-6 m); when mature, up to 30 ft (9 m)
❏ Spread 15-30 ft (4.5-9 m)
❏ Any good garden soil
❏ Deciduous broadleaf
❏ Hardy zones 5-9
❏ Features: profuse flowers and berries; fall foliage

The dogwoods range from prostrate creepers to medium-size shrubs and small single-stemmed trees. The blooms are striking bracts surrounding insignificant true flowers. They appear in clusters at winter's end before the foliage, or in midspring to late spring. The oval leaves are midgreen to dark green, often turning a rich red, yellow, and bronze in fall. The fruit, black or red berries, appears as the leaves turn.

Some species are now included in different genera but are still listed under *Cornus*. For shrubby dogwoods, see pages 86-88.

Popular species
Cornus florida (flowering dogwood), which grows up to 20 ft (6 m) high and wide, has tiered, sweeping branches and oval dark-green leaves that turn red to reddish-purple in fall, bearing blooms of four white bracts in early to midspring; red berries follow. It is hardy in zones 6-9. 'Cherokee Chief' bears ruby-red flowers; 'Golden Nugget' has gilt-edged leaves.

Cornus kousa is a bush or small bushy tree, 20-30 ft (6-9 m) high with an equal spread. The oval midgreen to dark green leaves have wavy edges turning bronze and crimson in fall. Large creamy white bracts appear in late spring to early summer; raspberry-like fruits follow. It is hardy in zones 6-8. The variety *chinensis* is taller and more open with larger leaves and bracts.

Cornus mas (Cornelian cherry) forms into a small tree, about 20-25 ft (6-7.5 m) high and 15-20 ft (4.5-6 m) wide, with dense branches and dark green oval leaves. Clusters of golden yellow flowers appear from late winter to early spring before the leaves, followed by red, semitranslucent, edible berries. It is hardy in zones 5-8. The heavy-flowering cultivar 'Golden Glory' is upright in form.

Cornus nuttallii (Pacific dogwood), forms a tree up to 25 ft (7.5 m) high and 15 ft (4.5 m) wide. It has dull green leaves with yellow or red fall tints. In late spring round white blooms open, surrounded by large creamy white bracts that later turn pink. The strawberry-like fruits are orange-red. It is not hardy north of zone 7.

Cultivation
Plant dogwood in midfall or early spring in an organically rich, well-drained, acid garden soil, preferably in a partially shaded spot. Wet soils or alkaline ones are not recommended.
Pruning It has no special needs.
Pests/diseases Anthracnose is fatal to *C. florida* in the North; other species are fairly pest free.

Cotoneaster
cotoneaster

Cotoneaster salicifolius

❏ Height at 25 years 6-15 ft (1.8-4.5 m); when mature, typically 20 ft (6 m)
❏ Spread 6-15 ft (1.8-4.5 m)
❏ Deciduous broadleaf
❏ Ordinary garden soil
❏ Hardy zones 6-8
❏ Features: berries; flowers; foliage

Though cotoneasters are better known as shrubs (see page 91), this large genus also includes small trees grown for their neat foliage, creamy white flower clusters, and dazzling show of red berries, carried in heavy bunches in fall and winter.

Popular species
Cotoneaster frigidus is a fast-growing deciduous or semievergreen small tree or large shrub up to 15 ft (4.5 m) high and wide with midgreen to dark green oblong leaves and white to pink flowers in early summer. The red berries last well into winter. It is hardy to zone 7.
Cotoneaster salicifolius (willowleaf cotoneaster) is a vigorous 10-15 ft (3-4.5 m) evergreen. Though usually treated as a shrub, in a small garden it may function as a small multistemmed tree. Bright red fruits persist through winter, setting off the purplish color of the winter foliage.

Cotoneaster frigidus

Cultivation
Plant in midfall or early spring to midspring in ordinary garden soil.
Pruning There are no special requirements.
Pests/diseases Canker and fire blight can kill branches or the whole tree; scale insects and spider mites may be troublesome.

CRAB APPLE — see *Malus*

Crataegus
hawthorn

Crataegus laevigata 'Paul's Scarlet'

❏ Height at 25 years 18-25 ft (5.4-7.5 m); when mature, 25-30 ft (7.5-9 m)
❏ Spread approximately equal to height
❏ Ordinary garden soil
❏ Deciduous broadleaf
❏ Hardy zones 3-8
❏ Features: flowers; fruits; foliage

Because of their thorny branches, hawthorns have long been used as hedging plants, as self-repairing substitutes for barbed wire. But with the heavy crops of scented flowers that they bear in spring and the rich foliage tints and clusters of colorful berries (haws) they provide in fall, hawthorns also make fine specimen trees. Care should be taken, however, not to plant them where their thorns will injure children or passersby.

The major drawback to hawthorns is their susceptibility to a variety of bacterial and fungal diseases such as fire blight and rusts. Check with your nursery about disease-resistant species and cultivars before you make your selection.

Popular species
Crataegus crus-galli (cockspur thorn) has branches armed with 2 in (5 cm) thorns and glossy green leaves that turn scarlet in fall. The white blooms appear in

Crataegus monogyna, haws

Crataegus laevigata plena, flowers

Crataegus laevigata rosea-plena

early summer, followed by red haws lasting until midwinter. The variety *inermis* is thornless. It is hardy in zones 3-7.

Crataegus laevigata (English hawthorn), syn. *C. oxyacantha*, has fragrant white flowers in late spring, followed by crimson oval haws. The dark green leaves have three or five lobes. Popular cultivars and varieties include 'Crimson Cloud' (red single flowers; foliage resistant to leaf blight), 'Paul's Scarlet' ('Coccinea Plena'; scarlet double flowers), *plena* (white double flowers, aging pink), and *rosea-plena* (pink double flowers).

Crataegus × lavallei (Lavalle hawthorn) is a dense leafy tree with glossy dark green foliage that turns bronze to coppery red in fall. The haws are orange-red and persist into winter. It is hardy in zones 5-7.

Crataegus mollis (downy hawthorn), from central North America, is up to 30 ft (9 m) high and wide with red haws as large as cherries. It is hardy in zones 3-6.

Crataegus monogyna (single-seed hawthorn) is a densely branched thorny tree up to 25 ft (7.5 m) high and 20 ft (6 m) wide. Suitable as a specimen tree and for hedging and screening, it has glossy dark green lobed and toothed leaves. Clusters of sweet-smelling white flowers cover the branches in late spring, followed in fall by small crimson haws in large clusters. The cultivar 'Stricta,' or 'Fastigiata,' is a narrow tree up to 18 ft (5.4 m) high and 8 ft (2.4 m) wide. It is hardy in zones 5-7.

Crataegus phaenopyrum (Washington thorn), originally from the southeastern US, has glossy, maplelike leaves with rich fall tints and crimson haws. It is hardy in zones 3-8.

Cultivation
Plant in midfall or early spring in any ordinary, well-drained garden soil. Hawthorn tolerates partial shade but prefers sun. It withstands exposure and air pollution.

When planting *C. monogyna* as a hedge, use plants 1-1½ ft (30-45 cm) high at intervals of 2 ft (60 cm). For screening, use 3-4 ft (90-120 cm) high trees at intervals of 2-3 ft (60-90 cm).

Pruning Trim hedges or screens of *C. monogyna* in early spring. Tall neglected hedges can be heavily pruned in midsummer.

Pests/diseases Aphids, caterpillars, scale, and mites will infest hawthorns. Fire blight blackens and shrivels leaves and tips of new shoots; cankers appear in bark as whole limbs die back. Leaf spot shows as small brown or black spots. Powdery mildew is a white coating on the leaves. Rust shows as yellow or orange swellings on young shoots, leaves, and fruits in early summer.

CUCUMBER TREE —
see *Magnolia*

Davidia
dove or handkerchief tree

Davidia involucrata

❏ Height at 25 years 18-25 ft (5.4-7.5 m);
   when mature, 20-40 ft (6-12 m)
❏ Spread 15 ft (4.5 m)
❏ Deciduous broadleaf
❏ Any good, moist garden soil
❏ Hardy zones 6-8
❏ Features: flower bracts

Dove tree *(Davidia involucrata)*, a good specimen tree, is a spectacular sight in bloom in midspring or late spring. The true flowers form dense round heads, concealed by two large, whitish flower bracts of uneven sizes. The bracts resemble dove wings or folded handkerchiefs among the bright green, heart-shaped, and veined leaves which are covered with gray down underneath. The young tree is narrow but later becomes rounded at the top.

Cultivation
Plant in any good moist garden soil in midfall or early spring. A lightly shaded site is best, but the dove tree will tolerate full sunlight in a moist soil.
Pruning It has no special needs.
Pests/diseases Generally trouble free.

DAWN REDWOOD —
see *Metasequoia*
DOGWOOD — see *Cornus*
DOVE TREE — see *Davidia*
ELM — see *Ulmus*
EMPRESS TREE —
see *Paulownia*

Fagus
beech

Fagus sylvatica 'Zlatia'

❏ Height at 25 years 10-30 ft (3-9 m);
   when mature, 50-100 ft (15-30 m)
❏ Spread 35-45 ft (10.5-13.5 m) or more
❏ Any good, well-drained soil
❏ Deciduous broadleaf
❏ Hardy zones 3-9
❏ Features: foliage color

In the wild, beech trees are stately and long-lived, demanding ample room, but in return lending nobility to the landscape with their dense, broad tops; massive, smooth gray trunks; pale green young foliage; and yellow and russet fall tints. Fortunately, smaller forms are also available, with narrow or weeping growth habits and green and gold foliage; these make good specimen trees. Notable among these are "copper beeches" with their outstanding purple foliage.

The pointed oval, sometimes toothed leaves, about 4 in (10 cm) long, cast deep shade. The insignificant flowers may be followed by woody, prickly fruits that open to reveal one to three triangular brown nuts (mast).

Popular species
Fagus grandifolia (American beech) soars to 100 ft (30 m) with an equal or lesser spread. The leaves open silver-green, changing to a dark green by midsummer. In fall the leaves fade to golden bronze and often hang on the branches well into winter. This tree's shallow roots and dense canopy make it impossible

Fagus sylvatica, fruit

Fagus sylvatica 'Purpurea Pendula'

Fagus sylvatica 'Fastigiata'

Fagus sylvatica 'Pendula,' fall

to grow grass beneath its branches — use it to frame a vista, not for shade. It is hardy in zones 3-9. *Fagus sylvatica* (European beech) is hardy in zones 5-7. It grows 50-60 ft (15-18 m) tall with a thick gray trunk and a rounded head 35-45 ft (10.5-13.5 m) wide. The wavy-edged leaves are bright green when young, maturing to mid- or deep green and developing rich yellow and russet tints in fall. This species makes an excellent tall hedge, retaining its russet leaves throughout winter if trimmed in late summer. Cultivars include 'Asplenifolia' (fern-leaved beech; narrow, deep-cut leaves), 'Aurea Pendula' (tall, narrow tree, to 15 ft/4.5 m high and 5 ft/1.5 m wide; pendent branches; golden yellow leaves; best in light shade), 'Fastigiata' ('Dawyckii'; columnar tree to 30 ft/9 m high and 7 ft/2 m wide, broadening with age), 'Pendula' (weeping beech; pendent branches or horizontal branches with pendent branchlets), 'Purpurea' (purple-red foliage), 'Purpurea Pendula' (weeping, round-headed, to 10 ft/3 m high and 6 ft/1.8 m wide; purple foliage), 'Riversii' ('Rivers' Purple'; deep purple leaves), and 'Zlatia' (young golden yellow leaves turning green).

Cultivation

Beech grows well in moist, well-drained, acid soils; European beeches tolerate alkaline soils. Plant in early spring in an open sunny spot.

For hedging, plant trees 1 ft (30 cm) high 1½-2 ft (45-60 cm) apart. Remove the upper quarter of all shoots after planting to encourage branching; repeat this tipping again the next year.

Pruning Trim hedges in late summer. Specimen trees require no pruning once established.

Pests/diseases Aphids produce tufts of white wax on the undersides of leaves and excrete sticky honeydew. Beech scale insects produce tufts of white wax. Severe infestations cause yellowing of foliage and loss of vigor. The insects also spread the fungal "beech bark disease," which penetrates the bark through the insects' puncture wounds, killing the tree afterward. Bleeding canker may attack beeches, causing a watery light brown or thick reddish-brown liquid to ooze from the bark. Bracket fungi may enter dead wood and cause rotting of the heartwood; later, large bracket-shaped fruiting bodies develop on the trunks of neglected trees. Caterpillars of several types, including tent caterpillars and hemlock loopers, may attack and devour beech foliage. Coral spot may develop on dead shoots and cause dieback; pink to red cushionlike spore pustules may appear at the base of dead wood. Powdery mildew may develop on foliage in late summer. Two-lined chestnut borers create cankers on sides of branches exposed to the sun; dark red liquid oozes from punctures at the cankers' centers.

FALSE ACACIA — see *Robinia*

Fraxinus
ash

Fraxinus excelsior, fruit

❏ Height at 25 years 20-30 ft (6-9 m); when mature, 20-120 ft (6-36 m)
❏ Spread equal to or more than height
❏ Deciduous broadleaf
❏ Hardy zones 3-9
❏ Features: elegant appearance; fine foliage

With its extensive root system and wide-spreading branches clothed with leaves divided into lance-shaped leaflets, the ash tree stands solid against the strongest winds. Many species in this fast-growing genus are too large for most gardens, but smaller forms are available, many with fine fall foliage of yellow or purple.

Fraxinus ornus, flowers

Fraxinus excelsior 'Jaspidea'

Popular species
Fraxinus americana (white ash) grows 50 ft (15 m) or more high (120 ft/36 m specimens are not unknown) with an equal spread. This excellent shade tree has furrowed bark. The midgreen leaves are divided into seven pointed oval leaflets, paler beneath. The foliage may develop amber, yellow, and purple fall tints. Female trees bear narrow winged fruits. Cultivars include 'Autumn Purple' (seedless; reddish-purple fall foliage) and 'Greenspire' (narrowly upright in form, dark orange fall foliage). It is hardy in zones 3-9.
Fraxinus excelsior (European ash) is up to 80 ft (24 m) high and 90 ft (27 m) wide. The long dark green leaves are up to 1 ft (30 cm) divided into 9 to 13 narrow oblong leaflets which turn yellow in fall. The roots are invasive. Cultivars are 'Diversifolia' (single, undivided leaves), 'Jaspidea' (golden ash; young leaves yellow; yellow fall tints), and 'Pendula' (weeping ash; pendent branches). *Fraxinus ornus* (flowering ash) is a handsome tree from southern Europe and Asia Minor. From

40-50 ft (12-15 m) high and wide, it is more suitable for small gardens than other species. It has a bushy rounded head with grayish-green leaves divided into seven oval leaflets. Dense, showy clusters, up to 4 in (10 cm) wide, of cream-white blooms appear in late spring. Hardy zones are 6-7. *Fraxinus velutina* (velvet ash) is 20-45 ft (6-13.5 m) high and wide with thick velvety leaves. It is hardy to zone 6 or 7 southward.

Cultivation
Plant ash in midfall or early spring in any ordinary garden soil in sun or partial shade. Do not plant *F. excelsior* close to buildings as the spreading roots may undermine foundations.
Pruning It has no special needs.
Pests/diseases Ash canker causes damage ranging from small swellings on the bark to large black cankers. Borers and scale insects may infest ashes. A disease called dieback may cause the death of unhealthy or stressed ashes in the Northeast. Leaf spot marks and scorches leaves in rainy springs, at times causing them to drop too soon.

Ginkgo
maidenhair tree

Ginkgo biloba 'Princeton Sentry,' fall

❏ Height at 25 years 25-30 ft (7.5-10 m);
   when mature, height 80 ft (24 m)
❏ Spread equal to half or more of
   height
❏ Fertile, well-drained soil
❏ Deciduous broadleaf
❏ Hardy zones 3-8
❏ Features: unique leaves; fall tints;
   tolerates air pollution

Ginkgo biloba, foliage

The maidenhair tree (*Ginkgo biloba*) is a primitive tree more closely related to conifers than to other broadleaf trees. The tree survived only in one region of China and was rescued about 50 years ago.

The Ginkgo's bright green fan-shaped leaves quickly turn a brilliant yellow in the fall. This slow-growing tree is conical when young and may broaden as it matures. It is suitable only for large gardens. 'Autumn Gold' is broadly conical and 'Princeton Sentry' is columnar.

Cultivation
Plant in midspring in fertile, well-drained soil.
Pruning Prune in spring.
Pests/diseases Trouble free.

Gleditsia
honey locust

Gleditsia triacanthos

❏ Height at 25 years 18-30 ft (5.4-10 m);
   when mature, 70 ft (21 m)
❏ Spread equal to height
❏ Deciduous broadleaf
❏ Any good garden soil
❏ Hardy zones 3-9
❏ Features: ornamental foliage and
   seedpods; tolerates air pollution

Grown for its handsome foliage, honey locust (*Gleditsia triacanthos*) is a large elegant tree native to central and eastern North America. This tree is highly resistant to air pollution and tolerates a wide range of soils and sites.

The species is up to 70 ft (21 m) high and wide. It has light green frondlike leaves, divided into 20 to 32 oblong to lance-shaped leaflets, with clear yellow fall tints. The shiny brown twisted seedpods remain on the tree throughout winter.

The branches of wild trees are armed with sharp thorns, which may measure up to 1 ft (30 cm) long. These can cause serious injury, so it is advisable to plant the thornless variety *inermis* or one of its cultivars.

Honey locust is fast-growing and the light shade its delicate foliage casts makes it an excellent shade tree for a large lawn. Its near-black trunk and branches look dramatic in winter.

Halesia
silverbell tree

Gleditsia triacanthos, foliage

Popular thornless cultivars
'Moraine' is a broad, rounded tree that may reach a height of 40-50 ft (12-15 m).
'Ruby Lace' has leaves that are purplish when young and become bronze-green as they mature.
'Shademaster,' an upright thornless form, has dark green foliage.
'Sunburst' produces golden new growth that gradually darkens to green.

Cultivation
Honey locust thrives in any good garden soil; plant in midfall or early spring in a sunny spot.
Pruning Remove dead wood in early spring.
Pests/diseases Fungal cankers may attack branches and trunks, killing trees if unchecked. Leaf spots are a serious problem in the South. Powdery mildew is common on honey locust foliage, though it rarely causes serious harm. Spider mites and webworms may also attack foliage.

GOLDEN CHAIN TREE —
see *Laburnum*
GOLDEN RAIN TREE —
see *Koelreuteria*

Halesia monticola, flowers

❑ Height at 25 years 15-35 ft (4.5-10.5 m); when mature, up to 80 ft (24 m)
❑ Spread 15-35 ft (4.5-10.5 m)
❑ Moist, lime-free soil
❑ Deciduous broadleaf
❑ Hardy zones 5-8
❑ Features: flowers

Beautiful specimen trees for gardens with acid soil, the silverbells bear profuse clusters of drooping silver-white bell-shaped flowers in early spring to midspring, often before the leaves emerge.

These wide-spreading trees have light green oval, pointed leaves, which turn clear yellow in fall. Cigar-shaped four-winged fruits follow the flowers.

Popular species
Halesia carolina, 40 ft (12 m) high and a spread of 5 ft (1.5 m), often has a multistemmed trunk. It is hardy in zones 5-8.
Halesia monticola may reach a mature height of 60-80 ft (18-24 m) and bears larger blossoms and fruits than *H. carolina*. It is hardy in zones 6–8.

Cultivation
Silverbells need moist and organically rich, acid soil, and a sunny or lightly shaded spot. They like woodland conditions. Plant in midfall or early spring.
Pruning Long shoots may be shortened after flowering.
Pests/diseases Trouble free.

HANDKERCHIEF TREE —
see *Davidia*
HAWTHORN — see *Crataegus*
HICKORY — see *Carya*
HONEY LOCUST —
see *Gleditsia*
HOP HORNBEAM — see *Ostrya*
HORNBEAM — see *Carpinus*
INDIAN BEAN TREE —
see *Catalpa*
IRONWOOD — see *Ostrya*
JUDAS TREE — see *Cercis*

Juglans
walnut

Juglans regia

Juglans nigra, foliage and fruit

Juglans regia, fruits

❏ Height at 25 years 25-40 ft (7.5-12 m);
  when mature, 40-75 ft (12-22.5 m)
❏ Spread approximately equal to height
❏ Any fertile, well-drained soil
❏ Deciduous broadleaf
❏ Hardy zones 3-9
❏ Features: attractive foliage; nuts

Walnut trees are a bit too coarse to make first-class specimen trees and are too large for small gardens. On large properties, the shade offered by their broad, dense tops is a relief in summer; their nuts are welcome, too.

The large midgreen to light green leaves, up to 3 ft (90 cm) long, are divided into many oval leaflets. These are aromatic when bruised. The tree bears catkins in spring. When pollinated, green fruits follow. These fruits open in fall to reveal wrinkled nuts.

Popular species
Juglans ailanthifolia (Japanese walnut), syn. *J. sieboldiana*, is up to 25 ft (7.5 m) high and wide and is hardy to zone 5. The leaves are up to 3 ft (90 cm) long.

Juglans cinerea (butternut), up to 40-60 ft (12-18 m) high with a spread of 30-50 ft (9-15 m) is hardy in zones 3-7. The hairy leaves are up to 20 in (50 cm) long.

Juglans nigra (black walnut) grows 50-75 ft (15-22.5 m) tall, with an equal spread. The glossy leaves are up to 2 ft (60 cm) long; the nuts have rough black shells. It is hardy in zones 5-9.

Juglans regia (English walnut), 40-60 ft (12-18 m) high with an equal or greater spread, is hardy only as far north as zone 6. The glossy leathery leaves are 8-18 in (20-45 cm) long; the nuts have wrinkled brown shells. The cultivar 'Carpathian Strain' is said to be hardy to -40° F (-40° C).

Cultivation
Buy walnut trees when they are small as they do not transplant easily. Plant in midfall or early spring in any fertile, well-drained soil in an open site.

Mulch annually in spring with well-rotted manure for the first few years until the tree is established. Trees do not fruit until they are at least 8 years old; for crops, several trees should be planted to ensure good cross-pollination.

Pruning Prune in late summer or fall; walnuts "bleed" profusely if cut in spring.

Pests/diseases Bacterial blight appears on leaves and young fruits as irregular black spots, causing a premature drop. Cankers, depressed areas ringed with callus tissue, may girdle stems, killing branches or whole trees. Caterpillars may attack and defoliate trees. Gall mites cause blisterlike pouches on the leaves. Birds and squirrels eat the nuts.

Koelreuteria
golden rain tree

Koelreuteria paniculata

❏ Height at 25 years 20 ft (6 m); when mature, 40 ft (12 m) or more
❏ Spread equal to or greater than height
❏ Good loamy soil
❏ Deciduous broadleaf
❏ Hardy zones 5-9
❏ Features: flowers; foliage; inflated seedpods

Golden rain tree (*Koelreuteria paniculata*), from China, is a beautiful and easy-to-care-for centerpiece for a sunny garden. Also known as varnish tree, it is quite spectacular in early summer, when hundreds of yellow star-shaped flowers, held in panicles up to 1 ft (30 cm) long, appear at the tips of the shoots, turning the dense, rounded head into a mass of color.

The fanlike midgreen leaves, up to 1½ ft (45 cm) long and divided into many deeply toothed oval leaflets, are tinted yellow in fall. The blooms are followed by bladderlike green fruits, which flush red as they ripen. The branches of golden rain tree are sparse when young but become compact and broadheaded with age.

Cultivation
Plant golden rain tree in midfall or early spring in good loamy soil in full sun. It is tolerant of air pollution and drought.
Pruning Prune during winter.
Pests/diseases Generally pest free. Coral spot fungus may enter through cuts and wounds, appearing as pink spots.

Koelreuteria paniculata, seedpods

Koelreuteria paniculata, flowers

Laburnum
golden chain tree

Laburnum x *watereri* 'Vossii,' flowers

❏ Height at 25 years 6-20 ft (1.8-6 m); when mature, 15-30 ft (4.5-9 m)
❏ Spread 3-15 ft (1-4.5 m)
❏ Any well-drained soil
❏ Deciduous broadleaf
❏ Hardy zones 5-7
❏ Features: flowers

The light and airy laburnum is an elegant feature in midspring to late spring with its long, drooping racemes of yellow pealike flowers.

The tree has small, oval midgreen to light green leaves. All parts, especially the seeds, are poisonous. In addition, its trunks or branches may die suddenly.

Popular species
Laburnum alpinum reaches a height of 20 ft (6m) and bears flower racemes 1 ft (30 cm) long or more. It is hardy in zones 5-7. The cultivar 'Pendulum,' up to 6 ft (1.8 m) high and 3 ft (1 m) wide, is slow-growing with a domed head and pendent branches.
Laburnum anagyroides (common laburnum) has flower racemes 4-10 in (10-25 cm) long. It is hardy in zones 6-7 and may grow 20-30 ft (6-9 m) tall.
Laburnum × *watereri*, 12-15 ft (3.6-4.5 m) high, has a spread of 9-12 ft (2.7-3.6 m). It has glossy leaves and slender flower racemes. 'Vossii' bears flower sprays up to 2 ft (60 cm) long and fewer seedpods. It is hardy in zones 6-7.

Cultivation
Plant in midfall or early spring in any deep, well-drained soil. Stake young trees.
Pruning Cut weak branches and seedpods after flowering.
Pests/diseases Leaf spot fungus may disfigure leaves. Twig blight may appear as brown lesions on twigs during wet springs, causing blighting of foliage above.

Laburnum anagyroides

Larix
larch

Larix decidua 'Pendula'

Larix kaempferi 'Nana'

❏ Height at 25 years 30-60 ft (9-18 m); when mature, 70-90 ft (21-27 m) or more
❏ Spread 15-40 ft (4.5-12 m)
❏ Any well-drained soil
❏ Deciduous conifer
❏ Hardy zones 1-7
❏ Features: foliage; flowers; cones

Fast-growing larch — one of the few deciduous conifers — is an elegant and graceful tree with wide-spreading, upward-curving branches. Its light twiggy outline makes it an attractive feature, even in winter. The needlelike leaves, which are softer than the foliage of other conifers, unfurl pale green in spring, turn bright green, and finally become golden or russet in autumn before they fall. They are borne in spirals on young shoots and in rosettes on spurs on older wood.

Male and female flowers occur in early spring on even young trees; the females are the most conspicuous — red, pale green, or yellow. They are followed by attractive, small red, violet, or brown rounded cones that remain on the tree until the following winter.

Popular species
Larix decidua (European larch), from the European Alps, is up to 75 ft (22.5 m) high and 30 ft (9 m) wide. It is conical when young,

Larix decidua, young cones

broadening with maturity. The cultivar 'Pendula' has downward-arching branches. It is hardy in zones 2-6.
Larix kaempferi (Japanese larch), syn. *L. leptolepsis*, up to 90 ft (27 m) high and 40 ft (12 m) wide, has young red shoots with sea-green foliage, broader than in the other species. The cultivar 'Nana' is compact and slow-growing, and 'Pendula' produces long, weeping branches. It is hardy in zones 2-7.
Larix laricina (eastern larch) from North America reaches a height of 40-80 ft (12-24 m) with a spread of 15-30 ft (4.5-9 m). At home in moist, acid soils and flourishing as far north as zones 1-6, it is an excellent tree for clothing otherwise difficult sites.
Larix occidentalis (western larch), from North America, is the tallest of the larches, reaching a height of 180 ft (54 m) in the wild. The yellow or pale orange shoots are clothed with glossy gray-green foliage; the purple-brown cones are oblong and have pointed bracts protruding from between the scales. It is hardy to zone 5.

Cultivation
Plant larch in any good, neutral to acid soil that is deep and well-drained in an open, sunny spot in late fall or early spring. Buy young trees under 2 ft (60 cm) tall. Larch grows well in windy and exposed sites; it does not, however, tolerate air pollution.
Pruning Prune competing leading shoots, to leave the strongest ones. On mature specimen trees, the lowest branches can be cut off flush with the bole for a neater appearance.
Pests/diseases Larch case-bearers eat into needles in midspring, causing them to brown. Sawfly larvae feed on shoots. Woolly larch aphids may eat leaves and stems, producing tufts of white waxy wool.

LINDEN — see *Tilia*

Liquidambar
sweet gum

Liquidambar styraciflua

- ❏ Height at 25 years 25 ft (7.5 m); when mature, 50-75 ft (15-22.5 m)
- ❏ Spread two-thirds height
- ❏ Deep, moist soil
- ❏ Deciduous broadleaf
- ❏ Hardy zones 6-9
- ❏ Features: foliage; fall colors

Few trees equal the fiery orange and red fall tints of the magnificent sweet gum tree. Growing in a column or pyramid shape when young, it spreads and branches as it matures. The maplelike leaves are glossy dark green with three, five, or seven lobes. Mature trees have rough gray furrowed bark.

Popular species

Liquidambar formosana may form a pyramid 50 ft (15 m) tall at maturity. The three- or five-lobed leaves are tinted red in spring and have red or crimson tints in fall. The tree is hardy in zones 7-9. *Liquidambar styraciflua*, from eastern North America, may reach a height of 75 ft (22.5 m) with a spread of 50 ft (15 m). The shiny dark green leaves develop five or seven lobes and turn brilliant shades of orange or scarlet in fall. Cultivars include 'Burgundy' (leaves turn wine color in fall), 'Moraine' (fast, uniform growth, brilliant red fall color), 'Palo Alto' (uniform growth, orange-red fall color), and 'Variegata' (striped and mottled with yellow). It is hardy in zones 6-9.

Cultivation

Plant sweet gum in deep, moist but well-drained soil in a sheltered site in early spring. It prefers slightly acid soil and full sun.

Pruning Remove unwanted and crossed branches during winter.

For a round-headed tree with a straight trunk, grow to the desired height, then cut off the tip of the leading shoot to encourage branch development.

Pests/diseases Bleeding necrosis causes profuse bleeding over bark and death of tree. Leaf spot fungi may spot leaves but cause no harm. Sweet-gum webworm wraps young leaves together with webs to make nests for larvae.

Liriodendron
tulip tree

Liriodendron tulipifera 'Arnold'

❑ Height at 25 years 25 ft (7.5 m);
when mature, 60-90 ft (18-27 m)
❑ Spread 35-50 ft (10.5-15m)
❑ Any good, well-drained soil
❑ Deciduous broadleaf
❑ Hardy zones 5-9
❑ Features:attractive foliage; flowers

Grown for its handsome foliage and flowers, the tulip tree (*Liriodendron tulipifera*) is an imposing specimen for larger gardens.The light green to midgreen leaves, tinted yellow in fall, have four pointed lobes with broad, squared-off tips. Mature trees bear lovely tulip-shaped flowers. Cultivars include 'Arnold' (broadly columnar) and 'Aureo-marginata' (leaves edged yellow or greenish yellow).

Cultivation
Plant in midfall or early spring in moist but well-drained garden soil in either sun or light shade.

Liriodendron tulipifera, flower

Pruning Prune in winter.
Pests/diseases Aphids may attack leaves, causing sooty mold. Cankers and powdery mildew on the foliage are also problems.

LOCUST — see *Robinia*

Magnolia
magnolia

Magnolia × soulangiana, flowers

❑ Height at 25 years 10-33 ft (3-10 m);
when mature, 12-80 ft (3.6-24 m)
❑ Spread generally equal to height
❑ Well-drained loamy soil
❑ Deciduous or semievergreen
broadleaf
❑ Hardy zones 3-9
❑ Features: flowers; attractive leaves

This genus of trees boasts the famous evergreen southern magnolia and many fine deciduous species. These have a handsome, broadly lance-shaped foliage and spectacular blossoms: the exquisitely formed chalice- or goblet-shaped flowers in shades of pink, purple, and white often open out flat to a width of 10 in (25 cm).

Most tree magnolias do not bloom until they are 15 to 20 years old. Shrubby magnolias (pages 110-112) bloom when young.

If planted to the north of their recommended range, many magnolias will survive, but their flowers are likely to fall prey to late frosts, so that the gardener rarely can enjoy the floral display.

Popular species
Magnolia acuminata (cucumber tree) is a fast-growing, spreading, alkaline-tolerant tree that may grow 50-80 ft (15-24 m) with an equal spread. The greenish-yellow flowers appear in early summer among the leaves, followed by cucumber-like purplish-red fruits. It is hardy in zones 5-8.
Magnolia campbellii (pink tulip

Magnolia campbellii 'Charles Raffill'

Magnolia denudata

tree) isn't hardy north of zone 8 but may become an 80 ft (24 m) tree in the Deep South. The pink flowers with paler insides appear before the leaves from late winter to early spring.

Magnolia cordata, also called *Magnolia acuminata cordata*, is a fast-growing small tree, eventually 25-30 ft (7.5-9 m) tall with a spread of 15-20 ft (4.5-6 m). An American native, it is hardy to zone 6. It bears canary-yellow flowers among the foliage in late

spring and flowers while young.

Magnolia denudata (Yulan magnolia), syn *M. heptapeta,* is a slow-growing tree taking many years to reach 30 ft (9 m) high and wide. The fragrant, cup-shaped white blooms open in profusion from early to late spring before the ovate leaves unfurl. These are midgreen above and white and downy beneath. 'Swada' has white flowers and is a compact plant. It is hardy in zones 6-8.

Magnolia 'Elizabeth' grows up to

30 ft (9 m) tall, in a conical shape, and is often admired for its fragrant, pale primrose-yellow flowers borne on naked branches in early spring to midspring. It requires neutral to acid soil.

Magnolia liliiflora, syn. *M. quinquepeta* is a small tree or large shrub up to 12 ft (3.6 m) high and wide. The narrow upright flowers are flushed purple on the outside, opening flat to reveal a cream-colored inside. They appear in midspring. All but strongly alkaline soils are suitable. It is hardy in zones 6-8.

Magnolia × loebneri is an alkaline-tolerant small tree or large shrub up to 25 ft (7.5 m) high and wide. In early spring profuse fragrant flowers have white strap-shaped petals; these appear before the leaves. It is hardy in zones 5-8.

Magnolia macrophylla is a spectacular tree of open habit from our southeastern states. Up to 40 ft (12 m) high, it has light green leaves which can grow up to 3 ft (90 cm) long. The fragrant, purple-marked ivory flowers are up to 1 ft (30 cm) wide and appear in late spring or early summer. Hardy to zone 6, it requires acid soil.

Magnolia salicifolia (anise or willow-leaf magnolia) is a broadly conical tree or large shrub up to 30 ft (9 m) high. It has willow-like leaves and bears creamy flowers in spring before the foliage; it flowers while young. When bruised, the leaves, bark, and wood smell of lemons. It needs acid soil and is hardy in zones 5-8.

Magnolia sargentiana is hardy only to the warmer parts of zone 7. It grows to 40 ft (12 m) high, blooming after about 15 years. The rose-pink, 8 in (20 cm) wide

Magnolia × loebneri 'Leonard Messel'

Magnolia x soulangiana

Malus
crab apple

Malus x robusta

❏ Height at 25 years 15-20 ft (4.5-6 m);
  when mature, about 25 ft (7.5 m)
❏ Spread 4-20 ft (1.2-6 m)
❏ Ordinary well-drained soil
❏ Deciduous broadleaf
❏ Hardy zones 2-8
❏ Features: flowers; fruit; fall tints

blooms, resembling nodding water lilies, appear in midspring, before the leathery leaves. *M.s. robusta* has larger, rosy crimson flowers at an earlier age. Both need lime-free soil.

Magnolia × soulangiana is a shrub or small tree with fragrant, purple-flushed, white flowers appearing before the leaves in midspring. Cultivars, which flower when young, are 'Alexandrina' (rose-purple outside, pure white within), 'Lennei' (large leaves; rose-purple flowers, cream white stained with soft purple inside; may bloom again in fall), and 'Lilliputian' (compact; light pink flowers). It is hardy in zones 5-9.

Magnolia × veitchii is a vigorous tree, 40 ft (12 m) or more high at maturity, with a spread of 25 ft (7.5 m). It flowers from the age of 10 years, bearing blush-pink, 10 in (25 cm) wide goblet flowers in early spring. The leaves appear later, opening purple and maturing to dark green, 10 in (25 cm) long. Best in acid soil, it is hardy to the southern reaches of zone 7.

Magnolia virginiana (sweetbay

magnolia) is hardy in zones 5-9. Just 10-20 ft (3-6 m) high and 10 ft (3 m) wide in the North, it may reach a height of 60 ft (18 m) in the South. Nearly evergreen in mild-winter regions, it is fully deciduous in the North; it tolerates alkaline soils. The fragrant, waxy, cream-white flowers last all summer long; red fruits follow.

Magnolia wilsonii, a large shrub or a small tree up to 24 ft (7.2 m) high and wide, has scented white flowers that are saucer-shaped with red stamens in midspring. It is hardy to zone 6.

Cultivation
Plant in early spring in well-drained, organically rich soil in a sunny or lightly shaded site. Most magnolias prefer acid soil.

Pruning Prune immediately after flowering.

Pests/diseases Black mildew may spread over leaves in the South; many fungi cause leaf spotting. Cankers cause cracks in the bark, followed by dieback of the affected parts. Magnolia scale may stunt leaves.

The flowering crab apple is a very beautiful garden tree. In full bloom it rivals, and is sometimes mistaken for, the outstanding ornamental cherry *(Prunus)*. The trees may be round-headed, weeping, narrow, or spreading.

The clusters of bowl-shaped single, semidouble or fully double flowers have golden anthers and cover the branches in white, pink, and purple from mid- to late spring. Round or oval bright red or yellow fruit (crab apples), as small as plump cherries or as big as golf balls, arrives in fall. These fruits may stay on the branches after the leaves have fallen. Many are fine for making into jelly.

Popular species
Malus baccata (Siberian crab) is hardy to zone 2. This rounded tree, 20-50 ft (6-15 m) high, has fragrant white flowers and red or yellow fruits.

Malus floribunda (Japanese crab), a rounded tree with long, arching branches, is hardy to zone 5 and one of the best for the South. Up to 15-25 ft (4.5-7.5 m)

Malus x purpurea

Malus tschonoskii, fall

high and wide, it bears midgreen, narrowly oval, coarsely toothed leaves and profuse blush-pink flowers. The fruits are yellow.

Malus hupehensis is 20-25 ft (6-7.5 m) tall and wide, with a vase-shaped profile and deep green, oval, serrated leaves. Pink buds open into scented white blooms in midspring; red-tinted yellow fruits follow. It is hardy to zone 5.

Malus × purpurea is up to 25 ft (7.5 m) high and 12 ft (3.6 m) wide with purple-flushed, midgreen oval leaves and rosy red single blooms in midspring. Its small fruits are dull purple. It is hardy to zone 5.

Malus × robusta (cherry crab apple), up to 40 ft (12 m) high, bears white or pinkish flowers and cherrylike red or yellow fruits about 1 in (2.5 cm) wide that stay on the tree into winter. It is hardy to zone 4.

Malus sargentii, an extremely compact (8 ft/2.4 m) tree, bears perfumed white flowers in midspring to late spring, followed by dark red fruits. A good choice for southern gardens, it is nevertheless winter hardy to zone 5.

Malus spectabilis, originally cultivated in China, is a small tree up to 15 ft (4.5 m) high and wide. It has glossy leaves and double blush-pink flowers up to 2 in (5 cm) wide, opening from deep rose-red buds. Cultivars include

'Riversii,' with upright branches and semidouble rosy pink flowers. *Malus tschonoskii* is a conical tree up to 30-40 ft (9-12 m) high. It has pinkish flowers and coarsely toothed leaves that in fall turn fine hues of orange, scarlet, and purple. The brownish fruits are insignificant.

Hybrids are commonly round-headed trees that reach a height of 15-20 ft (4.5-6 m) and a width of 10-18 ft (3-5.4 m). As noted in the following descriptions, some are considerably more compact, while others are vase-shaped,

columnar, or weeping in form. The best offer not only fine flowers and fruits but also a resistance to the fungal and bacterial diseases that plague crab apples. Highly resistant hybrids include 'Angel Choir' (an upright tree to 12 ft/3.6 m high; pale pink buds; white double flowers; red fruits), 'Baskatong' (dark purplish-red buds; large purplish-red flowers with white claw; large purplish fruits), 'Callaway' (pink buds; large white flowers; large and persistent maroon fruits; well adapted to the South), 'Centuri-

Malus floribunda

Mespilus
medlar

Malus x robusta, flowers

Malus 'Golden Hornet,' fruits

Mespilus germanica, fruits

❏ Height at 25 years 15 ft (4.5 m); when mature, 20 ft (6 m)
❏ Spread 18 ft (5.4 m)
❏ Ordinary well-drained soil
❏ Deciduous broadleaf
❏ Hardy zones 6-8
❏ Features: picturesque form; flowers; fruit

The medlar tree (*Mespilus germanica*) is picturesque even in winter with its wide-spreading, rather crooked and thorny branches. It makes an ornamental specimen tree for a lawn.

The finely toothed, dull green leaves develop rich russet and yellow tints in fall. Large saucer-shaped white flowers appear singly in late spring to early summer, followed by smallish apple- or pear-shaped brown fruits with five stiff leafy structures (calyxes). They are edible when softened by frost or storage.

Cultivation
Plant medlar in midfall or early spring in an open, sunny spot in ordinary well-drained but moisture-retentive soil, enriched with well-rotted manure. Stake until established and mulch annually in spring.
Pruning To train young trees, cut back all lateral shoots to two or three leaf buds in midfall or early spring. When the tree has reached the desired height, pinch the leading shoots to encourage bushy growth. After the basic form is established, no special pruning is required.
Pests/diseases Trouble free.

on' (upright, narrow tree to 25 ft/7.5 m tall; red buds; rose-red flowers; persistent cherry-red fruits), 'Harvest Gold' (columnar tree to 30 ft/9 m tall and 15 ft/4.5 m wide; pink buds; white flowers; golden fruits that persist through winter), 'Molten Lava' (weeping tree to 15 ft/4.5 m tall; red buds; single white flowers; red-orange persistent fruits; yellow winter bark), 'Prairiefire' (red buds; dark rose flowers; small but persistent red-purple fruits), and 'White Cascade' (10-15 ft/3-4.5 m tall; pendulous branches; deep pink buds; white flowers; small yellow fruits).

Some hybrids are susceptible to disease, but may have attractions that compensate for the fungicidal and antibacterial sprays they will need. Examples of these are 'Golden Hornet,' a white-flowered tree that produces outsized (1 in/2.5 cm) yellow fruits; and 'White Candle,' a narrowly columnar tree that reaches a height of 15 ft (4.5 m) with a width of only 3 ft (90 cm), so it fits in spaces too constricted for almost any other flowering tree.

Cultivation
Crab apple thrives in any ordinary well-drained soil enriched with organic matter. Plant in full sun in midfall or early spring. To obtain the best fruiting, plant several cultivars close together.

Stake until established. Mulch young trees annually in mid-spring with well-rotted manure. If grown on lawns, allow them a grass-free root run of 3-4 ft (90-120 cm) for several years.
Pruning Remove dead or straggly shoots in late winter; otherwise, prune immediately after flowering.
Pests/diseases Aphids infest shoots, leaves, and fruit. Woolly aphids cover branches and twigs with tufts of white waxy wool and often encourage the growth of ugly galls. Apple scab shows as dark scabs on the fruits and olive-green blotches on foliage. Small pimples develop on the shoots; they later crack the bark, leaving scabs. Cedar apple rust appears on leaves as orange spots. Fire blight scorches branch tips. Powdery mildew may show as a white powdery deposit on new growth. Severely diseased foliage may wither and fall.

MAPLE — see *Acer*
MEDLAR — see *Mespilus*

Metasequoia
dawn redwood

Metasequoia glyptostroboides

❑ Height at 25 years 40-50 ft (12-15 m);
  when mature, 70-100 ft (21-30 m)
❑ Spread 15-25 ft (4.5-7.5 m)
❑ Any fertile, moist, slightly acid soil
❑ Deciduous conifer
❑ Hardy zones 5-8
❑ Features: attractive form and foliage
  tints; shaggy bark

The first living specimen of the vigorous dawn redwood *(Metasequoia glyptostroboides),* known previously only as a fossil, was discovered in China in 1941. This decorative conifer forms a slim cone with shaggy cinnamon-brown bark. The feathery needle-like leaves are light green in spring, darkening to midgreen in summer; in fall they turn pink, then a deep rust color.

Cultivation
Dawn redwood likes any good, moist but well-drained, slightly acid soil; a hillside site that protects against early frosts is ideal. Plant trees 1-3 ft (30-90 cm) tall from late fall to early winter. Place where trees can be admired from a distance, since dawn redwoods put on height at an extraordinary rate.
Pruning This is seldom necessary; remove second leader should trunk fork.
Pests/diseases Canker may attack trunks, killing trees. Japanese beetles feed on foliage.

Morus
mulberry

Morus nigra

❑ Height at 25 years 15-25 ft (4.5-7.5 m);
  when mature, 30-50 ft (9-15 m)
❑ Spread equal or less than height
❑ Deep, rich moist soil
❑ Deciduous broadleaf
❑ Hardy zones 5-8
❑ Features: ornamental foliage; fruits;
  gnarled form

Though it lacks refinement, the indestructible mulberry tree is a practical choice for gardens with limited space or adverse conditions: mulberries thrive in seaside or urban locations where few other trees survive. In summer mulberries cast dense shade with canopies of rough heart-shaped leaves on branches that become increasingly gnarled and rugged.
    The insignificant green catkins are followed by fruits resembling blackberries — delicious in the black mulberry.

Popular species
Morus alba (white mulberry), a rugged-looking tree, 15-20 ft (4.5-6 m) high, was originally grown for its foliage, which is used to feed silkworms. It has heart-shaped or oval to lance-shaped leaves up to 6 in (15 cm) long. The sweet but insipid white fruits ripen to red-pink. It is hardy in zones 5-8. The cultivar 'Pendula' has dense, pendulous branches.
Morus nigra (black or common mulberry) is a long-lived tree up to 30 ft (9 m) high and wide. It becomes gnarled as it matures: its rough, coarsely toothed, heart-

Morus nigra, foliage and fruits

shaped leaves are up to 8 in (20 cm) long. The tasty dark red fruits are up to 1 in (2.5 cm) long. It is hardy to zone 6.

Cultivation
In fall, plant mulberry trees in deep, rich loamy soil that is well drained but moisture retentive.
Pruning Prune in winter, removing dead wood and any crossing branches from established trees.
Pests/diseases Bacterial blight attacks leaves and shoots. Mealybugs, scale insects, and mites may also infest mulberries.

MOUNTAIN ASH — see *Sorbus*
MULBERRY — see *Morus*

Nothofagus
southern beech

Nothofagus obliqua

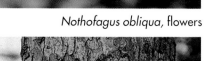

Nothofagus obliqua, flowers

Nothofagus obliqua, bark

❏ Height at 25 years 30-50 ft (9-15 m); when mature, 30-60 ft (9-18 m)
❏ Spread 15-30 ft (4.5-9 m)
❏ Well-drained, neutral to acid soil
❏ Deciduous broadleaf
❏ Hardy zones 7-10
❏ Features: glossy foliage; fall tints

Closely related to the beech tree (*Fagus*), but with smaller leaves, southern beech thrives in areas with cool, moist summers and mild winters. It performs best in the Pacific Northwest. There it is an ideal tree for large, sheltered gardens and for urban planting.

Deciduous southern beeches are rapid growers of upright columnar or broad-headed habit and make excellent specimen trees. The branches are densely covered with ovate or heart-shaped, toothed, glossy green leaves that assume handsome fall colors of yellow and red. Insignificant greenish flowers are followed by bristly fruit cases (mast) with three small nuts.

Popular species
Nothofagus antarctica (Antarctic beech) grows up to 40 ft (12 m) high and spreads 20 ft (6 m). The heart-shaped leaves turn yellow in fall. The trunk and branches may be twisted. It is hardy to zone 7.
Nothofagus obliqua (roble beech) is a fast-growing tree up to 50 ft (15 m) high and 30 ft (9 m) wide. It has arching branches and larger leaves than the other species. It is hardy to zone 8.
Nothofagus procera grows rapidly to 60 ft (18 m) high and 15 ft (4.5 m) or more wide. The oval, 4 in (10 cm) long leaves are veined and finely toothed; they take on golden yellow and scarlet fall colors. It is hardy to zone 8.

Cultivation
Plant in late fall or early spring in a fairly sheltered site. The trees grow in any good, well-drained soil. They do not like alkaline soil.
Pruning No special needs.
Pests/diseases Fungal root rots may afflict these trees.

Nyssa
black gum, pepperidge, sour gum, tupelo

Nyssa sylvatica, fall

❏ Height at 25 years 25-30 ft (7.5-9 m); when mature, up to 50 ft (15 m)
❏ Spread 15-30 ft (4.5-9 m)
❏ Moist, acid soil
❏ Deciduous broadleaf
❏ Hardy zones 3-9
❏ Features: fall foliage; pyramidal shape

With its glossy green foliage and pyramidal profile, tupelo — also known as sour gum, pepperidge or black gum — is a handsome tree and makes a fine street tree or specimen in the garden. It becomes truly spectacular, however, with the onset of fall, when the foliage turns to shades of scarlet, orange, and yellow.

This moisture-loving tree is one of the most reliable trees for fall color, seldom failing to mount a first-class display and typically turning before other trees. The insignificant flowers are followed by small blue-black fruits.

Popular species
Nyssa sinensis, a rare species from China, forms a small to mid-size tree 30-50 ft (9-15 m) tall. It bears narrow oval leaves up to 6 in (15 cm) long and 2 in (5 cm) wide. These are tinted red or purple when young and turn many shades of red and orange in fall. It is hardy in zones 7-9.

Nyssa sylvatica grows wild in eastern North America. In the wild it may grow to 100 ft (30 m); in cultivation it more typically stops at 30-50 ft (9-15 m). It has gleaming midgreen, oval leaves, which develop brilliant scarlet, red, and orange shades in fall. It is hardy in zones 3-9.

Cultivation
Tupelos are tap-rooted trees that are difficult to transplant. Move while still young, planting balled-and-burlapped stock (not bare-root specimens) in early spring. These trees prefer moist but well-drained, deep, acid soil in sun or partial shade. A site protected from the wind is best.

Pruning Prune, when necessary, in fall.

Pests/diseases There are no serious problems.

OAK — see *Quercus*

Ostrya
hop hornbeam

Ostrya carpinifolia, fruit

❏ Height at 25 years 20-25 ft (6-7.5 m);
   when mature, 20-60 ft (7.5-18 m)
❏ Spread two-thirds height
❏ Any well-drained soil
❏ Deciduous broadleaf
❏ Hardy zones 4-9
❏ Features: catkins; fruits; bark

Somewhat resembling true hornbeam *(Carpinus),* hop hornbeams are handsome ornamental trees. They are easy to grow and outstanding for their striking catkins in spring and for the hoplike fruits and fine foliage colors in fall.

Popular species
Ostrya carpinifolia (European hop hornbeam) grows about 25 ft (7.5 m) high and 20 ft (6 m) wide. The short trunk has rough bark beneath a dense, round head. The oval, toothed leaves are midgreen and about 4 in (10 cm) long; they take on clear yellow fall tints. In early spring the tree is decked with a profusion of drooping yellow-green male catkins; the pendulous hoplike fruit clusters add to the tree's attraction in fall. It is hardy to zone 6.
Ostrya virginiana (American hop hornbeam or ironwood) grows slowly, but eventually reaches a height of 25-40 ft (7.5-12 m) and

Ostrya virginiana

occasionally 60 ft (18 m). The spreading branches are slender but exceedingly tough and wind resistant, hence the common name "ironwood." It differs from the European hop hornbeam in having hairy shoots and leaves with fewer veins; the fall color is a warm golden yellow. The horizontal or drooping branches give this compact tree a graceful aspect. Well adapted to city conditions, this species has been neglected by the nursery trade, but offers a good choice for a street or specimen tree, and for parks, golf courses, and other large lawn areas.

Cultivation
Plant ostryas in early spring, in a slightly acid, well-drained but moisture-retentive soil in sun or light shade.
Pruning Remove any crossing or weak branches in late winter to early spring.
Pests/diseases Witches'-brooms, small bunches of twiggy growth, may form on branches.

PAGODA TREE — see *Sophora*

Parrotia
parrotia

Parrotia persica, autumn

- ❑ Height at 25 years 15 ft (4.5 m); when mature, 20-40 ft (6-12 m)
- ❑ Spread 15-30 ft (4.5-9 m)
- ❑ Well-drained loamy soil
- ❑ Deciduous broadleaf
- ❑ Hardy zones 5-8
- ❑ Features: fall foliage; bark; early-spring flowers

The lovely parrotia tree (*Parrotia persica*) provides interest all year with its spreading leafy top, fine fall tints, winter flowers, and flaking bark. Seldom seen in American gardens, parrotia is one of the finest small specimen trees.

This slow-growing tree develops a single short trunk or several stems. It can be pruned to a single trunk or left to grow into a spreading shrub. With age, the gray bark flakes off to reveal patches of silver-white or golden new bark beneath.

The oval midgreen leaves, up to 4 in (10 cm) long, develop beautiful amber, crimson, and gold tints before they fall. In late winter or early spring, flowers with prominent red stamens appear on the leafless branches. Though parro-

Parrotia persica, flowers

tia grows only 20-40 ft (6-12 m) tall, it needs space to spread out.

Cultivation
Plant in well-drained soil in early spring. The tree thrives in neutral to slightly acid soil but is also tolerant of alkaline soil. Although it will withstand full sun, it flourishes in a lightly shaded site.
Pruning Prune in spring; remove lower branches to expose the attractive bark.
Pests/diseases Japanese beetles may attack foliage.

Parrotia persica, bark

Paulownia
empress tree, princess tree

Paulownia tomentosa

Paulownia tomentosa, flowers

- ❏ Height at 25 years 30 ft (9 m); when mature, 30-60 ft (9-18 m) or more
- ❏ Spread 23-30 ft (7-9 m)
- ❏ Deep, well-drained loamy soil
- ❏ Deciduous broadleaf
- ❏ Hardy zones 6-9
- ❏ Features: foxglovelike flowers; foliage

The somewhat coarse empress tree is wonderful in bloom. In midspring the 2 in (5 cm) long, tubular flowers stand in upright sprays above the heart-shaped leaves. The blooms, which are pale violet with dark spots and yellow stripes inside, exude a sweet scent of vanilla.

Although the tree is hardy into New York state and the southern Midwest, the flowers may not be: the flower buds are formed in fall, and in northern regions they may be killed by winter frosts.

The trees may be pruned hard back to the ground ("stooled" or "pollarded") each year and grown as shrubs or accent plants. Treated this way, the vigorous shoots will grow up to 10 ft (3 m) high in a season, bearing leaves up to 2 ft (60 cm) wide — but no flowers.

The large leaves are heart-shaped and 10 in (25 cm) long. Their size may make fall raking a chore. The empress tree's fast growth also comes at a price: the soft, brittle wood is subject to breakage by storms, and older specimens may thus develop a misshapen appearance. The empress tree is delightful at the edge of a landscape, where it can be the focal point in spring.

Popular species
Paulownia tomentosa, syn. *P. imperialis*, will grow 15 ft (4.5 m) in 4 or 5 years, but commonly stops at 30-40 ft (9-12 m), with an equal spread. Specimens 50-60 ft (15-18 m) are not uncommon.

Cultivation
Plant in a sunny, sheltered spot in early spring in deep, well-drained loamy soil. Tolerant of pollution, the trees cast dense shade but litter the ground in fall with leaf pods and huge leaves.
Pruning Little pruning is needed. If grown as a stooled plant, the tree should be cut down to ground level each year in winter.
Pests/diseases Leaf spot shows as yellow-brown lesions, which later turn gray, or as spots with dark edges. Powdery mildew may attack foliage, and twig canker may cause the dieback of branch tips.

PEAR, ORNAMENTAL —
see *Pyrus*
PECAN — see *Carya*
PEPPERIDGE — see *Nyssa*
PLUM, ORNAMENTAL —
see *Prunus*

Populus
poplar

Populus trichocarpa

❏ Height at 25 years 25-60 ft (7.5-18 m); when mature, 50-100 ft (15-30 m)
❏ Spread to 75 ft (22.5 m)
❏ Ordinary garden soil
❏ Deciduous broadleaf
❏ Hardy zones 2-9
❏ Features: foliage; fast-growing

Poplars are fast-growing, ornamental (if coarse), and tolerant of pollution. They serve as windbreaks for exposed sites and are handsome as a small grove at the back of a landscape.

Popular species
Populus alba (abele or white poplar), up to 40-70 ft (12-21 m) high with a similar spread, has gray-green lobed leaves with white woolly undersides. Hardy in zones 3-8, it thrives on alkaline soil. 'Pyramidalis' ('Bolleana') is conical with erect branches.
Populus deltoides (eastern cottonwood), up to 75-100 ft (22.5-30 m) high and 50-75 ft (15-22.5 m) wide has light green deltoid leaves that are bright green on the undersides. A drought- and cold-resistant tree that is hardy in zones 2-9, it thrives in the Plains states.

Populus tremuloides

Populus × *canadensis* (Carolina poplar) is a group of hybrids that may reach 60 ft (18 m) in height. Columnar in shape, they include 'Eugenei' (young leaves coppery), 'Robusta' (young leaves coppery red), 'Serotina' (open habit; young leaves bronze), and 'Serotina Aurea' (young golden leaves mature through yellowish green to golden in fall). It is hardy in zones 3-9.
Populus lasiocarpa (Chinese poplar), up to 60 ft (18 m) high and 30 ft (9 m) wide, is hardy to zone 5. Its heart-shaped leathery leaves have red veins and stalks.
Populus tremuloides (quaking aspen) is a fast-growing, relatively short-lived native that grows 40-50 ft (12-15 m) high and spreads 20-30 ft (6-9 m) wide. The heart-shaped leaves show their silver undersides as they flutter in the slightest breeze; in fall the leaves turn a glorious yellow. It is hardy in zones 1-6.
Populus trichocarpa (black cottonwood) is similar to *P. balsamifera*, but grows rapidly to 60 ft (18 m) high and 20 ft (6 m) wide. It is hardy in zones 2-4.

Cultivation
Plant in any type of garden soil in a sunny, open spot from late fall to early spring. Position tallest types at least 100 ft (30 m) from buildings and drains, which can be damaged by the roots.
Pruning None is required.
Pests/diseases Bacterial canker, bracket fungus, rust, and silver leaf may cause problems.

PRINCESS TREE — see *Paulownia*

Prunus
almond, cherry, plum

Prunus padus, flowers

❏ Height at 25 years 12-40 ft (3.6-12 m); when mature, up to 40-60 ft (12-18 m)
❏ Spread 5-30 ft (1.5-9 m)
❏ Any well-drained soil
❏ Deciduous broadleaf
❏ Hardy zones 3-9, depending on species and cultivar
❏ Features: flowers; fall foliage

The large *Prunus* genus includes some of our most beautiful flowering trees, such as ornamental almonds, cherries, and plums. They bloom from late winter onward (depending on the local climate), before or at the same time as the leaves unfold, and many have outstanding fall colors.
Prunus species and cultivars make spectacular specimen trees, with types to suit the smallest gardens. For shrubby kinds, see pages 122-124.

Popular species
Ornamental almonds flower in early spring before the toothed lance-shaped leaves appear. The green fruits rarely ripen.
Prunus dulcis (common almond), syn. *P. amygdalus*, is up to 25 ft (7.5 m) high and wide with soft pink flowers. 'Alba' is white and 'Roseo-plena' has double pink flowers. It is hardy to zone 6.
Ornamental cherries have toothed, pointed oval leaves and bear dense clusters or sprays of flowers.
Prunus avium (mazzard or wild cherry), up to 40 ft (12 m) high and 30 ft (9 m) wide, has crimson fall tints. Pendent clusters of white flowers appear in midspring and are followed by dark red fruits. 'Plena' has profuse double flowers. It is hardy in zones 3-8.

Prunus serrula, bark

Prunus sargentii, autumn

Prunus avium 'Plena'

Prunus 'Kwanzan'

Prunus padus (bird cherry), up to 40 ft (12 m) high and 20 ft (6 m) wide, provides drooping sprays of small, white almond-scented flowers in late spring and black fruits. Cultivars include 'Albertii' (erect; profuse flowers), 'Colorata' (coppery young foliage; pale pink flowers), 'Plena' (double flowers), and 'Watereri' (flower sprays up to 8 in/20 cm long). It is hardy in zones 3-7.

Prunus sargentii, a round-headed tree up to 30 ft (9 m) high and wide, has rich brown bark. The foliage is bronze-red in spring and orange and crimson in early fall. The large, clear pink flowers appear from early spring. This tree does not tolerate air pollution. It is hardy in zones 5-7.

Prunus serotina (black or rum cherry), up to 50-60 ft (15-18 m) high and 30 ft (9 m) wide, has glossy, deep green leaves with yellow fall tints. Sprays up to 6 in (15 cm) long of white flowers appear in late spring. It is hardy in zones 3-9.

Prunus serrula is up to 15 ft (4.5 m) high and wide. It has glistening mahogany-brown flaking bark, narrow leaves, and small white flowers in midspring. It is hardy to zone 6.

Prunus serrulata hybrids, commonly called Japanese cherries, often reach a height of 20-25 ft (6-7.5 m) with an equal spread. The leaves are bronze when young, and the trees flower in midspring. It is hardy to zone 6. Cultivars include 'Amanogawa' (erect and narrow, to 20 ft/6 m high, 5 ft/1.5 m wide; pale pink semidouble flowers), 'Fugenzo' (dense, flat-topped tree; large, rose-pink double flowers), 'Jonioi' (white, especially fragrant flowers), 'Kiku-Shidare-Sakura' (weeping; deep pink double flowers), 'Kwanzan' (popular, vase-shaped tree; purple-pink double flowers), 'Mt. Fuji' (white, fragrant, semidouble flowers), 'Pink Perfection' (vase-shaped tree; clear pink flowers), 'Shirofugen'

Prunus 'Amanogawa'

Prunus subhirtella

Prunus cerasifera 'Atropurpurea'

(drooping branches; orange fall tints; large white double flowers that turn purple-pink in late spring), and 'Tai Haku' (robust tree; large, glistening white single flowers; young copper-red leaves).

Prunus subhirtella (spring cherry), grows up to 20-30 ft (6-9 m) high and wide, and bears profuse pale pink flowers in early spring before the leaves appear. The tree produces black fruits and often turns handsome colors in the fall. It is hardy in zones 5-8. Its cultivars include 'Autumnalis' (fall cherry, white or pale pink semidouble flowers in mild spells in late fall or early spring), 'Autumnalis Rosea' (pink semidouble flowers in late fall or early spring), 'Pendula Rosea' (drooping branches; blush-pink), and 'Pendula Rubra' (drooping branches; deep rose-pink).

Ornamental plums have oval, narrow purple leaves.

Prunus × blireiana is a small tree or large shrub up to 20 ft (6 m) high and 20 ft (6 m) wide. Rose-pink double flowers appear in early spring just before the bronze young leaves, which eventually turn green. It is hardy to zone 6.

Prunus cerasifera (cherry plum), a bushy tree that grows up to 30 ft (9 m) high and wide, is useful for hedging. It bears profuse white flowers in the early spring before the midgreen leaves appear. Mature trees will bear red or yellow small fruits. It is hardy in zones 5-8. Cultivars include 'Atropurpurea' ('Pissardii'; dark red young leaves turning deep purple; white flowers opening from pink buds) and 'Newport' (dark purple leaves; pale pink flowers).

Cultivation

Plant in early spring to midspring in any well-drained soil. The trees thrive in any good, moist but well-drained garden soil.

Pruning Prune immediately after flowering; remove crossing and damaged shoots.

Pests/diseases Black knot fungus causes black, roughly cylindrical galls to form on twigs of cherries and plums. Leaf spot fungi may cause "shot holes" to appear in leaves and will defoliate trees if not controlled. Peach tree borers may tunnel into trunks at their bases, killing trees if not controlled. Scale may infest trees. Tent caterpillars may weave their nests in cherries and plums. Troublesome diseases include canker, chlorosis, honey fungus, silver leaf, and witches'-brooms.

Pterocarya
Caucasian wingnut

Pterocarya fraxinifolia, fruits

❏ Height at 25 years 33 ft (10 m); when
mature, 50 ft (15 m) or more
❏ Spread similar to height
❏ Any moist, fertile soil
❏ Deciduous broadleaf
❏ Hardy zones 6-8
❏ Features: foliage; catkins; fruits

Caucasian wingnut (*Pterocarya fraxinifolia*, syn. *P. caucasica*) is not well known in the US but is a handsomer tree than its relative the walnut *(Juglans)*. The wingnut is a fast-growing tree with a broad, spreading top and has long, dangling strings of winged fruits in fall. It makes a good shade or specimen tree.

The 2 ft (60 cm) long leaves are divided into numerous finely toothed leaflets, each up to 8 in (20 cm) long. The greenish catkins, which appear in summer, are up to 20 in (50 cm) long. The tree usually has a short, thick trunk with deeply furrowed bark. It is likely to grow suckers at the base of the trunk; if these are not removed, the tree will form a thicket of several stems.

The hybrid *P. × rehderana* has long-lasting catkins and fruits.

Cultivation
Plant young Caucasian wingnuts in midfall or early spring in any fertile, deep, moist soil in an open site. These trees do well by water.
Pruning Remove suckers as they appear; prune in summer.
Pests/diseases Gall mites cause blisterlike pouches on the leaves.

Pyrus
ornamental pear

Pyrus salicifolia 'Pendula'

❏ Height at 25 years 10-25 ft (3-7.5 m);
when mature, up to 50 ft (15 m)
❏ Spread 6-35 ft (1.8-10.5 m)
❏ Any well-drained soil
❏ Deciduous broadleaf
❏ Hardy zones 3-8
❏ Features: foliage; flowers; fall tints

An ornamental pear is a fine sight in a lawn, flourishing even in cold areas and tolerant of sea winds and both wet and dry soils. The genus *Pyrus*, which includes the common fruiting pear, provides a range of beautiful specimen trees for large and small gardens, with their profuse clusters of snowy flowers and pale foliage.

The toothed leaves, up to 4 in (10 cm) long, are green or gray-green and sometimes glossy. Some species develop rich fall tints in shades of bronze, crimson, orange, or yellow. The five-petaled flowers are white or creamy white and appear in clusters in midspring, though *P. ussuriensis* blooms in early spring. The blooms are followed by small rounded or pear-shaped fruits, which are generally rather inconspicuous and mostly inedible.

Popular species
Pyrus calleryana, a Chinese tree that grows up to 50 ft (15 m) high and 35 ft (10.5 m) wide, has thorny branches and oval, glossy green, finely toothed leaves. The small fruits are brownish. The cultivar 'Autumn Blaze' is extremely cold hardy and turns an outstanding reddish purple in the fall; 'Bradford' is thornless and conical in profile, especially fast-growing, free-flowering, and resistant to fire blight; 'Capital,' a possible substitute for Lombardy poplar, is upright and its leaves turn a copper color in fall; 'Chanticleer,' which is more narrowly conical than 'Bradford' and also free-flowering and thornless, grows up to 35 ft (10.5 m) tall and 15 ft (4.5 m) wide; 'Redspire' is pyramidal, more graceful in form than 'Bradford' but slower-growing. It is hardy in zones 6-8.
Pyrus nivalis (snow pear) is up to 16 ft (4.8 m) high and wide. The profuse white flowers appear with the silvery gray young leaves. The small rounded fruits are yellowish green and taste sweet. It is hardy to zone 6.

Quercus
oak

Pyrus ussuriensis, flowers

Pyrus salicifolia (willow-leaved pear), a graceful tree from the Caucasus, is up to 25 ft (7.5 m) tall and almost as wide, with graceful arching branches. The narrow willowlike leaves are silvery at first, becoming gray-green. The creamy white flowers are followed by small brownish fruits. It is hardy in zones 5-7. The cultivars 'Pendula' and 'Silver Frost' have weeping branches, often right to the ground, and more silvery foliage.

Pyrus ussuriensis (Chinese pear) reaches a height of 40-50 ft (12-15 m). The oval or rounded leaves have bristly teeth and turn bronze-crimson in fall. Profuse white flowers appear in early spring, followed later by rounded yellowish fruits. It is hardy in zones 3-7.

Cultivation
Plant ornamental pear trees in any well-drained soil in a sunny spot in late fall or early spring. They are exceptionally tolerant of air pollution.

Pruning Prune to maintain shape in winter or early spring.

Pests/diseases Aphids may infest young growths. Black sooty mold grows on their sticky deposits, and young leaves are distorted. Fire blight blackens and shrivels the flowers and may kill the young shoots and branches. Leaves turn brown and shrivel, but do not fall. *Pyrus salicifolia* and *P. calleryana* 'Autumn Blaze,' 'Capital,' and 'Redspire' are particularly susceptible.

Quercus rubra 'Aurea'

☐ Height at 25 years 15-40 ft (4.5-12 m); when mature, up to 100 ft (30 m)
☐ Spread varies, usually equal to height
☐ Acid soils; some species are alkaline tolerant
☐ Deciduous broadleaf
☐ Hardy zones 3-9
☐ Features: foliage; fruits; attractive form

Synonymous with strength, the oak tree is one of the longest-lived and grandest additions to any landscape. The oak's branches may run straight out 50 ft (15 m) from the trunk, seemingly immune to gravity. But if the wood is tough, the roots are not, and oaks are typically sensitive both to transplanting and to disturbance of the soil in which they grow. When treated well, however, an oak tree is a premier shade tree, and many of the species grow surprisingly fast.

Popular species
Quercus alba (white oak) is an American species, growing 50-80 ft (15-24 m) tall with an equal spread. The horizontal branches bear oval, irregularly lobed leaves that, despite their name, open pinkish red, mature to soft green, and turn purple-crimson in fall. It is hardy in zones 3-9.

Quercus cerris (Turkey oak) grows to a height and spread of 40-60 ft (12-18 m). It is hardy in zones 6-8 and tolerates drought and clay soils. It has deeply lobed, hairy green leaves, and the acorns have mossy cups. The cultivar 'Variegata' ('Argenteo-variegata') has wide creamy white margins on the leaves.

Quercus coccinea (scarlet oak) reaches a height of 75 ft (22.5 m) with a spread of 50 ft (15 m) and tolerates alkaline soils. Its leaves are toothed, lobed, and glossy green. They turn scarlet in fall and persist well into winter. It is hardy in zones 5-9.

Quercus palustris (pin oak) is a fast-growing tree that reaches a height of 60-70 ft (18-21 m) with a spread of 25-40 ft (7.5-12 m). Its deeply cut leaves are glossy green, turning to bronze or russet in fall. It is easily transplanted and tolerates city conditions. It is hardy in zones 5-8.

Quercus phellos (willow oak) reaches a height of 40-60 ft (12-18 m) and a width of 30-40 ft (9-12 m). Its narrow, lance-shaped willowlike leaves are dark green, turning yellow-brown or russet in the fall. Easily transplanted, it is alkaline tolerant and is hardy in zones 6-9.

Quercus robur (English oak) is a slow-growing, long-lived species up to 60 ft (18 m) high and wide.

Quercus robur 'Concordia'

Quercus cerris 'Variegata,' foliage

Q. robur is alkaline tolerant; its midgreen to deep green leaves have rounded lobes and very short stalks. It is hardy in zones 6-8. Cultivars include 'Concordia' (golden oak; slow-growing, rounded tree to 15 ft/4.5 m high and wide; golden yellow leaves) and 'Fastigiata' (columnar).

Quercus rubra is a rounded tree up to 30 ft (9 m) high and wide. The leaves have deep, pointed lobes and develop red, yellow, and brown fall tints. The tree is moderately fast-growing and tolerates air pollution. The cultivar 'Aurea' has bright yellow young leaves; it does best in light shade. It is hardy in zones 3-8.

Cultivation

Grow oak trees in any rich, deep, and well-drained soil — preferably in an open site in full sun, though they tolerate partial shade. Plant in midfall or early spring. During the first few years apply an annual mulch of well-rotted organic matter.

Pruning Remove lower lateral branches in late winter when the trees are 2 to 3 years old to maintain a clean trunk.

Pests/diseases Anthracnose causes spotting of the leaves and in wet seasons may defoliate trees. Gypsy moth caterpillars favor oaks, defoliating trees when these insects are abundant. Shoestring root rot envelops roots with black fungal strands and surrounds trees with mushrooms, eventually killing the host. Scale insects may cause dieback of twigs or death of young trees.

REDBUD — see *Cercis*
REDWOOD — see *Metasequoia*

Rhus
sumac

Rhus typhina

Rhus typhina, fall colors

Rhus typhina, fruits

❏ Height at 25 years 15-20 ft (4.5-6 m); when mature, up to 25 ft (7.5 m)
❏ Spread 15-20 ft (4.5-6 m)
❏ Any ordinary garden soil
❏ Deciduous broadleaf
❏ Hardy zones 3-8
❏ Features: interesting foliage and bark; flowers; fall tints

Sumacs are outstanding small garden trees, with attractive foliage developing dramatic shades of red, orange, yellow, and purple in fall. In summer sumacs produce dense, fluffy upright sprays of creamy or greenish flowers, followed later on female trees by showy clusters of red fruits.

The leaves, which are 6-24 in (15-60 cm) long, are divided into many coarsely toothed leaflets.

For shrubby sumac, see page 128.

Popular species
Rhus chinensis (Chinese sumac) is a round-headed tree or large shrub from Japan, China, Korea, and southeastern Asia. Growing up to 24 ft (7.2 m) high and 15 ft (4.5 m) wide, it has leaves up to 6 in (15 cm) long with rich fall tints. The creamy white flower sprays are up to 10 in (25 cm) high and appear in late summer. This species does best in mild, sheltered gardens; late growths may be cut back by frost. It is hardy in zones 6-8.

Rhus typhina (staghorn sumac), from eastern North America, is a small tree or large shrub, eventually up to 25 ft (7.5 m) high and wide. It is flat-topped with sparse, spreading branches, giving it a gaunt appearance in winter. The young shoots, leaves, and fruits are covered with soft velvety hairs. The midgreen leaves are up to 2 ft (60 cm) long and divided into numerous toothed leaflets. From early fall they develop rich tints of orange, red, yellow, and purple. The upright flower clusters are greenish and up to 8 in (20 cm) high. On female trees they are followed by long-lasting red fruits. This species can be pruned back to the ground annually, so that it forms a thicket of lush foliage. It tolerates air pollution and will thrive in city gardens. 'Laciniata' is a female clone with deeply cut fernlike leaflets that turn orange and yellow in fall. It is hardy in zones 3-8.

Cultivation
Sumac thrives in any ordinary garden soil. Plant in midfall or midspring, preferably in a sunny spot.
Pruning None is essential. To obtain lush foliage, prune *R. typhina* to the ground each year in late winter to midspring. Remove suckering stems at the same time.
Pests/diseases No serious problems — though leaf spot may afflict leaves, and aphids, mites, and scales may infest stems and foliage.

Robinia
locust

Robinia pseudoacacia

Robinia pseudoacacia, flowers

Robinia pseudoacacia, bark

❏ Height at 25 years up to 30 ft (9 m); when mature, 40-50 ft (12-15 m)
❏ Spread 15-35 ft (4.5-10.5 m)
❏ Any ordinary soil
❏ Deciduous broadleaf
❏ Hardy zones 3-8
❏ Features: flowers; attractive foliage

Locusts are popular, fast-growing ornamental trees that thrive even in the polluted air and poor soil of city gardens. In summer they bear drooping clusters of scented pink or white pealike flowers. The fernlike leaves are divided into oval leaflets and cast light shade; the branches may have thorns. For shrubby *Robinia* see pages 129-130.

Popular species
Robinia × ambigua, a hybrid of *R. pseudoacacia* and *R. viscosa* grows up to 40 ft (12 m) high and 25 ft (7.5 m) wide. It has slightly sticky young growths and clusters of fragrant pink flowers in early summer. Cultivars are 'Idahoensis' (syn. 'Idaho'; large sprays of pink to purplish flowers) and 'Purple Robe' (dark pink flowers; reddish new growth).

Robinia pseudoacacia (black or common locust), from eastern North America, is up to 50 ft (15 m) high and 35 ft (10.5 m) wide. It has rugged blackish bark that is deeply furrowed. The leaves are divided into many light green oval leaflets and turn golden or rich orange in fall. White blooms, held in drooping sprays up to 8 in (20 cm) long, appear in early summer and attract bees. They are followed soon afterwards by poisonous brown fruits. Cultivars are 'Frisia' (red thorns and young growths; golden yellow leaves), 'Inermis' (thornless; compact growth; rarely flowers), 'Pyramidalis' (narrow columnar tree), 'Rozynskyana' (spreading branches, drooping at tips; drooping leaves), and 'Umbraculifera' (similar to 'Inermis'; dense umbrellalike canopy; virtually thornless; seldom flowers).

Cultivation
Plant in midfall or early spring in any ordinary well-drained soil in a reasonably sheltered, sunny spot. Robinias tolerate drought and thrive in poor or disturbed soils.
Pruning Suckering stems should be removed as soon as seen.
Pests/diseases Stem borers, leaf miners, and scale insects may infest the trees.

Salix
willow

Salix babylonica

Salix alba 'Chermesina,' winter

Salix matsudana 'Tortuosa'

❏ Height at 25 years 15-40 ft (4.5-12 m); when mature, 25-75 ft (7.5-22.5 m) or more
❏ Spread 8-50 ft (2.4-15 m)
❏ Moist soil
❏ Hardy zones 2-8
❏ Deciduous broadleaf
❏ Features: graceful form; catkins; winter shoots

Willows range from creeping alpines to lofty trees that make outstanding specimen trees for large gardens. They have a graceful form, fluffy early-spring catkins, and colored winter shoots. See also pages 131-132.

Popular species
Salix alba (white willow) is up to 75 ft (22.5 m) high and 50 ft (15 m) wide, with drooping branch tips and tapering, narrow, downy gray-green leaves. 'Chermesina' (syn. 'Britzensis') has orange-red winter shoots; 'Sericea' is slower growing with silvery leaves; *S. a. vitellina* has bright yellow shoots. *S. a.* 'Tristis,' the golden weeping willow, also sold as *S. a.* 'Vitellina Pendula' or *Salix* × *chrysocoma*, is a weeping tree up to 40 ft (12 m) high and 30 ft (9 m) wide. Hardy in zones 2-9, it has arching branches and slender yellow branchlets.
Salix babylonica (weeping willow) is up to 36 ft (10.8 m) high and 40 ft (12 m) wide, with narrow leaves on pendulous branches. 'Annularis' or 'Crispa' has twisted leaves. It is hardy in zones 6-8.
Salix caprea (goat willow) grows 15-25 ft (4.5-7.5 m) high with a 12-15 ft (3.6-4.5 m) spread. The 2 in (5 cm) long, silky male catkins appear in early spring, making this the best of the "pussy willows." It is hardy in zones 5-8.
Salix matsudana (Pekin willow) is up to 50 ft (15 m) high and 25 ft (7.5 m) wide and drought tolerant. It is usually conical with yellow shoots and pointed leaves that are gray beneath. Cultivars are 'Tortuosa' (corkscrew willow; twisted leaves and branches) and 'Umbraculifera' (bushy; 25-35 ft/7.5-10.5 m tall). It is hardy in zones 6-8.
Salix pentandra (bay willow) is a handsome upright tree up to 35 ft (10.5 m) high. The twigs and aromatic baylike leaves are glossy. It is hardy in zones 2-6.

Cultivation
Plant in midfall or early spring in deep, moist soil. Site them well away from buildings and drains.
Pruning Remove deadwood between late fall and late winter. Willows grown for their colored stems should be cut back hard annually or every other year in early spring.
Pests/diseases Aphids and sawfly larvae may infest leaves. Caterpillars and various beetle larvae may eat leaves. It is prone to many cankers.

SILVER BELL TREE — see *Halesia*
SNOWBELL — see *Styrax*
SNOWDROP TREE — see *Halesia*

Sophora
Japanese pagoda tree

Sophora japonica 'Pendula'

❏ Height at 25 years 20-25 ft (6-7.5 m); when mature, 50-75 ft (15-22.5 m)
❏ Spread comparable to height
❏ Any well-drained soil
❏ Deciduous broadleaf
❏ Hardy zones 4-8
❏ Features: foliage; flowers

The Japanese pagoda tree, *Sophora japonica*, from China, Korea, and Japan, is an elegant and ornamental tree whose graceful foliage casts light shade. It grows at a medium to fast rate, adding as much as 3 ft (90 cm) to its height each year while it is young and then rapidly developing into a good-sized, round-headed specimen tree.

The attractive midgreen foliage, up to 1 ft (30 cm) long, is divided into rounded to oval leaflets, arranged in pairs. Established trees, when they are 15 to 20 years old, bear a profusion of creamy white, pealike flowers that are held in pendent clusters up to 10 in (25 cm) long in late summer and midfall. The showy blossoms are followed by long bright green seedpods that turn yellow and remain on the branches well into winter.

The cultivar 'Pendula,' with its stiffly drooping branches and graceful outline in winter, makes a fine lawn specimen. 'Regent' is more vigorous and flowers at an earlier age than the species. 'Princeton Upright' is similar to 'Regent' but with a compact upright form.

Sophora japonica, flowers

Cultivation
Plant in early spring or midspring when the ground has warmed, in any good and well-drained but moisture-retentive soil. Transplant sophoras when young, as balled-and-burlapped specimens. Somewhat frost-tender when young, they acquire greater cold and drought hardiness with age.

They are also tolerant of heat and air pollution.

Pruning Lower branches can be removed in fall to give headroom and leave a clear section of trunk.

Pests/diseases Canker and twig blight may cause the dieback of branches. Leafhoppers may kill young stems, causing witches'-brooms to form.

Sorbus
mountain ash, rowan, whitebeam

Sorbus aucuparia, flowers

❏ Height at 25 years 12-25 ft (3.6-7.5 m); when mature, up to 50 ft (15 m)
❏ Spread equal to or less than height
❏ Any well-drained soil
❏ Deciduous broadleaf
❏ Hardy zones 5-7
❏ Features: foliage; fall tints; fruit

Sorbus is an important group of tough, hardy trees. Most have attractive foliage and produce a brief show of white flowers in late spring to early summer. But they come into their full glory in late summer to early fall, when the branches are hung with bunches of berries in shades of red, yellow, orange, pink, and white. Soon afterward these brilliant colors are complemented by fine fall foliage tints.

Mountain ashes will flourish where the weather is cool and moist. Where stressed, as in areas of extreme summer heat, they are so susceptible to pests and diseases (particularly borers and fire blight) that they may provide more aggravation than pleasure.

Popular species
Sorbus alnifolia grows 40-50 ft (12-15 m) high with a spread of 20-30 ft (6-9 m). Its oval, toothed leaves are shiny dark green in summer and turn yellow, orange, and golden brown in fall. The white flowers form flattened clusters up to 2-3 in (5-7.5 cm) wide in midspring. They are followed by spectacular bunches of orange-red to scarlet fruits. This is the

Sorbus aucuparia, fall

Sorbus aria

most borer resistant of the mountain ashes. *S. alnifolia* is hardy in zones 3-7.

Sorbus aria (whitebeam), from Europe, up to 45 ft (13.5 m) high, has compound — feathered — leaves of multiple toothed leaflets. Silvery white when young, the foliage later becomes glossy dark green with gray-white hairy undersides and turns russet and gold in fall. Creamy white flowers in clusters up to 5 in (13 cm) wide are followed by bunches of red fruits in early fall. Cultivars include 'Majestica' ('Decaisneana'; larger leaves and fruits). Hardy to zone 6, it thrives on alkaline soils.

Sorbus aucuparia (mountain ash, rowan), from Europe, 20-40 ft (6-12 m) tall, achieves a spread two-thirds its height. It has midgreen leaves that are gray beneath and divided into many sharply toothed leaflets. They turn yellow and red from midfall onward. White flower heads that are up to 6 in (15 cm) wide in midspring are followed by large bunches of edible orange-red fruits, which begin to ripen in late summer. The tree is short-

lived in shallow alkaline soils. Cultivars include 'Asplenifolia' (ferny leaves), 'Beissneri' (compact, upright; red young shoots; amber-orange bark; yellow-green leaves), 'Black Hawk' (columnar tree; large orange fruits), 'Cardinal Royal' (vigorous, upright tree; brilliant red fruits in late summer), 'Edulis' (larger leaves and fruits), and 'Fastigiata' (columnar; slow-growing). It is hardy in zones 3-7.

Sorbus cashmiriana, from Kashmir, is an elegant, open tree that grows to a height of 20-40 ft (6-12 m) with a similar spread. It has leaves similar to those of *S. aucuparia.* In late spring pale pink flowers appear in 4 in (10 cm) wide clusters, followed by glistening white, long-lasting fruits. It is hardy to zone 5.

Sorbus hupehensis, from western China, grows up to 20 ft (6 m) high and 12 ft (3.6 m) wide with ascending branches. It has blue-green leaves that are similar to those of *S. aucuparia,* and red or orange fall colors. White flowers borne in clusters up to 3 in (7.5 cm) wide appear in summer, followed by long-lasting loose

bunches of white or pink-tinged fruits.

Sorbus intermedia (Swedish whitebeam), from northwestern Europe, is up to 18 ft (5.4 m) high and wide. White flowers in 4 in (10 cm) clusters appear in late spring, followed by large, bright red fruits. It is hardy to zone 6.

Sorbus sargentiana, from western China, reaches a height of 30 ft (9 m) high. It has midgreen leaves up to 1 ft (30 cm) long, similar to those of *S. aucuparia* but with fewer, larger pointed leaflets. Felted and white underneath, they turn red in fall. The sticky bright red-brown winter buds open in late spring into white flower clusters, followed later by orange-red fruits in wide, flattened bunches. It is hardy to zone 7.

Sorbus vilmorinii, from western China, is a large shrub or small tree up to 18 ft (5.4 m) high and wide. It has midgreen leaves similar to those of *S. aucuparia* but with more and smaller ferny leaflets. They turn red and purple in fall. Loose white flower clusters appear in late spring, followed by loose bunches of rose-red fruits, which turn white, tinged pink, when ripe. It is hardy to zone 6.

Cultivation

Plant in any well-drained soil in midfall or early spring; a sunny or partially shaded spot is best.

Sorbus aucuparia, fruit

Trees are tolerant of cold winds, but leaves may scorch in areas of intense sunlight and summer heat. *Sorbus aucuparia* and its hybrids are unsuitable for alkaline soils.

Pruning There are no special requirements.

Pests/diseases Fire blight may devastate mountain ashes, particularly in areas where they are stressed by air pollution or heat. Crown gall may attack the base of trees, forming swollen knots of tissue, and leaf rusts may disfigure foliage, producing clusters of orange horn-shaped structures on leaves. Borers may tunnel into wood at the base of trunks, weakening or killing the tree. Aphids also commonly infest mountain ashes.

SOUTHERN BEECH —
see *Nothofagus*
STAGHORN SUMAC —
see *Rhus*

Sorbus vilmorinii

Stewartia
stewartia

Stewartia pseudocamellia, fall colors

❏ Height at 25 years 12-20 ft (3.6-6 m); when mature, up to 40 ft (12 m)
❏ Spread 12-30 ft (3.6-9 m)
❏ Well-drained, acid soil
❏ Deciduous broadleaf
❏ Hardy zones 5-9
❏ Features: flowers; fall tints; peeling bark

Related to the genus *Camellia,* stewartias are slow-growing trees and shrubs, with lovely flowers, rich fall tints, and attractive peeling bark.

The oval leaves develop brilliant yellow, red, and scarlet tints. The camellialike blossoms are white with golden centers. They are short-lived but are produced in succession throughout the summer.

Popular species
Stewartia koreana, from Korea, reaches a height of 20-30 ft (6-9 m), with an upright pyramidal profile. The dark green leaves turn reddish purple in fall, and the flowers measure 3 in (7.5 cm) wide. It is hardy in zones 6-7.
Stewartia malacodendron, also from Korea, is up to 15 ft (4.5 m) high and wide. The oval hairy leaves turn reddish purple in fall. The white flowers, 3 in (7.5 cm) wide, have purple stamens and bluish anthers. It is hardy in zones 7-9.
Stewartia pseudocamellia, from Japan, grows 20-40 ft (6-12 m)

Stewartia malacodendron, flowers

tall and 15-30 ft (4.5-9 m) wide, with yellow and red fall tints. The orange-brown bark peels away to reveal lighter orange bark beneath. The cup-shaped white flowers have yellow anthers. It is hardy in zones 5-7.
Stewartia sinensis, from China, reaches a height of 15-25 ft (4.5-7.5 m). It has crimson fall tints and fragrant white flowers up to 2 in (5 cm) wide. The bark is an attractive shade of brownish purple. It is hardy in zones 6-7.

Cultivation
Transplant when still small in early spring to a site with well-drained, acid soil and ideally some midday shade.
Pruning Rarely needed.
Pests/diseases Trouble free.

Styrax
snowbell

Styrax obassia

❏ Height at 25 years 20 ft (6 m); when mature, up to 30 ft (9 m)
❏ Spread equal to height
❏ Moist, well-drained, acid soil
❏ Deciduous broadleaf
❏ Hardy zones 5-8
❏ Features: foliage; flowers

Snowbells are handsome specimen trees that grow slowly with wide-spreading branches and deep green foliage. Pendent bell-shaped white flowers with yellow stamens appear in late spring.

Popular species
Styrax japonicus, up to 20-30 ft (6-9 m) high and wide, has drooping branch tips and glossy oval leaves. The mildly fragrant flowers come in drooping clusters.
Styrax obassia grows 20-30 ft (6-9 m) high. Its rounded leaves are velvety beneath and it bears long, loose sprays of fragrant flowers.

Cultivation
Plant snowbells in early spring in moist, well-drained and organically enriched, acid soil in a site protected from cold winds. They prefer partial shade.
Pruning It has no special needs.
Pests/diseases Trouble free.

SUMAC — see *Rhus*
SWAMP CYPRESS — see *Taxodium*
SWEET GUM — see *Liquidambar*
SYCAMORE — see *Acer*

Taxodium
bald or swamp cypress

Taxodium distichum, root projections

Taxodium distichum, fall colors

❏ Height at 25 years 25-35 ft (7.5-10.5 m); when mature, 50-80 ft (15-24 m)
❏ Spread 10-30 ft (3-9 m)
❏ Fertile, moist soil
❏ Deciduous conifer
❏ Hardy zones 5-9
❏ Features: fall tints

The pond cypress *(Taxodium ascendens)* is a conical or columnar tree up to 70-80 ft (21-24 m) high and 15-20 ft (4.5-6 m) wide. The awl-shaped leaves are bright green, turning rich brown in fall.

Swamp cypress *(Taxodium distichum)* is a wonderful ornamental tree for large gardens with permanently moist soil and plenty of space. It has distinctive features: flaming fall colors and kneelike root projections that appear above the ground when the tree is grown by water. The latter help the tree obtain adequate air.

This long-lived, slow-growing deciduous conifer is native to swampy sections of the South; many ancient specimens grow in the Florida Everglades.

Swamp cypress is a columnar to broadly conical tree, up to 35 ft (10.5 m) high and 16 ft (4.8 m)

wide after 25 years, and eventually reaching up to 70 ft (21 m) with a width of 30 ft (9 m). The bark is pale red-brown, rather stringy, and closely ridged with smooth, shallow fissures.

The tiny needlelike leaves are bright yellow-green above, with two gray lines beneath, and develop fox-red and then russet fall tints. They are arranged spirally on long shoots and in opposite pairs on short shoots. The short shoots are dropped along with the leaves in fall.

Mature trees produce male and female flowers together in winter. Male flowers are clustered in purple catkins up to 6 in (15 cm) long, which are held in groups of three on the tips of the shoots. The less noticeable female flowers may be followed by round green 1 in (2.5 cm) wide cones, ripening to midbrown.

The cultivar 'Pendens' is a weeping form with drooping branches and branchlets.

Cultivation
Swamp cypresses thrive in moist, acid soil; pond cypresses thrive in

Taxodium distichum, foliage

wet soils but also adapt to well-drained or even dry ones. They need a sunny, open site. Once well established, cypresses are virtually windproof, riding out hurricanes without being uprooted.

Pruning None is needed except to maintain a single leader. When trees fork, eliminate one leader.

Pests/diseases Twig blight may cause dieback of branch tips in wet seasons. Cypress moths tunnel into needles, bundling them with webbing in late summer.

Tilia
linden

Tilia petiolaris

Tilia platyphyllos, flowers

❏ Height at 25 years 25-40 ft (7.5-12 m);
   when mature, 50-100 ft (15-30 m)
❏ Spread half to two-thirds of height
❏ Any moist, well-drained soil
❏ Deciduous broadleaf
❏ Hardy zones 2-8
❏ Features: graceful form; scented
   flowers; attractive foliage

Lindens are tall, graceful trees with a fine head of heart-shaped or rounded foliage. In summer fragrant creamy white flowers appear in pendent sprays toward the top of the tree, attracting swarms of bees. The flowers are followed later by rounded pealike fruits, which persist into winter.

Untrimmed, lindens are too large for most gardens. However, they tolerate hard pruning and can be pollarded and pleached. They are often infested by aphids, which drop large amounts of honeydew, staining anything below.

Popular species
Tilia americana (American linden or basswood) is fast-growing, up to 60-80 ft (18-24 m) high. It has long coarse-toothed leaves. 'Redmond' is dense and conical. It is hardy in zones 2-8.
Tilia cordata (little-leaf linden), syn. *T. parviflora,* is up to 60-70 ft (18-21 m) high. The dark, glossy green heart-shaped leaves are up to 3 in (7.5 cm) long. 'Glenleven' is fast-growing with a straight trunk; 'Greenspire' is columnar. It is hardy in zones 3-7.
Tilia × *euchlora* is up to 40-60 ft (12-18 m) high with shiny dark green leaves on arching branches. It is hardy in zones 3-7.
Tilia × *europaea* (European linden), syn. *T.* × *vulgaris,* is up to 100 ft (30 m) high with midgreen heart-shaped leaves and is prone to aphids. It is hardy in zones 3-7.
Tilia petiolaris (weeping silver linden) is a beautiful wide-spreading tree up to 30 ft (9 m) high and 18 ft (5.4 m) wide. The rounded, long-stalked leaves are finely toothed and mid- to dark green. It is hardy in zones 6-7.
Tilia platyphyllos (broad-leaved lime) grows 60-80 ft (18-24 m) high. Hardy to zone 3, it has midgreen heart-shaped leaves. 'Aurea' has yellow young shoots and 'Laciniata' has a cut-leaf form.
Tilia tomentosa (silver linden) grows to a height of 50-70 ft (15-21 m) and is pyramidal in profile when young, becoming rounded as it ages. It tolerates heat and drought. 'Sterling' offers leaves with silvered undersides and resistance to gypsy moth and Japanese beetle. It is hardy to zone 6.

Cultivation
Plant in midfall or early spring in any ordinary, moist but well-drained garden soil.
Pruning Remove sucker shoots from the base and trunk. Pleaching and pollarding should be done in late winter and early spring.
Pests/diseases Aphids, caterpillars, leaf spot, and powdery mildew may infest leaves; scales and linden mites may be problems.

TREE OF HEAVEN —
see *Ailanthus*
TULIP TREE —
see *Liriodendron*
TUPELO — see *Nyssa*

Tilia cordata

Tilia platyphyllos, fruits

Ulmus
elm

Ulmus parvifolia

❏ Height at 25 years 12-30 ft (3.6-9 m); when mature, up to 35-100 ft (10.5-30 m)
❏ Spread varies with species, commonly half to two-thirds of height
❏ Any ordinary soil
❏ Deciduous broadleaf
❏ Hardy zones 2-9
❏ Features: stately specimen tree

One of the horticultural tragedies of the last generation was the loss of countless elms to the Dutch elm disease; boulevards, parks, and campuses all over the country were denuded by this epidemic. The disease still threatens surviving specimens, and infected elm trees should be removed immediately.

The good news is that there are many disease-resistant elm species and cultivars that offer a variety of attractive forms as well as the elm's characteristic fast growth and adaptability to a wide range of conditions. These elms make excellent shade trees and display fine fall colors.

Popular species
Ulmus americana (American elm) was this country's favorite street tree until the onset of Dutch elm disease. Hardy in zones 2-9, it reaches a height of 60-80 ft (18-24 m) with a spread equal to half or two-thirds its height. The toothed ovate leaves are 3-6 in (7.5-15 cm) long and turn yellow in fall; the branches have gracefully drooping tips. This species is very susceptible to

Ulmus americana

Ulmus glabra 'Camperdownii'

Ulmus pumila (Siberian elm), from Asia, is a fast-growing, extremely adaptable tree that reaches a height of 50-70 ft (15-21 m) with a spread three-fourths of that. The narrow and thin leaves are toothed and dark green, turning yellow in fall. Though resistant to Dutch elm disease, its wood is brittle, and branches break with every storm. It is hardy in zones 4-9.

Cultivation
Plant elms in midfall or early spring in any ordinary garden soil in full sun. They are excellent trees for cold, exposed sites and tolerate salty soil.

Pruning It is important to cut out any diseased branches at the first sign of trouble.

Pests/diseases Dutch elm disease manifests itself in yellowing and wilting leaves on individual branches, and is eventually fatal to infected trees. Phloem necrosis, which shows in the defoliation of branch tips and leaf curling, is equally deadly. A variety of aphids, beetles, scales, and borers may also afflict elms.

Dutch elm disease, but a number of resistant cultivars have been introduced, including 'Delaware #2' (vigorous with a broad, spreading crown), 'Liberty,' and 'Washington' (outstanding glossy foliage).

Ulmus carpinifolia (smooth-leaf elm), from Europe, North Africa, and Asia, grows to 70-90 ft (21-27 m) high, with a pyramidal shape. The branches, which often droop at the tips, are set with deep green, coarsely toothed leaves, oval to round and leathery in texture; they become chrome-yellow in late fall. The species is superseded by cultivars, including 'Homestead' (symmetrical, pyramidal crown; rapid growth; resistant to Dutch elm disease and phloem necrosis), 'Pioneer' (globe-shaped crown; resistant to Dutch elm disease and phloem necrosis), and 'Sapporo Autumn Gold' (upright form reminiscent of American elm; golden fall color). It is hardy in zones 5-7.

Ulmus glabra (Scotch elm, elm-wych), from northern Europe, grows to 80-100 ft (24-30 m) tall with a spread of 50-70 ft (15-21 m). The toothed ovate leaves are midgreen, turning golden yellow in fall. Hardy in zones 5-7,

it is excellent for cold, exposed sites, and one of the few elms to set seeds; these crowd the bare branches in spring. Outstanding cultivars include 'Camperdownii' (compact; weeping branches) and 'Pendula' (flat-topped; spreading branches; pendulous twigs). This species is not resistant to Dutch elm disease.

Ulmus × hollandica (Dutch elm) is a natural hybrid of *U. carpinifolia* and *U. glabra*. It grows rapidly to 35 ft (10.5 m) with a spread of 16 ft (4.8 m). The rounded to ovate leaves are glossy green and take on yellow fall tints. It is hardy to zone 5. Its cultivars include disease-resistant types such as 'Bea Schwarz' and 'Christine Buisman.'

Ulmus parvifolia (Chinese elm) is a round-headed tree that grows 40-50 ft (12-15 m) or more high, with pendent spreading branches. The small, glossy green leaves are leathery; they turn yellowish or reddish purple in fall and persist well into winter. This species is very disease and beetle resistant. It is hardy in zones 5-9. Cultivars include 'Dynasty' (vase-shaped) and 'True Green' (evergreen; hardy in zones 7-9).

WALNUT — see *Juglans*
WASHINGTON THORN —
see *Crataegus*
WHITEBEAM — see *Sorbus*
WILLOW — see *Salix*

Hydrangea blues In alkaline soil, blue-flowered hortensias, such as 'Blue Wave,' turn rose-pink.

A–Z of Deciduous Shrubs

Shrubs are an essential feature of the garden, furnishing it, together with trees, with a permanent framework around which more temporary plants can be grouped. Most deciduous shrubs are chosen for their flowers, which may be borne at almost any time of year, but it is worthwhile to consider a potential purchase for its other merits — foliage colors, leaf shapes, berries, and the pattern and color of its branches.

Some shrubby plants make outstanding specimens, such as the Japanese maples, hydrangeas, and magnolias; others, like forsythia and lilacs, are rather uninteresting in leaf and shape once the flowering display is over, and are better integrated in mixed borders, where their green leaf color can act as a uniform background for flowering plants. Several shrubs, such as berberis, are ideal for hedging, combining beautiful flowers, attractive leaf colors, and berries with dense, sturdy growth.

There are shrubs to suit every garden site — shrubby willows and azaleas for damp soil, and brooms and spireas for dry, shallow ground. Some shrubs, such as euonymuses and honeysuckles, thrive in light shade and against north-facing walls. There are neat-growing shrubs, like the hardy fuchsias, which are suitable for tubs and other containers, and shrubs that billow and spread to give quick cover, such as cotoneasters and callicarpas.

The main job in maintaining shrubs is pruning. Many need annual trimming to control their vigor and direct their growth, and to encourage flower and berry production as well as colored winter stems. The flowering habit dictates the time of pruning; generally, shrubs that flower on shoots made the previous year should be cut back when flowering has finished, while those that bear flowers on shoots of the current year's growth are pruned in early spring, before new growth begins.

VERSATILE SHRUBS

From prostrate and ground-hugging types to wall and tree-scrambling climbers, shrubs fulfill a variety of useful and decorative purposes.

By definition, a shrub is a woody multistemmed plant. Shrubs vary in growth habit from dwarf specimens through types with stiff, bushy or spreading branches to climbers whose weak stems need vertical support. Such diverse growth habits make shrubs ideal for a multitude of uses.

When choosing shrubs, consider not only their flowers, foliage, or berries, but also their performance as long-term plants. Their eventual shape and size are key factors in determining their use. Young shrubs look insignificant when you buy them, so they are often planted too close to other plants or in sites with inadequate space. As they develop, they must therefore be pruned constantly or they must be uprooted before their useful life is over. Another common mistake is to plant tall-growing shrubs beneath a window so that in a few years they block the view.

Dwarf shrubs are ideal for edging borders and paths, and compact types do well in rock gardens and raised beds. Tall shrubs, either flowering types or those with interesting foliage, look perfect against a background of trees or along boundary lines; those of medium size should occupy the middle ground.

Wall shrubs can enhance any house wall but should be chosen with care — vivid flowering types can often look garish against red brick and may have little to contribute when in leaf.

True climbers are marvelous for adding finishing touches; they take up little ground space and are invaluable for hiding fences and walls with flowers and foliage. Scented climbers can clothe arbors and pergolas, and rampant types are ideal for hiding eyesores.

▲ **Groundcover roses** If left to sprawl over the ground, climbing miniature roses will form a flowering carpet a couple of inches high but as much as 10 ft (3 m) across. This cultivar, 'Nozomi,' bears white blossoms once in early to midsummer, but others repeat their bloom throughout the growing season.

◄ **Prostrate or upright**
The familiar *Cotoneaster horizontalis* is an accommodating shrub. On level ground, its herringbone branches spread wide, but the shrub grows no more than 3 ft (90 cm) high. Against a wall, however, it can reach 8 ft (2.4 m). In fall the tiny leaves turn brilliant red, leaving ranks of bright red berries in their wake.

▲ Low-growing shrubs
While many brooms are tall-growing, *Cytisus* x *kewensis* reaches just 2 ft (60 cm) high, its lax arching branches spreading to 4 ft (1.2 m). It will tumble over a low wall or grow on a sunny bank, and its almost leafless stems are covered with cream-colored pealike flowers in late spring.

◄ Cinquefoils Strawberry-like foliage covered with silvery hairs distinguishes herbaceous cinquefoils, or potentillas, from the shrubby types. In either case, the leaves provide a good foil for the sprays of roselike flowers borne in summer and midfall on 1 ft (30 cm) high plants. 'Gibson's Scarlet,' which has single bright red flowers, spreads to 1½ ft (45 cm).

▲ **Tall shrub** The vigorous European cranberry bush (*Viburnum opulus*) is covered in mid- to late spring with flat, wide flower heads beautifully set off by maplelike leaves. In fall the foliage turns crimson, and the shrub is loaded with clusters of translucent red berries.

▶ **Shrub companions** The diversity of deciduous shrubs is evident in the tiered branched structure of white *Viburnum plicatum tomentosum* 'Mariesii' contrasted with a bushy weigela, whose rose-purple flowers are tempered by an erect silver-variegated cornus.

▲ **Fall scene** A mixed border of deciduous and evergreen shrubs and pyramidal conifers rises against a background of bare-branched trees, whose long shadows flit across the lawn.

◄ **Foliage colors** In early fall, deciduous foliage shrubs reach the peak of their performance. A few slender crimson trumpets still droop from a variegated *Fuchsia magellanica*, but they are eclipsed by the beautiful pale green foliage edged with silvery white. The fuchsia easily holds its own against the taller *Berberis thunbergii* 'Silver Beauty,' whose foliage changes during fall from creamy white and green to pink and orange or purple-red.

▶ **Happy wanderer** Using golden privet for a foothold, a slender *Clematis macropetala* parades its magnificent deep violet-blue flowers in late spring and early summer. By fall they will have turned into fluffy silky seed heads.

Abelia
glossy abelia

Acer
Japanese maple

Abelia x grandiflora

❏ Height 3-6 ft (90-180 cm)
❏ Spread equal to height
❏ Flowers early summer to early fall
❏ Well-drained, moist, acid soil
❏ Sunny spot protected from cold winds
❏ Hardy zones 6-9

Grown for its long floral display
— *Abelia × grandiflora* bears
lightly fragrant, funnel-shaped
blush-pink flowers from late
spring to early fall. It is a bushy
shrub reaching 6 ft (1.8 m) high
and wide. Perhaps its main attraction is the oval-shaped and
lustrous dark green foliage, which
persists into winter, turning
bronze-red.

Cultivation
Plant in early fall to midfall or
early spring to midspring in well-
drained but moist, acid soil. In
northern areas, set in a sunny
spot sheltered from cold winds;
this shrub increases in cold hardiness as it matures, but is vulnerable to frost when young.

Regular pruning is unnecessary, though overgrown shoots
can be thinned after flowering to
encourage new growth. Remove
deadwood in late winter.
Propagation Take 3-4 in (7.5-
10 cm) long cuttings of the current season's wood in midsummer. Root in a cold frame, and
plant out the following spring.
Pests/diseases There are no serious problems.

Acer japonicum 'Aureum'

❏ Height up to 25 ft (7.5 m)
❏ Spread up to 8-25 ft (2.4-7.5 m)
❏ Foliage shrub
❏ Well-drained, moist, cool soil
❏ Sunny or partially shaded site
❏ Hardy zones 5-8

Most maples are of treelike proportions, but two species and
their cultivars grow so slowly in
American gardens that they are
usually treated as shrubs.

Acer japonicum and *A. palmatum* are grown for their exceptionally beautiful foliage — lobed
green, red, or purplish leaves that
turn into magnificent fiery oranges, yellows, and reds in fall.

Both are hardy plants, though
they are susceptible to frost and
cold winds in spring and fall.
Avoid planting them in frost
pockets.

Popular species
Acer japonicum has soft green
leaves that turn crimson in fall. It
is hardy in zones 5-7. Its cultivars
include 'Aconitfolium' (deeply
lobed, toothed green leaves; up to
10 ft/3 m high and 8 ft/2.4 m
wide) and 'Aureum' (yellow leaves

with shallow lobes, turning green
in summer, then brilliant red and
orange in fall; up to 10-20 ft/3-6 m
high and wide; liable to scorch in
full sun). Both cultivars eventually develop into small trees but
may serve for many years as specimen shrubs in small gardens —
in a raised bed, a paved area, or
on a lawn. The cultivar 'Aureum'
also looks striking when cultivated in a tub.

Acer palmatum produces large,
intricately cut leaves in a range of
colors depending on the cultivar.
It forms a rounded bush, which
spreads with age. Its maximum
height in a garden is 15-25 ft (4.5-
7.5 m) with an equal spread. It is
hardy in zones 5-8. Popular cultivars and varieties include *atropurpureum* (purplish-red leaves),
'Aureum' (light yellow leaves,
deepening in fall), 'Bloodgood'
(rich purple-red leaves), *dissectum*
(intricately lobed green leaves
turning bronze-yellow), *dissectum
atropurpureum* (intricately lobed
purplish-red leaves), 'Osakazuki'
(finely toothed green leaves, turning fiery scarlet in fall), and 'San-
go Kaku' (syn. 'Senkaki'; coral-red

Actinidia
actinidia

Actinidia kolomikta

❏ Height 15-30 ft (4.5-9 m)
❏ Climber
❏ Flowers late spring to summer
❏ Well-drained, rich loam
❏ Sunny or partly shaded site
❏ Hardy zones 5-9

Actinidia species are hardy climbing shrubs of twining habit, ideal for covering walls and fences. Collectively they offer not only fragrant flowers but also decorative foliage — and if both male and female plants are grown together, delicious fruit.

Popular species
Actinidia arguta (bower actinidia) is a very vigorous vine that may send stems of glossy pointed leaves 20 ft (6 m) high in 2 years. Sweetly perfumed white flowers appear in late spring, followed by greenish, pleasantly flavored, 1 in (2.5 cm) long berries. It is hardy in zones 5-8.

Actinidia deliciosa (kiwifruit) is also a vigorous climber, growing some 30 ft (9 m) high with large, dark green heart-shaped leaves, 9 in (23 cm) long and 8 in (20 cm) wide. Clusters of small, fragrant cream white flowers appear in summer; these are followed by green-brown kiwifruits. It is hardy in zones 8-9.

Actinidia kolomikta (Kolomikta vine) has stunning foliage — dark green heart-shaped leaves with pink and white at the tips. This

Acer palmatum atropurpureum and *dissectum*

shoots; green leaves, turning yellow in fall).

Cultivation
Plant in well-drained but moist and cool soil in midfall or early spring. Maples tolerate sun and partial shade, but those grown for their fall colors do best in light shade and in a site sheltered from both prevailing winter winds and spring frosts.

Pruning is necessary to control growth in a restricted space. Remove entire branches to avoid spoiling the general appearance.

Propagation Maples are propagated by grafting, which is best done by the nursery.

Pests/diseases Spider mites may be troublesome.

Acer palmatum dissectum, fall colors

Actinidia deliciosa

Actinidia deliciosa, fruit

Aesculus
buckeye, horse chestnut

Aesculus parviflora, fall colors

❏ Height 8-20 ft (2.4-6 m)
❏ Spread equal to or greater than height
❏ Flowers late spring to early summer
❏ Any good soil
❏ Sunny or partially shaded site
❏ Hardy zones 5-8

The stately, long-lived horse chestnut trees belong in large parks and the countryside. They are not suitable in the average garden, but some shrubby species demand less space.

Popular species
Aesculus parviflora (bottlebrush buckeye), a hardy upright shrub 8-12 ft (2.4-3.6 m) high and wide, bears pink-white blooms in tall spikes in early summer. Smooth midgreen horse-chestnut-like leaves turn yellow in fall.
Aesculus pavia (red buckeye) is a round-headed shrub reaching 10-20 ft (3-6 m) high with an equal or greater spread. It bears erect spikes of red flowers in late spring or early summer. 'Atrosanguinea' has dark red flowers.

Cultivation
Plant buckeyes in early spring in any fertile garden soil in a sunny or partially shaded spot. If necessary, thin the shrubs from ground level in late winter.
Propagation Plant seed as soon as collected, and do not let dry out.
Pests/diseases Leaf spot may affect the foliage.

Aesculus parviflora

Aesculus pavia 'Atrosanguinea'

species climbs 15-20 ft (4.5-6 m) high and is hardy in zones 4-8. Fragrant white flowers are borne in late spring, followed by sweet 1 in (2.5 cm) fruits in late summer to early fall.

Cultivation
Plant actinidias in early spring in a sunny, sheltered site against a wall, fence, or trellis. Actinidias do best in a rich, well-drained but moist loam.

The male and female flowers of actinidias are borne on separate plants. So for fruits to form on the female shrub, plant a male nearby.

When plants are young, pinch the growing points to encourage a spreading habit. To keep them under control, thin the shoots and cut others back in late winter.
Propagation In mid- to late summer, root 3-4 in (7.5-10 cm) cuttings of half-ripened wood in potting soil, preferably in a mist propagator. When rooted, put them in 4-5 in (10-13 cm) pots, and plunge into an outdoor nursery bed until ready for planting out.
Pests/diseases Trouble free.

Amelanchier

Juneberry, serviceberry, shadbush

Amelanchier lamarckii

❑ Height 10-25 ft (3-7.5 m)
❑ Spread 10-20 ft (3-6 m)
❑ Flowers midspring
❑ Good, moisture-retentive soil
❑ Sunny or lightly shaded spot
❑ Hardy zones 4-9

Star-shaped white flowers held in loose upright clusters appear just as the shad run upriver to spawn — hence the name, "shadbush." Fleeting blooms appear just as the leaves unfold; orange to red fruits follow in summer, which darken to black or purple. In fall these shrubs' midgreen leaves turn bright red and golden.

Popular species

Amelanchier arborea grows to 15-25 ft (4.5-7.5 m). It may form a small tree but more often stays a multistemmed shrub. Cultivars are 'Cole' (exceptional red fall color) and 'Prince William' (compact; orange-red in fall).
Amelanchier lamarckii reaches 10 ft (3 m) high and wide.

Cultivation

Plant in late fall or early spring in any good garden soil that is well-drained but moisture retentive, in a sunny or partially shaded

Amelanchier lamarckii, fall colors

spot. Pruning is rarely needed. Cut out damaged shoots or crossing branches.
Propagation Dig up rooted suckers from midfall to early spring and replant.
Pests/diseases Rust attacks leaves and fruits; fire blight may blacken the flowers, causing them to shrivel. Leaf miners tunnel into leaves, and borers may tunnel into branches and trunks.

Aralia

Japanese angelica tree

Aralia elata 'Aureo-variegata'

❑ Height 30-50 ft (9-15 m)
❑ Spread 10 ft (3 m)
❑ Flowers midsummer
❑ Fertile, moist, well-drained soil
❑ Sheltered, lightly shaded site
❑ Hardy zones 3-9

The Japanese angelica tree is a suckering tree pruned as a shrub. It produces huge ornamental leaves and midsummer flowers. In spring the terminal buds begin to unfold great rosettes of leaves 2-4 ft (60-120 cm) long and wide, made up of many toothed leaflets on spiny branches. The leaves often take on handsome fall tints. Star-shaped flowers are borne in branched clusters in midsummer.

Popular cultivars

Two garden cultivars developed from *Aralia elata* are grown. 'Aureo-variegata' produces green leaves splashed and edged with yellow, changing to silvery white in summer.
'Variegata' has green leaves edged with white.

Cultivation

Plant in fall or spring in fertile, moist, but well-drained soil. The shrub thrives in full sun or partial shade and is well-suited to city gardens. Remove straggly growths in winter or spring to maintain compact growth.
Propagation Detach rooted suckers in early spring to midspring, and plant out.
Pests/diseases Trouble free.

AZALEA — see *Rhododendron*

Ballota
black horehound

Ballota pseudodictamnus

❏ Height 1-3 ft (30-90 cm)
❏ Spread 3 ft (90 cm)
❏ Flowers midsummer
❏ Ordinary well-drained soil
❏ Sunny site
❏ Hardy to zone 8

Ballota pseudodictamnus is a dwarf shrub from the Mediterranean. It is grown mainly for its foliage — heart-shaped silver-gray leaves — though it also produces whorls of lilac-pink flowers in midsummer. This low, spreading shrub is generally hardy, except during severe winters.

Cultivation
Plant in mid- to late spring in any ordinary, or even poor, soil as long as it is well drained; waterlogging in winter is likely to kill this shrub. The site must be in full sun. Prune back hard in midspring.
Propagation Take 4-6 in (10-15 cm) long heel cuttings of side shoots in late summer, and root in a cold frame. The following midspring transfer to nursery rows outdoors, and grow on for another year before setting in a permanent position.
Pests/diseases Generally trouble free.

BARBERRY — see *Berberis*
BEAUTYBERRY —
see *Callicarpa*
BEAUTYBUSH —
see *Kolkwitzia*

Berberis
barberry, berberis

Berberis x rubrostilla

❏ Height 2-7 ft (60-210 cm)
❏ Spread equal to height
❏ Flowers spring and summer
❏ Ordinary soil
❏ Sunny or lightly shaded site
❏ Hardy zones 3-8

The deciduous berberises are hardy, easily grown shrubs, popular for their rich fall colors and outstanding crops of brightly colored berries, which usually persist well into winter.

With their spiny stems, berberises make excellent barrier hedges; they also fit well into mixed borders, or they can be grown as specimen shrubs.

Popular species
Berberis koreana (Korean barberry) grows up to 4-6 ft (1.2-1.8 m) high, with a slightly lesser spread. It is a dense, rounded shrub, with dark green oval leaves; the new shoots are reddish, and the foliage turns to a deep reddish purple in the fall. The leaves may hang on the shrub well into November. The ¼ in (6 mm) drooping yellow flowers appear in late spring and are the showiest of any deciduous barberry. The fruit of the Korean barberry is a red berry that, like the leaves, is unusually persistent. It is hardy in zones 3-7.

Berberis × mentorensis (Mentor barberry) is a result of a cross between an evergreen species, *B. julianae,* and the deciduous Japanese barberry, *B. thunbergii.* The Mentor barberry is an upright shrub that reaches a height of 5 ft (1.5 m) with a spread of 5-7 ft (1.5-2.1 m). The lance-shaped leaves are 1-2 in (2.5-5 cm) long and leathery. Dark green in summer, they turn orange, yellow, or red in fall. The shrub bears yellow flowers in early spring to midspring, but no fruits. Adaptable to full sun or light shade and hardy in zones 6-8, it withstands the hot, dry summers of the Midwest better

Berberis thunbergii 'Crimson Pygmy'

than other barberries and so is the best choice for a barberry hedge in that region.

Berberis × rubrostilla has toothed leaves that turn ruby-red in fall. The yellow flower clusters open in late spring, giving way to coral-red berries. Reaching a height of 4 ft (1.2 m) and a spread of 6-8 ft (1.8-2.4 m), this species is hardy to zone 6.

Berberis thunbergii (Japanese barberry) is a rounded and compact species grown for its attractive fall foliage. Reaching a height of 3-6 ft (90-180 cm) and a spread of 4-7 ft (1.2-2.1 m), this shrub is hardy from zone 5 to 8. The leaves are small (1¼ in/3 cm long) and slender, but often very colorful, especially in the cultivars, which may be reddish or purplish in summer and a true orange, scarlet, or purple in fall. The small yellow flowers (up to ½ in/1.25 cm wide) appear in early spring to midspring and are followed by bright red fruits that show up quite well once the foliage has dropped in winter. Outstanding cultivars include 'Aurea' (yellow foliage turning greenish in late summer), 'Crimson Pygmy' (syn. 'Atropurpurea Nana,' com-

pact plant to 2 ft/60 cm tall and 3 ft/90 cm wide; purple leaves; color best in full sun), 'Crimson Velvet' (new foliage fuchsia-colored, darkening to smoky maroon; red fall foliage), 'Erecta' (similar to 'Atropurpurea,' but more upright), 'Gold Ring' (red-purple leaves edged with gold), 'Rose Glow' (young leaves purple and silver, turning bright rosy red and later purple), 'Sparkle' (arching, horizontal branches to 4 ft/1.2 m high and wide), and 'Thornless' (globe-shaped; 4-6 ft/1.2-1.8 m tall and wide; no thorns).

Cultivation
Plant berberis in midfall or early spring in a sunny site. Set hedging plants 1-2 ft (30-60 cm) apart. Prune old, lanky stems at ground level, or prune back to young shoots in late winter; in early summer and again (if necessary) at summer's end, trim young shoots to maintain shape.

Propagation Take heel cuttings from side shoots in late summer, and root them in a cold frame. The following spring transfer them to a nursery bed. After 2 years the plants should be moved

outside to their permanent positions.

Pests/diseases Bacterial leaf spot may cause purple-brown spotting on leaves and blighting of twigs; anthracnose may also cause leaf spotting. Wilt may cause leaves to brown and shrivel, eventually killing the whole plant. Aphids and scale insects infest barberries; barberry webworms weave together leaves and shoot tips with webs.

BLACK HOREHOUND —
see *Ballota*
BLACKTHORN — see *Prunus*
BLADDER SENNA —
see *Colutea*
BLUEBEARD — see *Caryopteris*
BLUEBERRY — see *Vaccinium*
BOSTON IVY —
see *Parthenocissus*
BRAMBLE, ORNAMENTAL —
see *Rubus*
BRIDAL-WREATH —
see *Spiraea*
BROOM — see *Cytisus*, *Genista*, and *Spartium*
BUCKEYE — see *Aesculus*
BUCKTHORN — see *Rhamnus*

Buddleia
butterfly bush

Buddleia davidii

Buddleia alternifolia

❏ Height 5-20 ft (1.5-6 m)
❏ Spread 4-15 ft (1.2-4.5 m)
❏ Flowers late spring to midfall
❏ Any good, well-drained soil
❏ Sunny site
❏ Hardy zones 5-9

Buddleias are excellent shrubs for providing an instant effect. The species and cultivars grow rapidly in any reasonable soil and bear a profusion of blossoms in plume-shaped clusters.

In the North, most buddleias (except *B. alternifolia)* die back to the ground in wintertime, sending up new shoots in spring. As a result, they are not satisfactory for a foundation planting or screen, but do fit easily into a perennial border.

Buddleia davidii, known as the butterfly bush, is a popular garden shrub, making a fine addition to a shrub or mixed border. As its name implies, the flowers are one of the great favorites of butterflies.

Popular species
Buddleia alternifolia is a graceful shrub with long arching branches. It grows 10-20 ft (3-6 m) high and 10-15 ft (3-4.5 m) wide, with narrow, lance-shaped pale green leaves. Its sweetly scented lavender-blue flowers appear in early summer and are borne in rounded clusters all along the branches of the previous year. It is hardy in zones 6-8.

Buddleia davidii (butterfly bush) grows rapidly to a height and spread of 10 ft (3 m). The mid-green leaves are lance-shaped and toothed. From early summer until frost, the shrub bears fragrant lilac-purple flowers arranged in slightly arching plume-shaped clusters. It is hardy in zones 5-9. Popular cultivars include 'Black Knight' (dark violet flowers), 'Border Beauty' (deep crimson-purple), 'Empire Blue' (violet-blue with orange eyes), 'Harlequin' (reddish-purple flowers; white variegated leaves), and 'Pink Delight' (deep pink, fragrant flowers).

Buddleia fallowiana has lavender-blue flowers similar to those of *B. davidii*, but the leaves are covered in white down and the shrub has a more weeping habit. It reaches 5-10 ft (1.5-3 m) high and has a spread of 4-6 ft (1.2-1.8 m). Hardy only through zone 9, it is best grown against a south-facing wall.

Cultivation
Plant buddleias in fall or spring in fertile soil and in full sun. Keep *B. davidii* and its cultivars under control by pruning before growth starts in early spring, cutting all new shoots back to within 2 in (5 cm) of the old wood. *B. alternifolia* should be pruned after flowering, reducing the stems by about one-third of their height.

Propagation Take heel cuttings of half-ripe lateral shoots in summer; take hardwood cuttings in midfall.

Pests/diseases Nematodes may attack roots in the South. Japanese beetles attack foliage.

CALIFORNIAN LILAC —
see *Ceanothus*

Callicarpa
beautyberry

Callicarpa bodinieri 'Profusion'

❑ Height 4-10 ft (1.2-3 m)
❑ Spread equal to height
❑ Flowers early summer to midsummer
❑ Any well-drained soil
❑ Sunny, sheltered site
❑ Hardy zones 6-8

Prized for their large clusters of violet or lilac berries, callicarpas make fine woody shrubs in the South but perform like herbaceous perennials in the North.

Popular species
Callicarpa bodinieri grows 6-10 ft (1.8-3 m) high and wide. Lilac flowers in early summer give rise to violet-purple berries in fall. The leaves turn purplish pink in fall. 'Profusion' fruits heavily.
Callicarpa japonica grows 4-6 ft (1.2-1.8 m) high and wide. Pink midsummer blooms are followed by lilac-mauve berries and golden fall foliage.

Cultivation
Plant in midfall or early spring in any good garden soil in a sunny, sheltered spot. For plenty of berries, plant in groups of three. In a cold garden, protect with evergreen boughs in winter. In the North, cut stems back to 4-6 in (10-15 cm) in early spring.
Propagation Take heel cuttings of lateral shoots in summer.
Pests/diseases Leaf spot may disfigure the foliage. Black mold may spread over leaves and twigs.

Campsis
trumpet vine or creeper

Campsis radicans

❑ Height 20-40 ft (6-12 m)
❑ Climber
❑ Flowers early summer to early fall
❑ Rich, well-drained soil
❑ Sheltered site in full sun
❑ Hardy zones 5-9

Trumpet vines are vigorous, rapid-growing climbers, excellent for covering large expanses of walls, fences, pergolas, or trees, to which they cling by means of aerial roots. The leaves are made up of numerous narrow leaflets; coarsely toothed and mid- or light green; they resemble those of the ash. From early summer onward, these climbers bear drooping clusters of large trumpet-shaped flowers, 2-4 in (5-10 cm) long, from the tips of the current year's shoots. After a warm summer and fall, long seedpods may be produced, remaining on the naked branches well into winter.

Popular species
Campsis grandiflora is the least hardy species, flourishing only from zone 7 to zone 9. But in a warm, sheltered site it may reach a height of 20 ft (6 m) or more. The deep orange and red trumpet flowers are outstanding, each measuring up to 3 in (7.5 cm) long.
Campsis radicans is hardier (zones 5-9) and more vigorous than *C. grandiflora*. It grows up to 40 ft (12 m) tall, with many self-clinging roots. The scarlet and orange blossoms, up to 3 in (7.5 cm) long, are tubular rather

Campsis x *tagliabuana* 'Madame Galen'

than trumpet-shaped and have wide-spreading lobes at the mouth. The cultivar 'Flava' bears rich yellow flowers.
Campsis × *tagliabuana* 'Madame Galen' is a hybrid between the two species. Hardy in zones 6-9, it climbs up to 30 ft (9 m) high if given initial support in the early stages. The salmon-red flowers resemble those of *C. radicans* in shape and size.

Cultivation
Plant in fall or spring in rich, moist, but well-drained soil. The plants will grow practically anywhere, but perform best in full sun. Apply an annual mulch over the root area in midspring, and protect the crowns with straw during winter until the plants are well established. Tie the shoots to supports until aerial roots appear.
After planting, cut all stems back to 6 in (15 cm) above ground to encourage side-branching from low on the plant. Control growth of mature plants with hard pruning in late winter or early spring, before new growth begins: cut shoots of the previous year back to about 2 in (5 cm) of their points of origin.
Propagation Increase the plants by layering long branches in fall; they should have rooted after a year, when they can be severed from the parent and planted out. Alternatively, take hardwood cuttings in fall and root in a cold frame.
Pests/diseases Fungal leaf spots, blight, and powdery mildew may disfigure leaves. Plant hoppers and scale insects may infest trumpet vines.

Caryopteris
bluebeard, caryopteris

Caryopteris x clandonensis

❏ Height 2-4 ft (60-120 cm)
❏ Spread equal to height
❏ Flowers late summer to early fall
❏ Ordinary well-drained garden soil
❏ Sheltered, sunny site
❏ Hardy zones 6-9

Fluffy clusters of small blue flowers and aromatic gray-green foliage are the distinguishing features of *Caryopteris × clandonensis*. The flowers appear in late summer and early fall and are particularly attractive to bees.

Popular cultivars
Several cultivars are available. 'Blue Mist' has powder-blue flowers and dull green leaves. It rarely grows taller than 2 ft (60 cm). 'Dark Knight' is also compact and bears deep purple-blue flowers. 'Longwood Blue' reaches a height and spread of 4 ft (1.2 m), bearing bluish-violet flowers with blue-black anthers.

Cultivation
Plant in fall or early spring in ordinary well-drained soil in a sheltered, sunny spot. The shrubs thrive in alkaline soils. In early spring, cut the previous year's growth back to young healthy buds and cut weak stems back to ground level.
Propagation In late summer or early fall, root 3-4 in (7.5-10 cm) long cuttings of half-ripened lateral shoots in a cold frame. The following spring, set them in an outdoor nursery bed; plant in permanent positions in spring.
Pests/diseases Trouble free.

Ceanothus
mountain lilac, wild lilac

Ceanothus gloriosus

❏ Height 2-10 ft (60-300 cm)
❏ Spread 2-12 ft (60-360 cm)
❏ Flowers late spring to early fall
❏ Well-drained, fertile soil
❏ Sheltered, sunny site
❏ Hardy zones 4-9

Because their showy blue or white blooms appear in spring, as do those of the European true lilacs (*Syringa* species), ceanothuses have been dubbed "wild" or "mountain" lilacs. In fact, ceanothuses are mostly western natives that flourish in dry, exposed conditions in warm-weather areas. While the majority of species are evergreen, there are also several fine deciduous ceanothuses. These tend to be less showy than the evergreen species, but their hardiness makes them useful over a greater range.

Popular species
Ceanothus americanus (New Jersey tea) is an eastern species. Growing 3-4 ft (90-120 cm) high and 3-5 ft (90-150 cm) wide, it is hardy in zones 4-8. Able to flourish in poor, sandy soils, it has ovate leaves 2-3 in (5-7.5 cm) long and bears small clusters of white flowers in late spring and early summer.
Ceanothus gloriosus (Point Reyes ceanothus) forms a prostrate shrub with small leathery leaves. The flowers are purplish to deep blue. It is hardy to zone 7.
Ceanothus ovatus (inland ceanothus) grows 2-3 ft (60-90 cm) high and wide; its glossy green leaves are 2½ in (6 cm) long. Clusters of red fruit follow white flowers. This species is hardy to zone 5.
Ceanothus sanguineus (wild lilac) reaches a height of 10 ft (3 m), bearing elliptical leaves 2¼ in (5.5 cm) long and white flowers. It is hardy to zone 5.

Cultivation
Plant in fall or spring in good, well-drained soil, in a sunny site. Shelter ceanothuses from winter winds.
Cut shoots back to 3 in (7.5 cm) long each midspring.
Propagation In midsummer root heel cuttings of side shoots in a propagating box; overwinter in a cold frame.
Pests/diseases Leaf spot and powdery mildew may cause minor damage to foliage.

Celastrus
climbing bittersweet, staff vine

Celastrus orbiculatus, fall colors

❏ Height 30 ft (9 m)
❏ Climber
❏ Fall foliage and fruit
❏ Any well-drained soil
❏ Tolerates shade; fruits best in full sun
❏ Hardy zones 3-8

These hardy, rampant climbers are grown for their decorative fall fruits. Borne in clusters and resembling small green peas, the seedpods split open to reveal scarlet seeds, which often last well into winter. The fall foliage is a greenish yellow. *Celastrus scandens* (American bittersweet) is the hardiest species, flourishing to zone 3; *C. orbiculatus* (Chinese bittersweet) doesn't thrive north of zone 5.

To obtain fruit you must buy hermaphrodite forms (plants with flowers of both sexes) or both a male and a female plant. This very vigorous vine is suitable for covering a wall or a shed, but it will strangle any tree it climbs.

Cultivation
Plant in fall or spring in well-drained soil. Acid and alkaline tolerant, bittersweet thrives in shade or sun. To keep bittersweet under control, thin unwanted growths, and cut back the main shoots to half their length in late winter.
Propagation Layer year-old growths in fall. They should have rooted a year later. Or take cuttings in midfall to late fall, and root in a propagating box.
Pests/diseases Scale insects sometimes infest the stems, and aphids attack foliage. Leaf spot and powdery mildew may also damage foliage.

Celastrus orbiculatus, flowers

Ceratostigma
Chinese plumbago

Ceratostigma willmottianum

❏ Height 1-4 ft (30-120 cm)
❏ Spread 15-48 in (38-120 cm)
❏ Flowers midsummer to late fall
❏ Well-drained, loamy soil
❏ Sunny or lightly shaded, sheltered site
❏ Hardy to zone 6 or 8

Vigorous and tolerant of poor soil, these subshrubs are useful as ground covers, brightening up areas where only weeds will grow. Growth starts in spring, when tiny coral-red buds open into narrow leaves along pink stems. Bristly flower heads appear from midsummer to fall. The midgreen leaves may turn red.

Popular species
Ceratostigma plumbaginoides, a shrubby perennial with a woody base and wiry stems, grows 1 ft (30 cm) high and 15 in (38 cm) wide. It bears clusters of blue flowers. It is hardy to zone 6.
Ceratostigma willmottianum, 4 ft (120 cm) high and wide, bears diamond-shaped hairy leaves that turn red in fall. Erect clusters of blue flowers bloom throughout the summer. It is hardy to zone 8.

Cultivation
Plant in spring in any well-drained, loose soil and in full sun or light shade, preferably with protection from winter winds.

Cut back frost-damaged stems to ground level in early spring.
Propagation In midsummer root 3 in (7.5 cm) long heel cuttings of half-ripe lateral shoots in a propagating box. Pot up rooted cuttings, and overwinter in a cold frame. Plant out in permanent positions in midspring.
Pests/diseases Trouble free.

Chaenomeles
flowering quince

Chaenomeles speciosa 'Moerloosei'

❑ Height 2-10 ft (60-300 cm)
❑ Spread 3-10 ft (90-300 cm)
❑ Flowers early spring to midspring
❑ Ordinary moisture-retentive soil
❑ Sunny site
❑ Hardy zones 5-8

Flowering quinces produce colorful saucer-shaped flowers in red, pink, salmon, or white. In the fall these shrubs often bear bright yellow-green fruits — quinces — which can be used to make jelly.

Flowering quinces are suitable for growing against sunny walls, as specimen shrubs in mixed borders, and as hedging plants.

Popular species

Chaenomeles japonica bears profuse orange-red bowl-shaped blossoms amid rounded, downy green leaves. It forms a low, spreading bush 2-3 ft (60-90 cm) high and 3 ft (90 cm) or more wide.

Chaenomeles speciosa, 6-10 ft (1.8-3 m) high and wide, has bowl-shaped flowers borne in small clusters. The small leaves are dark green and glossy. Popular cultivars include 'Cameo' (peach-pink flowers), 'Moerloosei' (pale pink and white), 'Nivalis' (white), 'Rubra Grandiflora' (spreading; dwarf; crimson), 'Spitfire' (upright; bright red flowers), and 'Toyo Nishiki' (upright; white, pink, and mixed-color flowers on the same stems).

Chaenomeles × superba is a free-flowering hybrid group; all reach 5 ft (1.5 m) high. Cultivars include 'Crimson and Gold' (crimson-red petals, yellow stamens),

Chaenomeles × superba 'Crimson and Gold'

Chaenomeles × superba, fruit

Chaenomeles speciosa

Chimonanthus
wintersweet

Chimonanthus praecox

❏ Height 10-15 ft (3-4.5 m)
❏ Spread 8-12 ft (2.4-3.6 m)
❏ Flowers winter to early spring
❏ Any well-drained soil
❏ Sunny or partially shaded, protected spot
❏ Hardy zones 7-9

The wintersweet (*Chimonanthus praecox*) is either a joy or a disappointment. When it blooms successfully, the perfume of its off-season flowers is particularly welcome, but too often (especially in the North) the buds fall prey to frost and never open at all. In a good year, though, the blossoms are so unusual and so exquisitely scented that they are worth the risk. Appearing around Christmas, if the weather is mild, and lasting until early spring, they are pale lime-yellow, stained with purple in the center.

Cultivation
In midfall or early spring plant in good, well-drained garden soil in a sunny site, ideally against a south-facing or west-facing wall.

Thin old and crowded wood after flowering. With shrubs espaliered against a wall, prune by cutting all flowered shoots back to just above the base.
Propagation Layer long shoots in early fall.
Pests/diseases Trouble free.

‘Jet Trail’ (white flowers; spreading shrub), ‘Knap Hill Scarlet’ (dwarf; spreading; orange-scarlet), and ‘Texas Scarlet’ (tomato-red; floriferous, spreading).

Cultivation
Plant in midfall or early spring in ordinary soil (flowering quince tolerates both acid and alkaline types), either in full sun or partial shade. For hedging, set the plants 2½-4 ft (75-120 cm) apart.

Freestanding shrubs need little pruning except to thin out crowded branches. Older specimens may become lanky and can be renewed by removing older, taller stems. Alternatively, cut the entire shrub back to a height of 6 in (15 cm).
Propagation Take 4 in (10 cm) long heel cuttings of lateral shoots in mid- to late summer, and root in a propagating box. Alternatively, layer long shoots in early fall — they should be ready for separating from the parent plant 2 years later.
Pests/diseases Leaf spot may

Chaenomeles japonica

cause defoliation in rainy springs and summers. Aphids may attack young growth. Fire blight may shrivel the flowers and cause dieback of the branches.

CHASTE TREE — see *Vitex*
CHERRY, ORNAMENTAL — see *Prunus*

CINQUEFOIL — see *Potentilla*

Clematis
clematis

Clematis macropetala

- ❏ Height 6-40 ft (1.8-12 m)
- ❏ Climber
- ❏ Flowers late spring to midfall
- ❏ Well-drained, alkaline to neutral soil
- ❏ Open, sunny site
- ❏ Hardy zones 4-9

The most popular of all hardy climbers, clematises are largely deciduous, producing their cup-, bell-, or urn-shaped flowers from late spring until fall, in shades of purple, mauve, red, pink, yellow, or white, often in bicolors.

There are more than 200 species of clematis worldwide, and almost 100 of these are cultivated in American gardens. But as beautiful as the wild types are, the public has always shown a taste for the larger blossoms and great color range of the hybrids and cultivars — there are dozens of these, too.

Clematises may be grown on trellises and fences, up walls and trees, and the species types especially are excellent for hiding a stump or other garden eyesore. If trained as climbers, these vines should be given firm support and protected at the base, since injury to the lower part of stems provides an entryway for diseases, and is a common cause for the loss of treasured specimens.

Popular species and cultivars
The enormous range of clematises includes species and their cultivars, as well as large-flowered hybrids. They can be divided according to flowering seasons.

Early-flowering types bloom between spring and midsummer. *Clematis alpina* bears drooping cup-shaped violet-blue flowers in mid- and late spring, with dark green leaves. It grows up to 6 ft (1.8 m) high. Cultivars include 'Pamela Jackson' (dark blue), 'Ruby' (rose-red), and 'Willy' (blush-white with pink center). *Clematis macropetala* is a slender climber, reaching 12 ft (3.6 m) high. The nodding light and dark bell-shaped flowers have centers of paler staminodes and appear in late spring and early summer. Cultivars include 'Maidwell Hall' (deep blue) and 'Markham's Pink' (lavender-pink). The species is hardy to zone 6.

Clematis montana is an easily grown, vigorous species that can reach up to 40 ft (12 m) high. The

Clematis viticella 'Purpurea Plena Elegans'

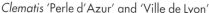
Clematis 'Perle d'Azur' and 'Ville de Lyon'

Clematis 'Alice Fisk'

Clematis florida sieboldiana

pure white flowers are carried in clusters in late spring among dark green leaves. Cultivars include 'Elizabeth' (pale pink) and 'Tetrarose' (lilac-rose flowers and bronze foliage). The species is hardy to zone 5.

Large-flowered hybrids are less vigorous than the species, reaching to 8-15 ft (2.4-4.5 m) high. They flower from late spring to early summer, and often will bloom again in late summer to early fall. Some popular cultivars include 'Alice Fisk' (wisteria-blue), 'Barbara Jackman' (violet-purple with plum stripes and white stamens), 'Bee's Jubilee' (pink with carmine stripes), 'Nelly Moser' (mauve-pink with crimson stripes), 'The President' (purple-blue with pale stripes), 'Vyvyan Pennell' (double violet-blue with carmine stripes), and 'Yellow Queen' (cream with yellow stamens). These hybrids are hardy in zones 5-8.

Late-flowering types bloom between midsummer and early fall. *Clematis florida* is sometimes evergreen, reaching 10 ft (3 m)

high. The flowers are cream-white with a green stripe on the reverse. The variety *sieboldiana* has semidouble cream flowers with a purple center. These types are hardy to zone 7.

Clematis orientalis is a vigorous, well-branched species reaching up to 20 ft (6 m) high. It has ferny green leaves and a wonderful display of nodding, scented, star-like yellow flowers. Silky, silver-gray seed heads are an added attraction. It is hardy in zones 6-9.

Clematis tangutica is similar to *C. orientalis*, reaching 15-20 ft (4.5-6 m) and with silver-gray foliage. It is best left to ramble freely over a support. Rich yellow, lantern-shaped flowers are followed by fluffy seed heads. It is hardy to zone 4.

Clematis texensis often dies back to the ground in winter. In summer it reaches a height of 6-12 ft (1.8-3.6 m). The leaves are blue-green, and the urn-shaped blossoms are scarlet. It is hardy to zone 5.

Clematis viticella grows 12 ft (3.6 m) high, though its growth

tends to die back in winter and should be pruned to 2 ft (60 cm) off the ground in late winter. It bears dark green divided leaves and nodding, bell-shaped violet or purple-red flowers. Cultivars are 'Purpurea Plena Elegans' (double violet-purple flowers) and 'Royal Velours' (velvet-purple). The species is hardy to zone 4.

Large-flowered hybrids that flower later have smaller blooms than the early-flowering hybrids. They reach 8-15 ft (2.4-4.5 m) high and are hardy in zones 5-8. Popular cultivars include 'Comtesse de Bouchard' (bright mauve-pink), 'Duchess of Albany' (bright pink), 'Ernest Markham' (glowing red), 'Gipsy Queen' (violet-purple), 'Gravetye Beauty' (crimson-red), 'Hagley Hybrid' (shell-pink), 'Jackmanii Superba' (purple), 'Mme. Edouard André' (wine-red), 'Mme. Julia Correvon' (small, wine-red), 'Niobe' (dark ruby-red), 'Perle d'Azur' (sky-blue), and 'Ville de Lyon' (carmine edged with crimson).

Dual-purpose clematis will flower in spring, summer, or fall,

Clematis 'Yellow Queen'

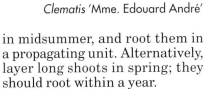

Clematis 'Mme. Edouard André'

depending on pruning. Light pruning produces large early flowers and late small flowers; hard pruning results in an impressive midsummer display. Favorites are 'W. E. Gladstone' (lavender-blue), 'Henryi' (cream-white), 'Mrs. Cholmondeley' (pale blue), and 'William Kennett' (lavender-blue with red stripes). This type is hardy in zones 5-8.

Cultivation

Plant midfall or spring in deep, well-drained, alkaline to neutral or slightly acid soil in an open, sunny site. A clematis needs shade over the base of its main stem and its roots. Mulch the root area annually in spring with well-rotted manure or compost. Water thoroughly during a dry spell.

Early-flowering species and hybrids do not require any regular pruning. To keep them under control, trim rampant shoots after flowering has finished.

Late-flowering species and hybrids should be cut back almost to ground level in late winter or early spring, leaving just one strong shoot.

Propagation Take stem cuttings in midsummer, and root them in a propagating unit. Alternatively, layer long shoots in spring; they should root within a year.

Pests/diseases Leaf spot (stem rot) appears as water-soaked spots on leaves, but eventually travels down stem, girdling and killing the plant. Black blister beetles attack clematis flowers and leaves; clematis borers tunnel into plants near the soil line. Root knot nematodes may attack roots, stunting them and crippling the plant.

Clematis 'Hagley Hybrid'

Clematis tangutica

Clerodendrum
clerodendron, glorybower

Clerodendrum trichotomum

❏ Height 6-15 ft (1.8-4.5 m)
❏ Spread equal to height
❏ Flowers late summer to early fall
❏ Fertile, well-drained soil
❏ Sheltered, sunny site
❏ Hardy zones 6-10

Clerodendrons are shrubs for a warm, sunny garden; most are very frost-sensitive, and only one species thrives in the North. They bear heads of pinkish-white flowers in late summer and early fall.

Popular species
Clerodendrum bungei is of semi-herbaceous habit, dying back to the ground in winter. It grows up to 6-8 ft (1.8-2.4 m) high and spreads by means of suckers. The heart-shaped leaves are dark green. It is hardy to zones 9-10. *Clerodendrum trichotomum* is hardier (zones 6-9), slow-growing, of bushy but open habit. The flowers are followed by turquoise berries. It is hardy in zones 6-9.

Cultivation
Plant in fertile, well-drained garden soil in early fall or midspring. The site should be sheltered and sunny. Remove any frost-damaged tips in spring.
Propagation Increase *C. bungei* by replanting rooted suckers in early fall or spring. This species and *C. trichotomum* can also be propagated from heel cuttings taken in late summer and rooted in a cold frame.
Pests/diseases Trouble free.

Clethra
summer-sweet, sweet pepper bush

Clethra alnifolia 'Rosea'

❏ Height 6-8 ft (1.8-2.4 m)
❏ Spread 4-6 ft (1.2-1.8 m)
❏ Flowers midsummer
❏ Acid, humus-rich, moisture-retentive soil
❏ Sunny or lightly shaded site
❏ Hardy zones 3-9

Summer-sweet (*Clethra alnifolia*) is aptly named, for its urn-shaped flowers perfume the air around the bush for 4 to 6 weeks in midsummer. Its 4 in (10 cm) long, lustrous green ovate leaves are attractive, too, especially when they turn golden yellow in fall. The adaptable summer-sweet thrives in wet soils, shade, or full sun and along the seashore.

Popular cultivars
'Paniculata' bears fine branched spikes of white flowers.
'Rosea' has spikes of red buds, which open into pink flowers.

Cultivation
Plant in early fall to midfall or early spring to midspring in acid soil with plenty of humus and moisture. Provide sunny or lightly shaded woodland conditions.
Propagation Take 3-4 in (7.5-10 cm) long heel cuttings of lateral shoots in mid- to late summer, and root in a propagating box. Pot the cuttings in lime-free compost, overwinter in a frost-free cold frame, and plant out the following year.
Pests/diseases Trouble free.

CLIMBING BITTERSWEET — see *Celastrus*

Colutea
bladder senna

Colutea arborescens

❏ Height 8 ft (2.4 m)
❏ Spread equal to height
❏ Flowers early summer to midsummer
❏ Any well-drained garden soil
❏ Sunny site
❏ Hardy zones 6-7

The hardy *Colutea arborescens* bears yellow pealike blossoms marked with red in early summer and continues for several weeks. The seedpods that follow give the plant its common name — bladder senna. They are 3 in (7.5 cm) long, inflated purses, flushed red.

Fast-growing bladder senna forms an open wide-spreading bush 8 ft (2.4 m) high. It is worth growing for its gray-green feathery foliage alone.

Cultivation
Plant in any well-drained soil in a sunny spot in fall or early spring. The root system is not very well branched, and container-grown stock adapts best to transplanting. Bladder senna does well in poor, sandy soils.

Remove spindly shoots in early spring, and cut back strong branches to within a few buds of the old wood.
Propagation Take 3-4 in (7.5-10 cm) long heel cuttings of ripe lateral shoots in early fall.
Pests/diseases Trouble free.

CORKSCREW HAZEL — see *Corylus*

Cornus
dogwood

Cornus kousa

- ❏ Height 2½-12 ft (75-360 cm)
- ❏ Spread 2½-15 ft (75-450 cm)
- ❏ Flowers early spring to early summer
- ❏ Moist or well-drained soil
- ❏ Sunny or partially shaded site
- ❏ Hardy zones 2-8

Some of the shrubby dogwoods are grown for their colored winter stems, while others have attractive flowers or stunning fall foliage. The flowers themselves are tiny but are surrounded by colored bracts resembling petals. They are often followed by colored fruits. (See also page 23.)

Popular species

Cornus alba is a suckering shrub up to 6 ft (1.8 m) high and 10 ft (3 m) wide. In winter the young stems are a glowing red. Its oval midgreen leaves turn red or orange in fall. The yellow-white flowers are carried in inconspicuous clusters from late spring to early summer and are followed by globular white berries. It is hardy in zones 2-8. Popular cultivars are 'Argenteo-marginata' (leaves edged with creamy white),

'Aurea' (leaves suffused with yellow; yellow fall color), 'Elegantissima' (leaves edged and mottled with white), 'Gouchaultii' (leaves edged with yellow and pink; centers green and pink), 'Sibirica' (shiny coral-red stems), and 'Spaethii' (golden variegated foliage).

Cornus alternifolia is grown for its attractive foliage. The red branches grow horizontally to form a large shrub about 10 ft (3 m) high and wide and may grow to 25 ft (7.5 m). The leaves are often brilliantly colored in fall. It is hardy in zones 3-7. The cultivar 'Argentea,' also listed as 'Variegata,' has small bright green leaves broadly edged with cream-white. They turn red in fall, when blue-black fruits also appear.

Cornus kousa, usually grown as a tree, may be maintained as a large shrub. Its small purple-green flower clusters are surrounded by white, large but slender, pointed bracts. They are carried along the top of the horizontal tiers of branches, creating a strikingly

Cornus alba 'Sibirica'

dramatic effect. The oval mid- to dark green leaves have wavy edges and turn reddish purple in fall, complementing the raspberry-like fruits. The shrub grows 10 ft (3 m) high and 8-10 ft (2.4-3 m) wide, eventually developing into a small tree.

Popular cultivars and varieties include *chinensis* (larger bracts; leaves crimson in fall), 'Dwarf

Cornus sericea 'Flaviramea'

Cornus alba 'Elegantissima'

Pink' (light pink bracts; low, spreading growth), 'Lustgarten Weeping' (weeping), and 'Summer Stars' (long-lasting flowers; purple-red fall color). These are hardy in zones 6-8.

Cornus racemosa (gray dogwood) grows 10-15 ft (3-4.5 m) high and wide. It bears dense bunches of white blossoms in midspring. In other seasons its twigs are of interest: the older twigs are a soft gray, and contrast nicely with the reddish brown of new growth. It is hardy in zones 5-8.

Cornus sericea (formerly *C. stolonifera*) is a vigorous suckering shrub 8 ft (2.4 m) high and 7-10 ft (2.1-3 m) wide. The willowlike stems are covered with attractive bright red bark. The flowers, like those of *C. alba,* are yellow-white, and insignificant. The dark green leaves turn red in fall. This species is very invasive and needs plenty of room. Some popular cultivars include 'Cardinal' (cherry-red stems), 'Flaviramea' (yellow stems), 'Isanti' (compact, with bright red stems), 'Kelseyi'

Cornus alba 'Spaethii'

Cornus racemosa

(compact, up to 2½ ft/75 cm tall; red stems), and 'Silver and Gold' (leaves edged creamy white; stems yellow).

Cultivation
Plant in fall or spring, in a sunny or lightly shaded spot. Species that are cultivated for their colorful bark *(C. alba, C. alternifolia, and C. sericea)* prefer moist soil and should be cut back within a few inches of the ground every year in midspring. Species that are grown for their flowers, such as *C. kousa,* prefer well-drained soils and do not require any regular pruning.

Propagation All species can be increased in mid- to late summer by rooting 3-4 in (7.5-10 cm) long heel cuttings of half-ripe shoots. Place them in a propagating case with a temperature of 61°F (16°C). Pot up the rooted cuttings and overwinter in a cold frame. Set out in nursery rows in late spring. Grow on for 2 or 3 years before transplanting to permanent positions.

Or, layer long shoots in early fall. *C. alba, C. alternifolia,* and *C. sericea* can be severed from the parent plant the following midfall; the other species usually take a couple of years to root. Suckering species may also be increased by removing and replanting rooted suckers in early spring.

Pests/diseases Blights, leaf spot, and powdery mildew may attack foliage. Borers attack stressed specimens, often causing severe damage or death. Leaf miners cause blisters on the undersides of leaves — in adult form, they skeletonize leaves.

Coronilla
scorpion senna

Coronilla emerus

- ❏ Height 6-8 ft (1.8-2.4 m)
- ❏ Spread 4-5 ft (1.2-1.5 m)
- ❏ Flowers late spring or early summer
- ❏ Well-drained soil
- ❏ Sunny site
- ❏ Hardy to zone 5

Elegant fronds of soft green foliage — rather like rue but without that herb's strong, pungent smell — clothe this hardy Mediterranean shrub. Under suitable conditions, it grows into a scandent shrub 6-8 ft (1.8-2.4 m) high and will scramble up walls.

The coronillas — or small crowns — of golden pealike flowers resemble those of the brooms *(Cytisus).* The one deciduous species, *Coronilla emerus,* is sometimes called scorpion senna because the tips of its slender seedpods resemble a scorpion's tail. Coronillas may reach up to 8 ft (2.4 m) high and approximately 5 ft (1.5 m) wide. The yellow blossoms are tinged with reddish brown at the tips. They are held in clusters in late spring or early summer.

Cultivation
Plant in early fall to midfall, or in midspring, in ordinary well-drained garden soil in a sunny site. Coronillas tolerate alkaline soils and will thrive in seaside gardens.

Prune the plants to shape after flowering by shortening the long shoots and thinning straggly stems.

Propagation Take semiripe cuttings in late summer or early fall; root them in a cold frame. Pot on as necessary, and plant out in permanent sites in fall or the following spring.

Pests/diseases Generally trouble free.

Corylopsis
winter hazel

Corylopsis spicata

❏ Height 5-15 ft (1.5-4.5 m)
❏ Spread similar to or greater than height
❏ Flowers early spring to midspring
❏ Rich, acid soil
❏ Sunny, sheltered site
❏ Hardy zones 5-8

Corylopsis is a genus of shrubs and trees native to China and Japan. Like witch hazel, it flowers early in the year on leafless branches. The bell-shaped fragrant blooms are borne in pendent clusters.

Popular species
Corylopsis glabrescens grows 8-15 ft (2.4-4.5 m) high and wide. It bears sweetly scented yellow flowers. It is hardy in zones 5-8.
Corylopsis pauciflora reaches 6 ft (1.8 m) high and 6-10 ft (1.8-3 m) wide. It is a densely branched shrub with bright green leaves and pale yellow flowers. It is hardy in zones 6-8.
Corylopsis spicata, is 5-6 ft (1.5-1.8 m) high and wide; its upright, spreading branches have gray-green leaves and green-yellow flowers. It is hardy in zones 5-8.

Cultivation
Plant in midfall or early spring, ideally in moist, neutral to acid soil. The site should be sheltered, in sun or partial shade. Pruning is rarely necessary.
Propagation Layer shoots in midfall; separate 1 or 2 years later.
Pests/diseases Trouble free.

Corylus
filbert, hazel

Corylus avellana 'Contorta'

❏ Height 10-20 ft (3-6 m)
❏ Spread equal to height
❏ Catkins in early spring
❏ Any well-drained soil
❏ Open, sunny or lightly shaded site
❏ Hardy zones 4-8

The yellow catkins of hazels and filberts are a pleasant source of color in early spring, and the leaves have attractive fall color.

Popular species
Corylus avellana (European filbert) reaches up to 20 ft (6 m) high and 15 ft (4.5 m) wide. Ornamental garden cultivars include 'Contorta,' the corkscrew hazel, a slow-growing shrub with twisted branches and leaves.
Corylus maxima filbert is 10-20 ft (3-6 m) high and wide. Similar to *C. avellana*, it is more robust and has larger leaves. The variety *purpurea* has purple leaves. It is hardy to zone 5.

Cultivation
Plant in midfall and early spring in well-drained soil, in a sunny or partially shaded site, sheltered from cold east winds.
In early years, cut back the

Corylus maxima purpurea

previous year's growth by half. When flowering starts after 4 or 5 years, shorten old growth after flowering in early spring. Remove suckers from below ground.
Propagation Layer in fall, and separate from the parent after 1 year.
Pests/diseases Caterpillars and sawfly larvae feed on the leaves; leaf spot and powdery mildew may also afflict foliage.

Cotinus
smoke tree

Cotinus coggygria 'Atropurpureus'

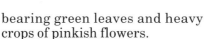

Cotinus coggygria, flower

❏ Height 10-15 ft (3-4.5 m)
❏ Spread equal to height
❏ Flowers in early summer
❏ Ordinary well-drained soil
❏ Sunny site
❏ Hardy zones 5-8

This shrub derives its common name, "smoke tree," from the summertime display of fluffy flowers. Coming in shades of pink, purple, or gray, they are surrounded by clouds of silky hairs, which remain a feature well into fall.

There are other reasons for finding room for a smoke tree in a garden. In fall its oval, light green leaves turn red or yellow before falling to the ground. Some cultivars have spectacular colored foliage in summer and are popular with flower arrangers.

Popular cultivars
Cotinus coggygria (syn. *Rhus cotinus*) has given rise to several outstanding cultivars.
'Atropurpureus' has purple flowers and green leaves that turn yellow in fall.
'Daydream' forms a dense bush bearing green leaves and heavy crops of pinkish flowers.
'Royal Purple' has purple flowers and deep wine-red leaves, turning deeper in fall.
'Velvet Cloak' has dark purple leaves that turn purple-red in fall.

Cultivation
Smoke trees are easy shrubs to grow in ordinary well-drained garden soil in a sunny site. They thrive in poor soils — in rich soils the leaves do not color as well in fall.

Regular pruning is unnecessary, but straggly growths can be shortened or removed entirely in early spring.
Propagation Layer long shoots in early fall, and separate from the parent plant after a year. Alternatively, take 4-5 in (10-13 cm) long softwood cuttings of lateral shoots in early summer.
Pests/diseases Rust and leaf spot may disfigure foliage; verticillium wilt may cause death of branches or whole trunks.

Cotinus coggygria, autumn

Cotoneaster
cotoneaster

Cotoneaster horizontalis

❏ Height 2-15 ft (60-450 cm)
❏ Spread 5-15 ft (1.5-4.5 m)
❏ Flowers late spring to early summer
❏ Ordinary garden soil
❏ Sunny site
❏ Hardy zones 5-8

This large genus of hardy shrubs includes deciduous and evergreen species. These shrubs may be low and spreading, bushy, arching, or mound forming. Grown for their berries and fall foliage, they have small pink or white flowers.

Cotoneaster frigidus

Popular species
Cotoneaster frigidus is a deciduous or semievergreen shrub, with a height and spread of 12-15 ft (3.6-4.5 m), bearing oblong dark green leaves. Large clusters of crimson berries (sometimes yellow) persist for a long time.
Cotoneaster horizontalis produces branches arranged in herringbone fashion. It grows 2-3 ft (60-90 cm) high and 5-8 ft (1.5-2.4 m) wide. The leaves are glossy green in summer and reddish purple in fall. The pink flowers open in late spring; bright red fruits follow, persisting from midsummer well into fall. It is hardy in zones 7-8. 'Variegatus' has leaves variegated with cream-white and tinged pink.

Cultivation
Plant in midfall or early spring in ordinary soil in full sun. To maintain shape, prune in early spring. **Propagation** Root semi-hardwood cuttings in midsummer in a cold frame. Grow on rooted cuttings outdoors; transplant to permanent sites after 2 years. **Pests/diseases** Leaf spot may disfigure foliage; canker and fire blight may kill branches or whole plants. Aphids and spider mites may attack foliage and stems.

Cytisus
broom

Cytisus x *beanii*

❏ Height 1-10 ft (30-300 cm)
❏ Spread 3-10 ft (90-300 cm)
❏ Flowers midspring to midsummer or midsummer to early fall
❏ Ordinary or poor, well-drained soil
❏ Sunny site
❏ Hardy zones 6-8

Cytisus, commonly known as broom, forms a large genus of hardy shrubs, which though seldom seen in the US, are grown in Europe for the profusion of flowers they bear in midspring to late spring and early summer, sometimes later. Resembling sweet peas in shape, the blossoms are yellow, cream, scarlet, or purple.

The bushy brooms are ideal for growing in borders against walls, while the low, spreading ones make excellent ground cover in large rock gardens.

Their tolerance for poor, dry soil makes brooms good choices for stabilizing a sandy bank. Their tolerance for salt spray also makes them excellent plants for seaside gardens.

Because they are not long-lived and are sensitive to cold, brooms do not perform well as specimen plants, especially in the North where an unusually cold winter may finish even a healthy plant. Brooms shine in mass plantings, often self-seeding when they find a hospitable site.

Popular species
Cytisus albus (Portuguese broom), syn. *C. nuttiflorus,* grows into a graceful upright shrub that has a height and spread of 5 ft (1.5 m). It produces white blossoms in late spring or early summer and bears small gray-green leaves on its arching branches. It is hardy to zone 6 or 7.
Cytisus × *beanii* is a dwarf hybrid 1½-2 ft (45-60 cm) high with a

Cytisus x *kewensis*

Cytisus 'Allgold' and 'Burkwoodii'

spread of 3 ft (90 cm). Golden yellow flowers are borne either singly or in small clusters in midspring. It has midgreen hairy leaves and makes a good rock garden plant. It is hardy to zone 6.
Cytisus × *kewensis* grows 1-2 ft (30-60 cm) high, but as the lax branches eventually spread to 4 ft (1.2 m) wide, it is ideal for growing over a sunny ledge or as ground cover. Its mass of cream-colored flowers appear in mid- or late spring, and the leaves are midgreen. It is hardy to zone 6.
Cytisus nigricans differs from other brooms in bearing its bright yellow upright flower spikes in midsummer and into early fall. This erect shrub, with a height and spread of 3-4 ft (90-120 cm) bears trifoliate midgreen leaves. It is hardy to zone 6.
Cytisus × *praecox* (Warminster broom) is an arching species capable of reaching a height and spread of 5-6 ft (1.5-1.8 m). Cascades of creamy white flowers appear in midspring before the gray-green leaves. Unfortunately, the foliage has a slightly acrid smell. It is hardy to zone 7. Popular cultivars are 'Albus' (white), 'Allgold' (deep yellow), and 'Gold Spear' (bright yellow).
Cytisus purpureus, syn. *Chamaecytisus purpureus*, a low, spreading species 1-2 ft (30-60 cm) high and 4-5 ft (1.2-1.5 m) wide, has dark green leaves and purple

Cytisus x *praecox*

Cytisus x praecox 'Allgold'

Daphne
daphne

Daphne mezereum

❑ Height 3-5 ft (90-150 cm)
❑ Spread 2-3 ft (60-90 cm)
❑ Flowers late winter to midspring
❑ Fertile, well-drained soil
❑ Sunny or partially shaded site
❑ Hardy to zone 6

flowers, which appear in mid- to late spring. It is hardy to zone 6. 'Albus,' a dwarf cultivar, has white flower clusters. 'Atropurpureus' is a deeper purple than the species.

Cytisus scoparius (common broom) is a European native that has naturalized in many areas along the Atlantic and Pacific coasts of North America. It forms an upright bush 8 ft (2.4 m) high and wide, with bright green branches giving it an evergreen appearance in winter. The deep golden butterfly-like flowers appear in mid- to late spring. It is hardy in zones 6-8. Numerous cultivars, often bicolored, have been developed and include 'Andreanus' (yellow and chocolate-brown flowers), 'Burkwoodii' (crimson-red), 'Cornish Cream' (cream and white), 'Firefly' (yellow and bronze), 'Golden Sunlight' (rich yellow), 'Killiney Red' (rich red and dark red), 'Lena' (red and yellow), and 'Zeelandia' (lilac, pink, and cream).

Cultivation
It is best to plant them as container-grown specimens, since *Cytisus* dislikes root disturbance. Plant in fall or spring in well-drained ordinary or poor soil in full sun. Alkaline soils are tolerated, but may shorten the plant's life span.

Regular pruning is not usually necessary, but to restrict size, prune brooms that flower on the previous year's growth — all except *C.* × *praecox* — by removing two-thirds of all growth immediately after flowering. *C.* × *praecox* — which flowers on the current year's growth — can be pruned in spring. Take care not to cut into old wood, or dieback will result. Old overgrown shrubs do not respond well to pruning and are best discarded.

Propagation Take 3-4 in (7.5-10 cm) long heel cuttings of lateral shoots in late summer to early fall, and root in pots in a cold frame. Transplant them to the final spots in early fall to midfall. Species can easily be raised from seed.

Pests/diseases Gall mites may disfigure new growth. Leaf spot and blight can kill whole plants.

The flowers of deciduous daphnes have a heady fragrance. Although hardy, the shrubs are slow-growing and may be difficult to establish; hard frosts may cause severe dieback, but they usually recover.

February daphne (*Daphne mezereum*), an upright shrub up to 5 ft (1.5 m) high and 2-3 ft (60-90 cm) wide, is a popular deciduous species. From late winter to midspring, purple-pink to violet-red blooms clothe the bare upper branches; poisonous red berries follow amid light green leaves. 'Alba' has white flowers; 'Autumnalis' bears pink ones in fall.

Cultivation
Daphnes resent root disturbance. Plant in containers in early fall or midspring in good, well-drained soil and full sun or light shade. Mulch annually in late spring. Pruning is rarely necessary.

Propagation From midsummer to early fall, root 2-4 in (5-10 cm) heel cuttings in pots in a cold frame. Plunge the pots outdoors in spring, grow on for 2 years, and transplant to permanent sites.

Pests/diseases Aphids, mealybugs, and scale insects may infest young growth; leaf spot may attack foliage.

Deutzia
deutzia

Deutzia x rosea

❏ Height 2-10 ft (60-300 cm)
❏ Spread 3-8 ft (90-240 cm)
❏ Flowers late spring to midsummer
❏ Ordinary well-drained soil
❏ Sunny or lightly shaded site
❏ Hardy zones 5-8

Deutzias are especially rewarding shrubs for small gardens. All are hardy and most grow no higher or wider than 8 ft (2.4 m). The entire shrub is smothered with small white to pale purple-pink flowers in early summer.

Popular species

Deutzia × elegantissima has fragrant, star-shaped pink to pale purple-pink flowers in late spring and early summer. It is an upright shrub, 4-5 ft (1.2-1.5 m) high and wide, with green lance-shaped leaves. It is hardy to zone 6. 'Rosealind' has deep carmine-pink flowers.
Deutzia gracilis is a low and spreading shrub that can form a mound 2-4 ft (60-120 cm) tall and 3-4 ft (90-120 cm) wide. It blooms in midspring, bearing pure white blossoms up to ¾ in (1.9 cm) wide. It is hardy in zones 5-8. Cultivars include 'Nikko,' a shrub that reaches only 2 ft (60 cm) high but spreads to 5 ft (1.5 m), with

foliage that turns wine-red in fall. *Deutzia × magnifica* bears dense clusters of white, double pompon-like flowers in late spring. It is a vigorous hybrid 8-10 ft (2.4-3 m) high with a spread of 6-8 ft (1.8-2.4 m). It is hardy to zone 6.
Deutzia × rosea grows into a compact bush 3 ft (90 cm) high and wide, bearing soft rose-pink flowers in early summer to midsummer. It is hardy to zone 6.
Deutzia scabra is a popular species. It is bushy and upright, up to 6-10 ft (1.8-3 m) high and 4-6 ft (1.2-1.8 m) wide. It bears lance-shaped pale green to midgreen leaves. The cup-shaped flowers are white (also flushed with pink) and appear in upright clusters in late spring to early summer. It is hardy to zone 5. 'Candidissima' has pure white double blossoms; 'Plena' has white double flowers, suffused with rose-purple.

Cultivation

Plant in midfall or early spring in ordinary well-drained garden soil. Deutzias grow well in full sun, though cultivars with bright flowers retain their color better in light shade.

Remove old blooming stems at ground level after flowering in

Deutzia scabra 'Plena'

order to encourage new growth.
Propagation Take 3-4 in (7.5-10 cm) long cuttings of semihardened lateral shoots in mid- to late summer, and root in a cold frame. In mid- to late spring the following year, plant the rooted cuttings in nursery rows outdoors, and grow on until the following fall, when they can be planted in the permanent site. Or, take 10-12 in (25-30 cm) long hardwood cuttings of lateral shoots in midfall.
Pests/diseases None are serious.

DOGWOOD — see *Cornus*
DYER'S GREENWEED — see *Genista*

Elaeagnus
elaeagnus

Elaeagnus commutata

Elaeagnus umbellata

❏ Height 6-18 ft (1.8-5.4 m)
❏ Spread equal to height
❏ Flowers midspring to early summer
❏ Ordinary, even poor, well-drained soil
❏ Sunny site
❏ Hardy zones 2-8

Elaeagnus species are grown for their elegant foliage, which has an almost metallic sheen. These hardy shrubs are reliable, easily grown, and tough enough to form hedges and windbreaks in coastal gardens.

All the deciduous species blossom from midspring to early summer. The blooms are not showy but possess a sweet fragrance; they are followed in fall by clusters of berries much loved by birds.

Popular species
Elaeagnus angustifolia (Russian olive) bears attractive willowlike silvery leaves. With a height and spread up to 10-15 ft (3-4.5 m), it achieves near-treelike proportions and thus is most suitable for planting in a large garden. In mid- to late spring, small fragrant silvery flowers appear, followed by silvery amber berries. It is hardy in zones 2-7. The cultivar 'Red King' bears especially showy, rust-red fruits.

Elaeagnus commutata (silverberry) is one of the slower-growing species. Reaching 6-12 ft (1.8-3.6 m) high and wide, it is of suckering habit. The red-brown stems are upright and carry deep silver-green leaves. Silver flowers appear in midspring, followed by silver fruits. *E. commutata* is hardy to zones 2-6.

Elaeagnus multiflora is sometimes called cherry elaeagnus. It grows 10 ft (3 m) high and as much wide; the ovate leaves are dark green above, silvery beneath. The pale yellow flowers in midspring are followed by drooping clusters of edible cherrylike red berries. The shrub is resistant to air pollution and thus is ideal for city gardens. *E. multiflora* is hardy to zones 5-7.

Elaeagnus umbellata is a large shrub that grows up to 12-18 ft (3.6-5.4 m) tall and wide, with arching branches and young silvery shoots. The lance-shaped leaves are glossy green above, silvery underneath. Fluffy, highly fragrant, small white flowers appear in late spring or early summer, followed by fruits that ripen from silver to orange-scarlet. This is a good specimen shrub for a lawn. *E. umbellata* is hardy in zones 3-8.

Cultivation
Plant in midfall or early spring. These shrubs grow in ordinary, even poor soil, including shallow alkaline soils and sandy soils. All do best in full sun. For hedging, set the plants 3-5 ft (90-150 cm) apart.

Long, straggling shoots can be shortened in mid- to late spring. Trim established hedges in early summer and again in early fall if necessary.

Propagation Increase elaeagnus from seed sown in early fall. Seedlings should be grown on for at least 2 years before being planted out. Alternatively, increase by cuttings taken in late summer and rooted in a cold frame. Pot the rooted cuttings in spring and place them outdoors until midfall, when they can be planted out.

Pests/diseases Leaf spot may cause brown blotches on the leaves. Verticillium may cause the wilting and death of branches or whole trunks.

ELDER — see *Sambucus*

Enkianthus
enkianthus

Enkianthus campanulatus

- ❏ Height 5-15 ft (1.5-4.5 m)
- ❏ Spread 3-8 ft (90-240 cm)
- ❏ Flowers in mid- to late spring
- ❏ Rich, acid soil
- ❏ Semishaded, sheltered site
- ❏ Hardy zones 5-7

A profusion of small bell-like flowers and brilliant fall foliage make *Enkianthus* outstanding garden shrubs. Native to Japan, these hardy-growing shrubs have an upright habit. They make good companions for rhododendrons, requiring the same conditions — acid soil and dappled shade.

Popular species
Enkianthus campanulatus has bell-shaped cream-yellow flowers with red veining. They are borne in drooping clusters in late spring. The shrub reaches 8-15 ft (2.4-4.5 m) high and has a spread of 3-8 ft (90-240 cm). Clusters of dull green toothed leaves are carried at the end of smooth red shoots. They turn brilliant red in fall. It is hardy in zones 5-7.
Enkianthus cernuus rubens bears deep red flowers in midspring. A shorter shrub, reaching just 5-10 ft (1.5-3 m) high, its broad dull green leaves turn orange in fall. It is hardy to zone 6.

Cultivation
Plant in mid- to late fall or early spring in acid soil enriched with compost or peat moss. The site should be lightly shaded.
Propagation Take 3 in (7.5 cm) long heel cuttings of lateral shoots in summer, and root in pots in a cold frame. In mid- to late spring move to a nursery bed outdoors and grow on for 2 or 3 years before planting out.
Pests/diseases Trouble free.

Euonymus
euonymus, spindle tree

Euonymus europaeus 'Red Cascade'

- ❏ Height 5-30 ft (1.5-9 m)
- ❏ Spread 4-25 ft (1.2-7.5 m)
- ❏ Foliage shrub
- ❏ Ordinary garden soil
- ❏ Sun or partial shade
- ❏ Hardy zones 3-8

Euonymus is one of the most accommodating shrubs; it is fully hardy, easy to grow in any kind of soil, and spectacular in fall, with colorful berries and rich foliage colors.

Popular species
Euonymus alata is a slow-growing shrub reaching 15 ft (4.5 m) high. The small, insignificant green-yellow flowers, which appear in late spring, are followed by purple berries with scarlet seeds. But it is the leaves that make the species outstanding, turning from brilliant crimson to rose-red in fall. It is hardy to zones 4-8. The cultivar 'Compacta' is somewhat smaller, growing only 10 ft (3 m) tall.
Euonymus europaea (European spindle tree) grows 12-30 ft (3.6-9 m) tall and 10-25 ft (3-7.5 m) wide. It looks splendid when its rose-red capsules split open in fall to reveal orange seeds. It is hardy to zones 3-7. 'Aldenhamensis' bears extra-large and showy seed capsules, and 'Red Cascade' has large rose-red fruits.
Euonymus hamiltoniana yedoensis, syn. *E. yedoensis*, is a strong-growing large shrub or small tree up to 15 ft (4.5 m) high and 10 ft (3 m) wide. The ovate glossy green leaves turn yellow and red in fall. Pink, orange-seeded fruits hang from the branches long after the leaves have fallen. It is hardy to zone 4.
Euonymus latifolia is a 20 ft (6 m) high shrub with a spread

Euonymus latifolius

of about half to two-thirds its height. The midgreen leaves assume brilliant red tints in the fall. Clusters of drooping rose-red fruits produce orange seeds which appear in late summer. It is hardy to zone 6.

Cultivation

All *Euonymus* species and cultivars thrive in ordinary garden soil. Plant in midfall or early spring in sun or partial shade. Pruning is rarely necessary, but shoots may be thinned or shortened to shape the shrub in late winter.

Propagation Take heel cuttings of lateral shoots in late summer.

Pests/diseases Aphids, scale insects, and caterpillars can be problems. Euonymus may also be affected by leaf spot, powdery mildew, and crown gall.

Exochorda
exochorda

Exochorda × macrantha 'The Bride'

❑ Height 3-15 ft (90-450 cm)
❑ Spread 7-15 ft (2.1-4.5 m)
❑ Flowers midspring
❑ Well-drained, moisture-retentive soil
❑ Sheltered, sunny or lightly shaded site
❑ Hardy zones 5-8

Even among the other spring-flowering shrubs, exochordas always catch the eye. Their branches bear dense clusters of large white flowers. The spectacular display lasts only 7 to 10 days in midspring.

These hardy shrubs have a bushy habit. Growing up to 3-15 ft (90-450 cm) high and 7-15 ft (2.1-4.5 m) wide, they should be given plenty of room.

Popular species

Exochorda giraldii is a tall, upright shrub 15 ft (4.5 m) high and wide. The pink young shoots are distinctive in spring. It is hardy to zone 6. The variety *E. g. wilsonii* bears the largest flowers, up to 2 in (5 cm) wide.

Exochorda × macrantha 'The Bride' forms a compact mound of weeping branches 4 ft (1.2 m) high and 7 ft (2.1 m) wide. It is free-flowering and hardy to zone 5.

Exochorda racemosa (syn. *E.* *grandiflora*) is a bushy, spreading species 15 ft (4.5 m) high and wide. It tends to be chlorotic in alkaline soils. It is hardy in zones 5-8.

Cultivation

Plant container-grown specimens in fall or spring in fertile, well-drained but moisture-retentive soil; they are generally unsuitable for shallow, alkaline soils. Choose a sunny or lightly shaded position, sheltered from cold winds. The short floral display will last slightly longer if the shrubs are in partial shade. After flowering, remove weak shoots from the base, and tip the remainder to encourage strong side shoots.

Propagation Take cuttings in summer and root under glass, or use larger long shoots in fall; they should have rooted after a year.

Pests/diseases Trouble free.

FALSE ACACIA — see *Robinia*
FALSE SPIREA — see *Sorbaria*
FILBERT — see *Corylus*
FLEECE FLOWER —
see *Polygonum*
FLOWERING QUINCE —
see *Chaenomeles*

Forsythia
forsythia

Forsythia x *intermedia* 'Spectabilis'

❏ Height 4-10 ft (1.2-3 m)
❏ Spread equal to height
❏ Flowers early spring to midspring
❏ Ordinary garden soil
❏ Sunny or partially shaded site
❏ Hardy zones 5-8

With their modest cultural requirements and spectacular display of yellow flowers, it is not surprising that the hardy forsythias are among the best-loved spring-flowering shrubs. The yellow flowers smother bare stems from early spring to midspring, before the fresh green leaves unfurl.

Popular species
Forsythia × *intermedia* is a vigorous shrub with a height and spread of 4-10 ft (1.2-3 m). Its clusters of golden yellow flowers appear in abundance between early spring and midspring. 'Spectabilis' is a commonly grown cultivar that makes a good hedging shrub. Other cultivars include 'Beatrix Farrand' (canary-yellow) and 'Lynwood' (broad petals, rich yellow).
Forsythia suspensa has drooping branches, which give it a rambling appearance. Long streamers of pale lemon-yellow flowers open in early spring to midspring. The variety *sieboldii* is a weeping form.

Cultivation
Plant in midfall or midspring in ordinary garden soil in sun or partial shade.

Forsythias flower on shoots of the previous year's growth; after flowering, remove old or damaged shoots and prune about a third of the remainder back to 4 in (10 cm) off the ground.

Propagation From May to September, take 10-12 in (25-30 cm) long hardwood cuttings of strong shoots of the current season. *Forsythia suspensa* can also be layered.

Pests/diseases Late freezes may destroy the young flower buds.

Forsythia x *intermedia* 'Lynwood'

Fothergilla
fothergilla

Fothergilla major

❏ Height 2-10 ft (60-300 cm)
❏ Spread 3-10 ft (90-300 cm)
❏ Flowers early spring to midspring
❏ Moist, rich, acid soil
❏ Sunny site
❏ Hardy zones 5-8

Fothergillas are grown as much for their brilliant fall colors as for their spring flowers — fragrant bottlebrush-like spikes consisting of numerous long cream-white stamens.

Popular species
Fothergilla gardenii has a slender, upright growth habit and reaches about 2-3 ft (60-90 cm) high and 3-4 ft (90-120 cm) wide. Its oval midgreen leaves turn red and crimson in fall. The flowers are carried in erect spikes in early spring to midspring. It is hardy in zones 5-8.
Fothergilla major reaches 6-10 ft (1.8-3 m) high with a similar spread. The oval leaves, which are dark green above and gray-green below, assume brilliant orange-yellow or red fall tints. Erect spikes of white flowers open in early spring to midspring. It is hardy in zones 5-8.

Cultivation
Plant in midfall to late fall or in early spring in moist, acid soil with plenty of organic matter. The site should be sunny.

Propagation Layer long shoots in early fall; separate from the parent after 2 years when they should have rooted.

Pests/diseases Trouble free.

Fuchsia
fuchsia

Fuchsia 'Mrs. Popple'

Fuchsia 'Gracilis Variegata'

❏ Height 6-72 in (15-180 cm)
❏ Spread 6-48 in (15-120 cm)
❏ Flowers early summer to midfall
❏ Well-drained, rich soil
❏ Sunny or lightly shaded site
❏ Hardy zones 6-10

Originally from South America and New Zealand, most of the popular fuchsias are hybrids developed from a few species. Many cannot tolerate frost or extreme heat and are suitable for cultivation only in the most temperate regions of the US, such as the Pacific Coast, although in cold winter regions they may be cultivated as summer-flowering annuals. A few fuchsias, however, exhibit considerable cold hardiness and will survive as more or less permanent plantings as far north as New York City or central Illinois. Even these hardy types must be planted in a spot protected from winter winds, and in severe winters they are often cut to the ground, but they will usually sprout again from the base.

The pendent flowers that make fuchsias such popular ornamental shrubs appear from early summer into midfall. They vary enormously in size and come in shades of red, pink, purple, blue, white, and cream — most are bicolored. All are set off by small lance-shaped green leaves.

Fuchsias have a wide range of uses in the garden. The large shrubby types make excellent informal hedges, or they can be grown against walls. Others can be trained as standards. The low, trailing fuchsias are shown off to best effect when grown in hanging baskets, window boxes, or other containers.

Popular cultivars

Fuchsia magellanica is the cold-hardiest fuchsia, flourishing in zone 6 with winter protection, and is much used as a hedging shrub in mild coastal gardens. It is a bushy shrub with an average height of 3 ft (90 cm) in the northern part of its range, and it may reach 6 ft (1.8 m) to the south. The small flowers are carried on slender stems. They have crimson tubes, a spreading skirt of crimson sepals, and purple petals. Some popular cultivars include the following:

'Alba' (also known as *F. m. molinae*) has pale pink flowers and bright green leaves.
'Gracilis' carries numerous slender red-and-purple flowers and has narrow leaves.
'Gracilis Variegata' has red-and-purple flowers and leaves edged with cream and flushed pink. It is less hardy than 'Gracilis.'
'Pumila' is a miniature cultivar just 6 in (15 cm) high with tiny, narrow red-and-purple flowers.
'Riccartonii' is exceptionally vigorous and hardy, with scarlet-and-purple flowers.
'Versicolor' carries slender red-and-purple flowers. It is chiefly grown for its leaves variegated with gray-green, cream, or yellow, and tinged pink.
Garden hybrids, derived chiefly from *F. magellanica* and *F. fulgens*, offer an enormous range of habits, flower sizes, and colors. Grown as free-standing shrubs that rarely exceed 2 ft (60 cm) high and wide, they are not reliably hardy outside of zone 9, although they may survive winters farther north if given a thick blanket of protective mulch.
'Abbe Farges' has cerise-and-lilac-pink semidouble flowers. It is hardy to zone 7.
'Alice Hoffman' has purple-tinted leaves and small double flowers with carmine sepals and white petals.
'Beacon Rosa' has pink flowers. It is hardy to zone 7.
'Corallina,' of strong spreading habit, has red-and-purple flowers.
'Lena' has large semidouble flowers of white, pink, and mauve. It is hardy to zone 7.
'Madame Cornieliesen' has semidouble flowers with red sepals and white petals.

Genista
broom, woadwaxen

Genista tinctoria

Fuchsia 'Tom Thumb'

'Mrs. Popple' is a particularly hardy cultivar. Its arching stems bear flowers with red sepals and purple petals.

'Mrs. W. P. Wood' has small but profuse white flowers, tinged pink.

'Tom Thumb' is usually less than 1 ft (30 cm) high and wide. It is heat tolerant and has cherry-red sepals and mauve petals.

Cultivation
Plant in late spring in a sheltered spot in full sun or light shade. Any well-drained garden soil is suitable, preferably enriched with organic matter. In all but the mildest areas, treat the shrubs as perennials, cutting them back to near ground level in late fall; cover the crowns with a deep winter mulch. In spring, trim unpruned shrubs if necessary, pruning dead and damaged twigs.

Propagation Take 3-4 in (7.5-10 cm) long tip cuttings in spring.

Pests/diseases Aphids and whiteflies may infest foliage. Botrytis blight may damage leaves, covering them with gray mold, and verticillium wilt may cause dieback of stems or whole plants.

❑ Height 3-48 in (7.5-120 cm)
❑ Spread up to 3-8 ft (90-240 cm)
❑ Flowers late spring to early summer
❑ Any well-drained soil
❑ Sunny site
❑ Hardy zones 5-8

Two large genera of plants are called brooms, *Cytisus* and *Genista*. *Genista* species have wiry stems, which may be spiny, and small leaves. Profuse pea-shaped yellow flowers appear in late spring and early summer. These hardy, easy-to-grow plants tolerate poor, dry soils. Tall types make fine specimen plants; others are good for ground cover.

Popular species
Genista hispanica (Spanish broom), a dwarf but wide-spreading shrub, is only 2-4 ft (60-120 cm) high but 8 ft (2.4 m) wide. In early summer the flowers are so profuse that the shrub takes on a golden yellow hue. This many-branched species has dense prickles and small, deep

green leaves. It is hardy to zone 6. *Genista lydia* is of elegant habit, with slender, arching spine-tipped stems. It reaches 2-3 ft (60-90 cm) high with a spread of 6 ft (1.8 m). It is excellent for training over walls, for covering banks, or for large rock gardens. Bright yellow

Genista sagittalis

Hamamelis
witch hazel

Genista lydia

flowers appear in late spring —
the small leaves are gray-green. It
is hardy in zones 7-9.

Genista sagittalis is a ground-
hugging species with slender,
almost prostrate stems. It grows
only 8 in (20 cm) high but spreads
to 3 ft (90 cm). Its green leaflike
"wings" give it an evergreen appearance. The small heads of yellow flowers appear in late spring.
It is hardy to zone 5.

Genista tinctoria (dyer's greenweed) has a varied habit and is
hardy in zones 5-7. It may grow
as a low, spreading shrub or as
an erect shrub. It reaches from
3-36 in (7.5-90 cm) high and up
to 6 ft (1.8 m) wide. The yellow
flowers are borne amid dark
green leaves in early summer.
'Royal Gold' has sprays of golden
yellow flowers.

Cultivation
Plant container-grown shrubs in
midfall or early spring to midspring in ordinary well-drained
soil. They thrive in poor soil in
full sun.

Encourage bushy growth by
pinching the growing points on
young plants after flowering.
Thin the crowded shoots of mature bushes after flowering.

Propagation Take heel cuttings
of lateral shoots in late summer.

Pests/diseases Trouble free.

GLORYBOWER —
see *Clerodendrum*
GRAPE VINE — see *Vitis*
GUELDER ROSE —
see *Viburnum*

Hamamelis mollis

❏ Height 10-20 ft (3-6 m)
❏ Spread equal to height
❏ Flowers late winter to early spring
❏ Neutral or acid, moist soil
❏ Sunny, sheltered site
❏ Hardy zones 5-8

Hardy witch hazels are invaluable shrubs for winter interest, as
they flower abundantly between
late winter and early spring. The
spider-like flowers are carried on
bare branches and range in color
from yellow to red. Many witch
hazels are fragrant. In fall the
leaves turn rich shades of red and
orange or yellow.

Popular species
Hamamelis × intermedia is a hybrid between *H. japonica* and *H.
mollis*. Growing 15-20 ft (4.5-6 m)
high and wide, it can be distinguished by the flowers, which
have twisted and crinkly yellow
or copper-tinted petals. They appear in late winter or very early
spring. The oval midgreen leaves
turn yellow in fall. It is hardy to
zone 5. Cultivars are 'Arnold
Promise' (yellow blooms nestled
in reddish cups; yellow fall foliage), and 'Diane' (coppery red
flowers; good fall color).

Hamamelis japonica, 10-15 ft
(3-4.5 m) high and wide, flowers
in late winter and early spring; it
has twisted and crinkly yellow
petals, sometimes tinged red. It is
hardy in zones 6-8.

Hamamelis mollis (Chinese witch
hazel) grows 10-15 ft (3-4.5 m)
high and wide. It may bloom as
early as midwinter in mild regions, but more commonly in late
winter or early spring, bearing
rich golden yellow flowers that
are flushed red at the base and
sweetly scented. It has green felted leaves. It is hardy in zones 6-8.
'Pallida,' a popular cultivar, carries sulfur-yellow blooms.

Cultivation
Plant in suitable weather in midfall or early spring in neutral or
acid, moisture-retentive soil. If
the soil is heavy, enrich it with organic matter. The site can be sunny or lightly shaded, but it should
be sheltered from cold east winds.

Cut back straggly branches after flowering.

Propagation Layer long shoots
in early fall; separate from the
parent plant 2 years later.

Pests/diseases Trouble free.

HARDY ORANGE —
see *Poncirus*
HAZEL — see *Corylus*

Hibiscus
hibiscus

Hibiscus syriacus 'Woodbridge'

❏ Height 6-12 ft (1.8-3.6 m)
❏ Spread 4-10 ft (1.2-3 m)
❏ Flowers late summer to midfall
❏ Well-drained, fertile soil
❏ Sunny, sheltered site
❏ Hardy zones 5-8

Though they produce spectacular flowers, most hibiscuses are subtropical or tropical plants that cannot tolerate frost. One species, however, does flourish throughout most of the US, offering brilliant blossoms all summer.

Hibiscus syriacus is a well-branched shrub with upright stems, up to 12 ft (3.6 m) tall and 10 ft (3 m) wide. Cultivars are 'Blue Bird' (blue with a white eye), 'Hamabo' (white with a crimson eye), 'Lady Stanley' (semidouble white flowers, tinted pink), and 'Woodbridge' (rose-pink). The National Arboretum has recently released a series of excellent cultivars that include 'Aphrodite' (pink flowers with dark red eyes), 'Diana' (large, pure white flowers that stay open at night), 'Helene' (white flowers with reddish-purple bases), and 'Minerva' (lavender flowers with dark red eyes).

Cultivation
Plant in midfall or early spring in well-drained, fertile soil in a sheltered border in full sun. Shorten long branches after flowering.
Propagation Take heel cuttings of half-ripe nonflowering shoots in midsummer.
Pests/diseases Aphids can infest growth.

HIMALAYAN HONEYSUCKLE—
see *Leycesteria*

Hippophae
sea buckthorn

Hippophae rhamnoides

❏ Height 8-10 ft (2.4-3 m)
❏ Spread equal to height
❏ Grown for its berries
❏ Any well-drained soil
❏ Sunny or partially shaded site
❏ Hardy zones 4-7

The sea buckthorn (*Hippophae rhamnoides*) is an uncommon but useful shrub: it thrives along roadsides and in seaside gardens, looking very effective when planted in masses. It is an exceptionally adaptable plant — it will grow equally well inland.

The scaly bark is covered with the sharp spines that give the plant its name, and the upright stems are clothed with elongated, willowlike silver leaves that glisten in the sun. But the sea buckthorn's true glory appears in fall, when the leaves fall, displaying shining bright orange-gold berries that often remain all winter long. For female plants to produce berries, a male specimen is essential — ideally one male to every six females.

Cultivation
Plant in midfall or early spring in well-drained soil in a sunny or partially shaded site. It is excellent in poor soils. Cut back straggly growths in midsummer.
Propagation Seed propagation takes many years, so buy new stock from a nursery.
Pests/diseases Trouble free.

Hoheria
hoheria

Hoheria glabrata

❏ Height 10-15 ft (3-4.5 m)
❏ Spread 8-10 ft (2.4-3 m)
❏ Flowers in midsummer
❏ Good, well-drained soil
❏ Sunny or partially shaded site, sheltered from cold winds
❏ Hardy to zone 8

Hoheria glabrata (syn. *H. lyallii),* is not hardy throughout most of the central US but thrives in the warmer areas of the Pacific Coast and in the southern states, especially if given a warm, sheltered spot. It is one of the loveliest white-flowered shrubs. The foliage is downy gray, turning soft yellow in fall. In midsummer the branches are weighed down with clusters of faintly fragrant, creamy white flowers.

Cultivation
Plant in mid- to late spring in good, well-drained soil, preferably against a sunny, sheltered wall.

Cut out the dead and damaged wood, and prune back any straggly shoots in early spring to midspring.
Propagation Layer long shoots in early fall, and separate from the parent plant a year later.
Pests/diseases Trouble free.

HONEYSUCKLE —
see *Lonicera*
HORSE CHESTNUT —
see *Aesculus*

Hydrangea
hydrangea

Hydrangea macrophylla 'Nikko Blue'

- ❏ Height 3-50 ft (.9-15 m)
- ❏ Spread 3-15 ft (90-450 cm)
- ❏ Flowers summer to early fall
- ❏ Loamy, moisture-retentive soil
- ❏ Sun or light shade; shelter
- ❏ Hardy zones 3-9

Hydrangeas are excellent shrubs for providing color in the late-summer garden — climbing types flower in early summer. Moderately cold hardy, these shrubs are ideal for town and seaside gardens, as they tolerate pollution and salt spray.

Popular species
Hydrangea anomala petiolaris is a vigorous, hardy climber up to 5 ft (1.5 m) high — it clings by aerial roots. The cream-white lace-cap flowers appear in early summer. It is hardy in zones 5-7.
Hydrangea arborescens reaches 3-5 ft (90-150 cm) high and wide. It is hardy in zones 4-9 and usually represented by the cultivar 'Grandiflora,' with large, pure white flowers in rounded clusters that are borne throughout the summer. The bright green leaves are oval and pointed.

Hydrangea macrophylla is the species from which most garden cultivars have been developed. Hardy in zones 6-9, it grows to a height and spread of 3-6 ft (90-180 cm) or more. The color of the flowers — blue or pink — is largely determined by soil type. In alkaline soils flowers are pink-red or purple-red; in acid soils they are blue. Cultivars divide into mop heads (hortensias) and lace caps. Both flower in summer.

Mop-head hydrangeas have 5-8 in (12-20 cm) wide heads of sterile flowers. They include 'All Summer Beauty' (rich blue to pink flowers on new growth), 'Domotoi' (large, pale pink or blue double flowers), 'Forever Pink' (compact bush; pink flowers that darken to red in cool weather), 'Goliath' (brick-red or purple-blue), 'Nikko Blue' (vigorous

Hydrangea anomala petiolaris

shrub to 6 ft/1.8 m; large blue flowers), and 'Westfalen' (crimson-red or purple-blue).

Lace-cap hydrangeas have delicate, flat heads 4-6 in (10-15 cm) wide with tiny, fertile inner flowers and sterile outer florets. Popular cultivars include 'Blue Wave' (blue, mauve, or pink), 'Lanarth White' (fertile flowers pink or

Hydrangea 'Blue Wave,' acid soil

Hydrangea 'Westfalen'

Hydrangea paniculata 'Grandiflora'

blue; sterile florets white), 'Mar-iesii' (rich pink or blue), 'Tricol-or' (pale pink to blue; variegated foliage), and 'Variegata' (blue flowers; leaves edged with cream). *Hydrangea paniculata* is a hardy 12-25 ft (3.6-7.5 m) high species with arching stems bearing conical clusters of white flowers that turn pink with age. They appear in summer. It is hardy in zones 3-8. 'Grandiflora' has 1½ ft (45 cm) long flower spikes; the smaller-flowered 'Praecox' is just 6 ft (1.8 m) high and wide.
Hydrangea quercifolia is distinguished by lobed, oak-leaf-like foliage that assumes brilliant fall tints. It grows 6 ft (1.8 m) high and wide. Upright white flower spikes appear in summer. It is hardy in zones 5-9.
Hydrangea serrata, syn. *H. macrophylla serrata*, grows up to 3 ft (90 cm) high and wide. Cultivars include 'Bluebird' (blue lace-cap flowers) and 'Preziosa' (salmon-pink to red flowers; young reddish-brown leaves). It is hardy in zones 6-7.

Cultivation

Plant in midfall or midspring in good, loamy, moisture-retentive soil. Choose a sheltered site, in sun or partial shade. Give hydrangeas an annual mulch of well-composted manure in midspring.

Deadhead hydrangeas after flowering. Remove weak or winter-killed shoots in early spring. Cut the previous year's shoots on *H. arborescens* and *H. paniculata* back by half. On *H. macrophylla* thin out 2- or 3-year-old flowering shoots at ground level.
Propagation Increase shrubby hydrangeas by 4-6 in (10-15 cm) cuttings in early summer to midsummer, and climbing species by 3 in (7.5 cm) cuttings.
Pests/diseases Aphids, mites, and scale insects may feed on the stems and leaves; bacterial wilt, bud blight, leaf spot, and powdery mildew attack twigs and foliage.

Hypericum
St.-John's-wort

Hypericum 'Hidcote'

Hypericum androsaemum

Forming a dome 5 ft (1.5 m) high and wide, it is covered with golden flowers throughout summer. It is hardy in zones 6-9.

Hypericum × inodorum 'Elstead' is a semievergreen 4 ft (1.2 m) high shrub with a spread of 5 ft (1.5 m). From midsummer on, it bears a profusion of gold flowers followed by salmon-red berry clusters. It is hardy to zone 8.

Hypericum × moseranum is a dwarf shrub, 1-2½ ft (30-75 cm) high, and spreading to 3-4 ft (90-120 cm). Clusters of yellow flowers appear between midsummer and midfall. The cultivar 'Tricolor' has green-and-white variegated leaves with red margins. It is hardy to zone 7.

Cultivation
Plant in midspring in any fertile, well-drained soil in a sunny spot.

Trim the plants to shape in early spring, and at the same time prune some of the oldest shoots at ground level to encourage the formation of new stems.

Propagation To increase small species and hybrids, take 2 in (5 cm) softwood cuttings in late spring to early summer, and root in a cold frame.

Propagate taller shrubs (*H. frondosum* 'Hidcote,' and *H. inodorum* 'Elstead') from 4-5 in (10-13 cm) long heel cuttings of nonflowering lateral shoots between midsummer and early fall. *H. calycinum* is best propagated by softwood cuttings taken in early summer.

Pests/diseases Rust shows as orange spots on the leaves; leaf spot and powdery mildew also afflict foliage.

❏ Height 1-5 ft (30-150 cm)
❏ Spread 2-6 ft (60-180 cm)
❏ Flowers early summer to fall
❏ Fertile, well-drained soil
❏ Sunny site
❏ Hardy zones 6-9

The shrubby St.-John's-worts include hardy evergreen and deciduous plants, the latter often semievergreen in mild-weather regions. Though fairly cold hardy and heat tolerant, they may be relatively short-lived.

St.-John's-worts are valued for their midsummer flowers. They come in shades of yellow and are cup-shaped, often opening out flat to reveal a central boss of golden stamens. In some species and hybrids, the flower display is followed by bright berries.

Easily grown, St.-John's-worts spread quickly and are excellent for providing summer color in plantings of shrubs or as ground cover in borders and on banks.

Popular species
Hypericum androsaemum (Tutsan), 2-3 ft (60-90 cm) high and wide, is free-flowering with clusters of small yellow flowers. Its chief attraction is its fall berries, which are red-purple at first, then turn dark crimson. It is hardy in zones 6-8.

Hypericum calycinum (aaronsbeard) is a semievergreen shrub 1-1½ ft (30-45 cm) high and 2 ft (60 cm) wide. A decorative, fast-growing ground cover, it bears brilliant yellow flowers from midsummer into fall. It is hardy in zones 6-8.

Hypericum frondosum is an upright shrub that reaches a height and width of 4 ft (1.2 m). The foliage is blue-green, and the exfoliating bark is reddish brown. The golden yellow flowers appear in early summer to midsummer. It is hardy in zones 6-8.

Hypericum 'Hidcote' is one of the most popular St.-John's-worts.

Indigofera
indigo, indigofera

Indigofera gerardiana

❑ Height 2-4 ft (60-120 cm)
❑ Spread similar to height
❑ Flowers early to late summer
❑ Good, well-drained soil
❑ Sheltered, sunny site
❑ Hardy zones 5-8

Even in their hardy zones, indigos are vulnerable to an unusually hard frost, which may cut them to the ground. But they grow fast and soon shoot up again from their bases. They have elegant gray-green fernlike foliage and profuse clusters of pealike flowers they bear all summer.

Popular species
Indigofera gerardiana, syn. *I. heterantha*, grows 2-4 ft (60-120 cm) tall and wide. The attractive gray-green foliage appears in early summer; rose-purple flowers follow. It is hardy through zone 7.
Indigofera kirilowii is hardier, flourishing from zone 7 up into zone 5. It forms a 3 ft (90 cm) tall, dense shrub with bright green foliage and rose-colored flowers that are borne in early summer.

Cultivation
Plant in early fall to midfall or midspring in good, well-drained soil that is not too rich. In midspring remove all weak and winter-killed shoots. To maintain shape, shorten strong shoots of the previous season by half.
Propagation Increase by seed.
Pests/diseases Trouble free.

JAPANESE ANGELICA TREE —
see *Aralia*
JAPANESE KERRIA —
see *Kerria*

Jasminum
jasmine

Jasminum nudiflorum

❑ Height 6-30 ft (1.8-9 m)
❑ Climber
❑ Flowers in winter and summer
❑ Any well-drained soil
❑ Sun or shade
❑ Hardy zones 6-10

Including both shrubs and climbers, this genus is usually trained up or over a wall and is cultivated mainly for its flowers — slender trumpet-shaped flowers that can be white or yellow and are often fragrant.
Jasminum nudiflorum, the winter-flowering jasmine, needs support for its floppy stems, but the common white jasmine will clamber over arbors and pergolas.

Popular species
Jasminum nudiflorum (winter jasmine) grows 15 ft (4.5 m) high against a wall, given support. The bright yellow flowers are produced from late winter to early spring on sprawling green stems. It is hardy in zones 6-10.
Jasminum officinale (common white jasmine) is a vigorous climber reaching 30 ft (9 m) high. Its twining stems carry clusters of sweetly scented white flowers from early summer to midfall. It is hardy in zones 8-10. Cultivars are 'Affine' (syn. 'Grandiflorum';

Jasminum officinale

large flowers, pink in bud) and 'Aureum' (yellow-blotched leaves).

Cultivation
Plant in midfall or early spring in any well-drained soil in a protected spot.
After flowering, cut the stems of *J. nudiflorum* back to within a few inches of the base. Thin the shoots of *J. officinale* after flowering, but do not shorten them.
Propagation Layer in early fall to midfall and separate from the parent plant a year later.
Pests/diseases Trouble free.

JUNEBERRY —
see *Amelanchier*

Kerria
Japanese kerria

Kerria japonica 'Pleniflora'

❏ Height 3-6 ft (90-180 cm)
❏ Spread 6-12 ft (1.8-3.6 m)
❏ Flowers mid- to late spring
❏ Ordinary garden soil
❏ Light shade or sun
❏ Hardy zones 5-9

During mid- to late spring, the shaggy buttercup-yellow flowers of *Kerria japonica* — Japanese kerria — are a familiar sight in gardens. Most specimens are the hardy, double-flowered form 'Pleniflora,' which has long, flexible stems ideal for training against a wall and wedge-shaped, toothed, bright green leaves that turn golden yellow in fall. It may reach up to 6 ft (1.8 m) high and 12 ft (3.6 m) wide. The species has single flowers and grows into a thicket of slender arching stems of similar size.

Cultivation
Plant during suitable weather in midfall or early spring in ordinary garden soil in a partially shaded spot or in full sun. In cold areas plant the shrubs against a wall with a south-facing or west-facing exposure.

After flowering, cut back all flowered shoots to new strong growth. Thin the new shoots of 'Pleniflora' to encourage vigorous young basal shoots.
Propagation Divide and replant shrubs with numerous stems in midfall or early spring.
Pests/diseases Trouble free.

Kolkwitzia
beautybush

Kolkwitzia amabilis 'Pink Cloud'

❏ Height 6-12 ft (1.8-3.6 m)
❏ Spread 4-10 ft (1.2-3 m)
❏ Flowers late spring to early summer
❏ Ordinary well-drained garden soil
❏ Sunny site
❏ Hardy zones 5-8

The apparently fragile-looking flowers of the beautybush (*Kolkwitzia amabilis*) belie the hardiness of this shrub, which grows into a thicket up to 12 ft (3.6 m) high. In late spring to early summer, the branches arch over with the weight of its many clusters of pink, yellow-throated flowers. The cultivar 'Pink Cloud' has an abundance of clear pink flowers.

The dark green leaves are oval, hairy, and toothed. Another distinguishing feature is the peeling brown bark.

Cultivation
Plant in midfall to late fall or in early spring in ordinary well-drained soil in a sunny site.

After flowering, remove some of the older flowering stems at ground level.
Propagation Take 4-6 in (10-15 cm) long heel cuttings of lateral nonflowering shoots in early summer, and root in a cold frame.
Pests/diseases Trouble free.

KOLOMIKTA — see *Actinidia*

Lavatera
tree mallow

Lavatera olbia 'Rosea'

❏ Height 6-8 ft (1.8-2.4 m)
❏ Spread 5 ft (1.5 m)
❏ Flowers early summer to late fall
❏ Ordinary, well-drained garden soil
❏ Sunny, sheltered site
❏ Hardy zones 8-9

With its hollyhock-like flowers, tree mallow (*Lavatera olbia*) has an old-fashioned cottage-garden appearance and is prized for its long flowering season.

It forms a 6-8 ft (1.8-2.4 m) high bush of pithy stems clothed with soft gray-green leaves. From early summer to late fall, it bears a succession of pink flowers. The cultivar 'Barnsley' is very pale pink with red clusters; 'Rosea' has red-pink flowers.

Sensitive to frost, the short-lived tree mallow is best grown in warm, sheltered sites and coastal areas. It thrives in any soil, even poor shallow types, and flourishes in alkaline soils.

Cultivation
Plant in early fall or in spring in any well-drained garden soil that is not too rich. The site should be sunny and sheltered from cold winds.

In fall, prune the shoots by half to avoid wind damage during the

Lavatera olbia

winter. Cut back hard in spring to maintain shape.

Propagation Take semiripe cuttings in late summer, and root in a cold frame.

Pests/diseases Leaf spot shows as yellow-brown spots on leaves, leaf stalks, and stems. Rust appears as orange spores that later turn brown. Japanese beetles may do serious damage to the foliage.

Leycesteria
Himalayan honeysuckle

Leycesteria formosa

❏ Height 6 ft (1.8 m)
❏ Spread 5 ft (1.5 m)
❏ Flowers mid- to late summer
❏ Any well-drained soil
❏ Full sun or light shade
❏ Hardy to zone 7

Himalayan honeysuckle (*Leycesteria formosa*) will grow in almost any soil in full sun or shade. It is a highly distinctive shrub with arching 6 ft (1.8 m) high stems that bear pendent spikes of white tubular flowers in mid- to late summer. Each bloom is partially concealed by a purple bract.

In fall the flowers are followed by shiny purple-black berries — the purple bracts remain. As the nights become colder, the leaves turn a similar color and then fall, to reveal sea-green shoots.

Cultivation
Plant in midfall or early spring in any well-drained soil. It is shade tolerant but flowers more freely in a sunny site. This is a good shrub for coastal gardens as it tolerates salt spray. In early spring, cut to the ground all the shoots that bore flowers that year; at the northern end of the shrub's hardy range, cut all branches back near to the ground in fall.

Propagation In midfall insert 6 in (15 cm) hardwood cuttings in a nursery bed. Grow on for a year before planting out in permanent sites in early fall to midfall.

Pests/diseases Trouble free.

LILAC — see *Syringa*

Lonicera
honeysuckle

Lonicera periclymenum 'Graham Thomas'

Lonicera periclymenum 'Serotina'

❏ Height 2-30 ft (60-900 cm)
❏ Spread 4-10 ft (1.2-3 m)
❏ Flowers throughout the year
❏ Fertile, well-drained soil
❏ Sunny or partially shaded site
❏ Hardy zones 3-8

Honeysuckle is the familiar vine of scented yellow and red flowers — and a vast range of deciduous and evergreen shrubs, both hardy and frost tender, as well. Climbing honeysuckles will grow up walls, fences, and archways. Those described here are deciduous or sometimes semievergreen. The blooms are often fragrant; berries follow. The deciduous shrubby honeysuckles are good for mixed borders; several are useful as ground-cover plants.

Popular species
Lonicera alpigena (Alps honeysuckle) grows 4-8 ft (1.2-2.4 m) high. Its leaves are oblong and dark, glossy green; the yellow blooms, tinged red, are borne on long flower stalks in midspring. It is hardy in zones 6-7.
Lonicera × brownii (scarlet trumpet honeysuckle), sometimes semievergreen, climbs 10-15 ft

(3-4.5 m) high. The orange-scarlet blooms appear in early summer and then return in late summer. It is hardy to zone 6. 'Dropmore Scarlet' has scarlet-red flowers and a longer flowering period.
Lonicera fragrantissima, a shrubby winter-flowering honeysuckle, is a loosely branched, partially

evergreen shrub, 6-10 ft (1.8-3 m) high and wide. Its sweetly scented ivory-white flowers appear from late winter to early spring. In late spring, red berries follow. It is hardy in zones 5-8.
Lonicera periclymenum (woodbine) will reach 15-20 ft (4.5-6 m) when grown over a wall. The sweetly fragrant, pale yellow flowers flushed with purple-red open from early to late summer; bright red berries follow. Several superior garden cultivars with a longer flowering period are available, including 'Belgica,' or early Dutch honeysuckle (a bushy climber with purple-red and yellow flowers in late spring and early summer); 'Graham Thomas'

Lonicera x brownii 'Dropmore Scarlet'

Lonicera x tellmanniana

Magnolia
magnolia

Magnolia x loebneri 'Leonard Messel'

❏ Height 6-25 ft (1.8-7.5 m)
❏ Spread 5-25 ft (1.5-7.5 m)
❏ Flowers early spring to late summer
❏ Well-drained, loamy soil
❏ Sun or dappled shade; sheltered
  from wind
❏ Hardy zones 5-8

(cream and yellow flowers in mid- to late summer); and 'Serotina,' or late Dutch honeysuckle (purple-red and cream-yellow flowers from midsummer to midfall). It is hardy in zones 5-8.

Lonicera tatarica (Tatarian honeysuckle) grows 12 ft (3.6 m) high and 10 ft (3 m) wide. The foliage is blue-green; the flowers, which appear in midspring, are pink to white. Red berries adorn the shrub all summer. Cultivars include 'Alba' (pure white flowers), 'Hack's Red' (red-purple blossoms), and 'Rosea' (rosy pink flowers). It is hardy in zones 3-8.

Lonicera × *tellmanniana* will climb vigorously over walls in semi- or full shade, where it may grow 15 ft (4.5 m) high. Large clusters of copper-red and yellow flowers appear in early summer and midsummer. It is hardy in zones 6-7.

Cultivation
Grow honeysuckles in any well-drained soil, enriched with humus for the climbing species. All will grow in sun or partial shade, but climbers do better in light shade. Plant in early fall or early spring.

On established climbers, thin all crowded stems by removing about one-third of the shoots from ground level in early spring every year. Shrubby honeysuckles need little pruning; to encourage new shoots from the base, they can be thinned in spring.

Propagation Increase climbing species and cultivars by rooting 4 in (10 cm) long stem cuttings (taken in mid- to late summer) in a cold frame. The following mid- to late spring pot the rooted cuttings and plunge them outside. Plant out in the permanent flowering sites in early to midfall.

Shrubby and climbing honeysuckles can be increased by layering between late summer and late fall. Separate from the parent plant about a year later.

Pests/diseases Aphids, whiteflies, flea beetles, looper caterpillars, and mealybugs attack foliage and twigs. Leaf spot may disfigure foliage and may cause dieback; powdery mildew shows as a powdery white deposit on the leaves.

This genus contains some of the most spectacular flowering shrubs and trees (see also pages 36-38). The magnificent blooms appear between early spring and late summer. All the shrubby magnolias are deciduous, with the early-flowering types carrying their blooms on bare branches.

To show magnolias off to best effect, grow them on their own as specimen shrubs. They need shelter from strong, drying winds and early-morning sun in spring, such as that afforded by a south-facing or west-facing wall.

Popular species
Magnolia liliiflora (lily magnolia) syn. *M. purpurea* has red-purple chalice-shaped flowers, which open in midspring. Its oval leaves are midgreen above and paler beneath. Average height is 8-12 ft (2.4-3.6 m), with a similar spread. It dislikes alkaline soils. It is hardy in zones 6-8. 'Nigra,' a more compact cultivar, has deep purple-red flowers.

Magnolia × *loebneri* bears profuse fragrant, star-shaped white flowers in early spring to midspring before the lance-shaped midgreen leaves appear. It can grow up to

Magnolia liliiflora 'Nigra'

25 ft (7.5 m) high and wide, and tolerates limy soils. It is hardy to zone 5. Cultivars are 'Leonard Messel' (lilac-pink flowers) and 'Merrill' (white flowers).

Magnolia sieboldii, syn. *M. parviflora,* has pendent bowl-shaped flowers with white petals and conspicuous claret-red stamens. The perfumed blooms appear in late spring, recurring off and on all through summer. The shrub grows 10-15 ft (3-4.5 m) high and wide, and bears dark green lance-shaped leaves that are downy beneath. Striking seed capsules open in fall to reveal orange seeds. The species is intolerant of alkalinity. It is hardy in zones 6-8.

Magnolia stellata is a slow-growing tree, usually treated as a shrub although it can eventually reach a height of 15-20 ft (4.5-6 m) with a spread of 10-15 ft (3-4.5 m). Its fragrant, star-shaped white flowers open in early spring. The lance-shaped leaves are pale green to midgreen. This species is hardy from zones 5-8. Cultivars are: 'Rosea' (pink buds with flowers fading to white),

Magnolia stellata 'Rosea'

Magnolia x loebneri 'Merrill'

Menziesia
menziesia

Menziesia ciliicalyx

- ❏ Height 3-6 ft (90-180 cm)
- ❏ Spread 1½ ft (45 cm)
- ❏ Flowers late spring to early summer
- ❏ Lime-free soil
- ❏ Sunny or partially shaded site
- ❏ Hardy to zone 6

This small shrub genus belongs to the heather family. Often planted along with rhododendrons as they like the same conditions, they are also good in a large rock garden. The urn- or bell-shaped flowers look like those of heather, but the leaves are different: oval, pale green, and bristly.

Popular species
Menziesia ciliicalyx is slow-growing with pinkish-purple flowers in late spring and early summer. *M. purpurea* has larger, purple-red and later blooms.

Cultivation
Plant in midfall or early spring in acid, organically rich soil in sun or partial shade, with shelter from strong winds. Mulch annually in spring with acid material such as composted pine bark.
Propagation Heel cuttings require several years to produce plants sturdy enough to plant out. Root in summer in a propagating box.
Pests/diseases Trouble free.

'Royal Star' (large white blooms), and 'Waterlily' (pale pink buds and many-petaled white flowers).

Cultivation
Plant in early spring to midspring in well-drained, loamy soil. The site can be in full sun or dappled shade, but it should be sheltered from drying winds and early morning sun which can damage the blooms of early-flowering species after night frost.

Avoid disturbing the soil around the shrubs, as their roots grow close to the soil surface. Every midspring top-dress with leaf mold, compost, or shredded bark. Pruning is not necessary.
Propagation Take 4 in (10 cm) heel cuttings of half-ripened shoots in midsummer and root in a propagating box at a temperature of 70°F (21°C). Pot the rooted cuttings in 3 in (7.5 cm) pots, and overwinter in a cold frame. The following late spring, plant in a nursery bed, and leave them for 2 or 3 years before planting in the permanent positions.
Pests/diseases Magnolia scale attacks new growth, stunting leaves. Leaf blight and leaf spot also attack foliage; canker may cause cracking of bark and the dieback of branches or whole trunks.

MALLOW, TREE —
see *Lavatera*
MAPLE — see *Acer*

MEZEREUM — see *Daphne*
MOCK ORANGE —
see *Philadelphus*

Paeonia
tree peony

Paeonia 'Age of Gold'

Paeonia lutea

❑ Height 4-7 ft (1.2-2.1 m)
❑ Spread equal to height
❑ Flowers late spring to early summer
❑ Well-drained, rich soil
❑ Sunny, sheltered site
❑ Hardy zones 5-8

Despite their name, tree peonies do not reach treelike proportions but grow as medium-size shrubs clothed with ornamental foliage. They are cold hardy but start growing in early spring, when frosts can damage the buds unless the shrubs are grown in a sheltered site. The blooms on tree peonies are as spectacular as those on their herbaceous relatives. Appearing in late spring, tree peony blossoms may be single, semidouble, or double and come in yellows, whites, pinks, and reds.

When the flowers are over, the deeply divided lush green leaves provide an ornamental backdrop for summer-flowering plants in mixed borders.

Popular species

Paeonia delavayi is a suckering shrub with an open, branching habit growing 6 ft (1.8 m) high and wide. It has doubly divided dark green leaves and deep red cup-shaped flowers with yellow anthers in late spring. It is hardy to zone 5. The popular 'Black Pirate' has striking deep crimson-maroon flowers. These shrubs thrive on deep alkaline soils.

Paeonia lutea is a 4-6 ft (1.2-1.8 m) high shrub with deeply divided pale green leaves. Its single yellow flowers, which have a lilylike fragrance, appear in early summer. It is hardy to zone 6.

Paeonia suffruticosa (Moutan peony) syn. *P. arborea*, bears large, 6 in (15 cm) wide bowl-shaped flowers in late spring, ranging in color from rose-pink to white, usually with a magenta blotch at the base of each petal. This species attains a height and spread of 5-7 ft (1.5-2.1 m) and produces pale green to midgreen leaves. It is hardy to zone 5. An outstanding cultivar is 'Rock's Variety' (single, very pale pink to silvery white with maroon blotches).

Popular hybrids Crosses between species have produced the cultivars treasured by gardeners. Many of the best are Japanese in

Paeonia suffruticosa 'Rock's Variety'

Parrotia
parrotia

Paeonia 'Jitsugetsu-nishiki'

Parrotia persica

❏ Height 10-40 ft (3-12 m)
❏ Spread 10-30 ft (3-9 m)
❏ Foliage shrub
❏ Well-drained, loamy soil
❏ Sunny or lightly shade site
❏ Hardy zones 5-8

Fall foliage in magnificent tints of amber, crimson, and gold makes *Parrotia persica* a shrub worth planting in the garden. Though eventually it develops into a tree, parrotia is slow-growing and will function as a shrub for many years, perhaps standing 10 ft (3 m) tall at the end of 10 years.

The trunk is covered in gray bark which on mature specimens flakes away to create attractive patterns — for this to be shown off to best advantage, remove the lower branches.

In early spring to midspring clusters of tiny, inconspicuous flowers appear. They have red stamens but no petals and are carried on bare twigs before the oval midgreen leaves unfurl.

Cultivation
Plant in any well-drained, loamy soil in sun or light shade in midfall or early spring. Parrotia tolerates limy soils.

Pruning is rarely required, but if a better view of the bark is desired, lower branches may be removed in early spring.
Propagation Layer in early fall, and sever from the parent plant 2 years later.
Pests/diseases Trouble free.

origin, including such favorites as 'Godaishu' (semidouble, white), 'Hana-kisoi' (fully double, medium rose), 'Jitsugetsu-nishiki' (semidouble, scarlet), 'Kamadanishiki' (double flowers, lilac-purple petals edged with white), 'Kaoh' (semidouble, scarlet), and 'Taiyo' (semidouble, crimson). Many outstanding hybrids also belong to the strain first developed by Professor A. P. Saunders of Clinton, New York, and further developed by William Gratwick and Nassos Daphnis; these include 'Age of Gold' (double, fragrant golden blossoms), 'Boreas' (semidouble, brilliant scarlet with a golden center), 'Hesperus' (single, rosy orange-red), 'Tria' (single, yellow with hint of red at center), and 'Zephyrus' (semidouble, apricot-pink with red at center).

Cultivation
Plant in midfall or early spring in any deep well-drained soil enriched with organic matter. Set the graft union 3 in (7.5 cm) below the soil surface. The site should be in sun or light shade and sheltered from late-spring

Paeonia delavayi

frosts. Every spring mulch with well-rotted manure or compost.

Cultivars with heavy double blooms may need staking. Deadhead as the flowers fade — regular pruning is not advisable. Water regularly in dry weather.
Propagation Shrubby peonies are grafted by professionals.
Pests/diseases Trouble free.

Parthenocissus
Virginia creeper

Parthenocissus quinquefolia

Parthenocissus tricuspidata 'Veitchii'

❑ Height 25-70 ft (7.5-21 m)
❑ Climber
❑ Foliage plant
❑ Fertile, well-drained soil
❑ Sunny or shaded site
❑ Hardy zones 4-9

Virginia creeper is an excellent climber for rapidly covering a sunny or shaded wall with fresh green leaves in summer and magnificent fiery reds in fall. Though usually grown against walls or fences, it can also be trained up an arch, pergola, trellis, or old tree, where it can grow to 25-70 ft (7.5-21 m). The species vary in hardiness, but all are self-supporting, clinging to any surface by means of sticky pads.

Though grown mainly for their foliage, parthenocissuses also bear minute yellow-green flowers between late spring and midsummer. Sometimes these are followed by blue-black berries.

Popular species
Parthenocissus henryana (silver vein creeper) produces dark, velvety green "fingered" leaves that are veined silver-pink. This variegation is most pronounced when the plant is grown on a shady wall. In fall the leaves turn bright

red; dark blue fruits follow hot summers. The creeper reaches 25-30 ft (7.5-9 m) high and flourishes best on a sheltered wall, as it is not cold tolerant — it is hardy only in zones 7-8.

Parthenocissus quinquefolia (Virginia creeper) is a very vigorous species, growing up to 70 ft (21 m) high. The leaves consist of three or five serrated leaflets that turn crimson in fall. It has tiny yellow-green flowers in late spring and early summer, sometimes followed by small, round blue-black berries. It is hardy in zones 4-9.

Parthenocissus henryana

Parthenocissus tricuspidata 'Veitchii' (Boston ivy) grows up to 50 ft (15 m) high. It clings to walls and other flat surfaces, where it establishes itself rapidly. Leaves usually have three lobes. In summer small yellow-green flowers appear; small black berries covered with a silvery bloom may follow. It is hardy in zones 5-8.

Cultivation
Plant container-grown specimens in late fall or early spring. Sun or shade suits most species, though *P. henryana* needs warmth and shelter. Set in planting pockets 2 ft (60 cm) square and 1½ ft (45 cm) deep, filled with moist, loamy soil and a dressing of well-rotted manure or compost.

Support young growth with twiggy sticks until the stems become self-clinging. Pinch growing tips to encourage side branching on wall-grown climbers.

Remove unwanted or overcrowded shoots during the summer. Prune to maintain or restrict growth in fall.

Propagation Take 10-12 in (25-30 cm) hardwood cuttings in late summer, and root in a sheltered border outdoors.

Pests/diseases Scale insects infest the stems and make the plants sticky and sooty. Leaf spot fungi may seriously disfigure foliage in rainy seasons; powdery mildew can also be a problem.

Perovskia
Russian sage

Perovskia atriplicifolia 'Blue Mist'

❑ Height 3-5 ft (90-150 cm)
❑ Spread 1½ ft (45 cm)
❑ Flowers late summer to early fall
❑ Any well-drained soil
❑ Sunny site
❑ Hardy zones 6-8

This hardy subshrub, which from a distance resembles a tall, leggy lavender, is excellent for growing in alkaline soils and coastal gardens. Spikes of violet-blue flowers, which appear in late summer to early fall, are its main attraction. They are set off by coarsely toothed gray-green leaves smelling of sage. Russian sage looks most effective in a mass planting.

Popular cultivars
Cultivars developed from *Perovskia atriplicifolia* have flowers in varying shades of blue.
'Blue Mist' has light blue flowers from midsummer onward.
'Blue Spire' has deep violet-blue flowers in late summer to early fall and daintily cut foliage.

Cultivation
Plant in late fall or early spring in any well-drained soil in a sunny site.
　In spring, cut the stems down to 1-1½ ft (30-45 cm) above the ground.
Propagation Take 3 in (7.5 cm) long heel cuttings of lateral shoots in midsummer, and root in a cold frame.
Pests/diseases Trouble free.

Philadelphus
mock orange

Philadelphus x virginalis 'Minnesota Snowflake'

❑ Height 3-12 ft (90-360 cm)
❑ Spread equal to height
❑ Flowers late spring to early summer
❑ Ordinary well-drained soil
❑ Full sun or partial shade
❑ Hardy zones 5-8

The common name for *Philadelphus* is mock orange, because the scent of its flowers resembles that of orange blossom. In late spring or early summer, the branches of these hardy shrubs are weighed down with sprays of sweetly fragrant flowers that are white or cream, sometimes with a pale cerise blush at the base of each petal.
　Mock oranges are easily grown free-flowering shrubs with oval, prominently veined midgreen leaves unless otherwise stated.

Popular species and hybrids
Philadelphus coronarius, a dense bushy shrub, has a height and spread of 6-12 ft (1.8-3.6 m). The cream-colored flowers have prominent yellow stamens. It is hardy in zones 5-8. 'Aureus' is a popular cultivar whose young foliage is a bright yellow color, becoming green-yellow in summer. The leaves retain their color best if grown in shade or semishade.
Philadelphus × cymosus is a hybrid that forms an open, leggy shrub. It is hardy in zones 5-6. The cultivar 'Norma,' a shrub up to 5 ft (1.5 m) high and wide, has arching branches that produce white flowers with only a slight fragrance.
Philadelphus × lemoinei is a group of hybrids that are hardy to zone 6 and bear highly perfumed flowers. 'Belle Etoile,' which grows 8-10 ft (2.4-3 m) high and 10-12 ft (3-3.6 m) wide, has large white single flowers with purple central blotches. 'Enchantment,' which rarely grows more than 6 ft (1.8 m) high and wide, has clusters of sweetly scented white double flowers, borne on arching stems. 'Sybille,' which grows 4 ft (1.2 m) high and 3 ft (90 cm) wide, bears a profusion of white single flowers with purple markings on arching branches.
Philadelphus microphyllus is the smallest mock orange. Growing

Philadelphus 'Belle Etoile'

3 ft (90 cm) high and wide, it has small bright green leaves and masses of sweetly scented white flowers. It is hardy to zone 6.

Philadelphus × virginalis is another group of hybrids, whose members are typically hardy to zone 6. Cultivars include 'Bouquet Blanc,' which grows 4-6 ft (1.2-1.8 m) high and wide and bears large clusters of double white flowers. 'Minnesota Snowflake,' which grows 4-6 ft (1.2-1.8 m) high and wide, bears white double flowers. 'Natchez' bears large quantities of perfumed (to 1½ in/3.75 cm wide) white flowers. 'Virginal,' which has a strong upright growth habit and reaches up to 10 ft (3 m) high and 5 ft (1.5 m) wide, carries richly scented white double or semidouble flowers in large clusters.

Miscellaneous cultivars of uncertain parentage include 'Galahad,' a compact, rounded shrub to 5 ft (1.5 m) high with fragrant white single flowers, and 'Miniature Snowflake,' a shrub that is just 3 ft (90 cm) tall with fragrant double flowers and disease-resistant foliage.

Cultivation
Plant in midfall or early spring in any ordinary well-drained soil in sun or light shade.

Thin old wood from the base after flowering. Be careful not to remove young shoots, which will flower the following year.

Propagation Take 4 in (10 cm) softwood cuttings from lateral shoots in early summer, and root in a cold frame. Set out the rooted cuttings in a nursery bed the following spring, and transfer to their permanent planting positions from midfall onwards.

Or, take 1 ft (30 cm) hardwood cuttings in fall or early spring, and root in an outdoor nursery bed. Plant out a year later.

Pests/diseases Leaf spot may

Philadelphus coronarius 'Aureus'

cause circular yellow blotches with darker edges on the foliage. Powdery mildew may also attack leaves.

Polygonum
fleece flower

Polygonum baldschuanicum

Polygonum aubertii

- Height 40 ft (12 m)
- Climber
- Flowers midsummer to early fall
- Any well-drained ordinary garden soil
- Sunny or lightly shaded site
- Hardy zones 5-8

Fleece flowers (*Polygonum* species) are ideal vines for gardeners with little time to spare. Extremely vigorous (spreading 10-15 ft/3-4.5 m a year), these hardy climbers will tumble over anything in their path, making further gardening in that area unnecessary — and impossible. In addition, the vines may spread by means of rhizomes, which are underground stems. For this reason they should be planted where there is plenty of room.

From midsummer to early fall these lofty plants become impressive, their massed bright pale green foliage foaming with long flower sprays of white or pale pink on the current year's growth.

They can be encouraged to climb up wires, trellises, hedges, and tall trees and are perfect for screening an unsightly shed or other garden eyesore. Remember, however, that being deciduous, they will form an attractive cover only during the growing season; in winter the bare stems can look ungainly.

Popular species

Polygonum aubertii, syn. *Bilderdykia aubertii,* scrambles its twining, slightly scaly stems to a height of 40 ft (12 m). They are clothed with small, ovate, glossy bright green leaves that are pale green and red-tipped when they are young. From late summer onward, the climber becomes a billowing mass of small white to greenish-white flowers.

Polygonum baldschuanicum, syn. *Bilderdykia baldschuanica,* closely resembles *P. aubertii,* though the pale green leaves are heart-shaped and the stems smooth. These two species are frequently confused, *P. baldschuanicum* being less common. It can be distinguished by the pink tinge to the huge panicles of late-summer flowers.

Cultivation

Plant young container-grown specimens in early spring to mid-spring in any type of soil, including alkaline and dry ones, in sun or shade. Support the young growth with stakes or a trellis after pinching the growth tips to encourage branching. Pinch young plants two or three more times during the summer.

Pruning is virtually impossible among the tangled mass of stems, but shoots can be thinned or shortened during the dormant season. In windy sites, they often break off naturally.

Propagation If necessary, take heel cuttings 3-4 in (7.5-10 cm) long from half-ripe wood during mid- to late summer. Root them in a cold frame, then pot them up and plunge outdoors until the following spring, when they can be planted out in their permanent positions.

Pests/diseases Aphids may infest and distort young growth; Japanese beetles may ravage foliage.

POMEGRANATE — see *Punica*

Poncirus
hardy orange, trifoliate orange

Poncirus trifoliata

❏ Height 8-20 ft (2.4-6 m)
❏ Spread equals two-thirds of height
❏ Flowers midspring
❏ Fertile, well-drained soil
❏ Sunny site
❏ Hardy zones 6-9

As the common name — hardy orange — implies, this shrub belongs to the citrus family. It is reliably hardy only in milder areas and flourishes in coastal gardens, where it is often grown as a hedge — the spiny stems making a formidable barrier.
Poncirus trifoliata, syn. *Citrus*

Poncirus trifoliata, fruits

trifoliata, makes an exotic specimen shrub in areas where other citruses will not survive — and its vivid green stems and persistent fruits make it an outstanding source of interest for the fall or winter garden. *Poncirus* has a dense angular habit, with olive-green stems that are covered with long, pointed spines. Clusters of sweetly scented white flowers appear in midspring, just before the leaves unfurl. In late summer, aromatic fruits resembling small tangerines begin to ripen from green to yellow. Though too bitter to eat raw, they can be used for marmalade.

Cultivation
Plant in fall or spring. Fertile, well-drained soil and a sunny site provide the best growing condition for hardy orange.
   Remove all dead and damaged growth in spring. If growing hardy orange as a hedge, clip it into shape in midspring after flowering has finished.
Propagation Take softwood cuttings in summer, and root in a propagator.
Pests/diseases Trouble free.

Potentilla
cinquefoil, potentilla

Potentilla fruticosa 'Tangerine'

❏ Height 1-4 ft (30-120 cm)
❏ Spread 3-5 ft (90-150 cm)
❏ Flowers early summer to midfall
❏ Any well-drained soil
❏ Sun or light shade
❏ Hardy zones 2-7

Potentillas, or cinquefoils, are among the most useful of flowering shrubs. They are prized for the succession of brightly colored flowers they produce from early summer into midfall. The single or double blooms are saucer-shaped and borne in small terminal clusters.
   Shrubby potentillas are suitable for the front of a border or a sunny bank; they will have the greatest impact when planted in groups of at least three. Prostrate types make excellent ground-cover plants.
   Few species are grown, but numerous garden cultivars have been developed, offering flowers in shades of yellow, orange, red, pink, and white.

Popular species
Potentilla davurica bears small, rich yellow flowers between late spring and late summer. It is a prostrate shrub with a height of 2 ft (60 cm) and a spread of 5 ft (1.5 m). The small, finely divided leaves are pale green to midgreen and covered with silky bronze hairs. 'Beesii,' an old cultivar, has silvery leaves.
Potentilla fruticosa has golden

Potentilla fruticosa 'Red Ace'

Potentilla fruticosa 'Elizabeth'

Potentilla fruticosa 'Abbotswood'

yellow flowers, which appear in succession between early summer and midfall. It grows to 3-4 ft (90-120 cm) high and wide, forming a small twiggy bush. The midgreen leaves are deeply cut. A large number of cultivars have been developed from this species; they include 'Abbotswood' (dwarf shrub with white blossoms and dark green leaves), 'Daydawn' (small bushy shrub with peach-pink flowers suffused with cream), 'Elizabeth' (tall and spreading to 4 ft/1.2 m, with rich canary-yellow flowers), 'Goldfinger' (bushy with deep yellow flowers and blue-green foliage), 'Katherine Dykes' (vigorous bushy shrub with primrose-yellow flowers), 'Moanely's' (gray-green foliage, yellow flowers with darker centers), 'Primrose Beauty' (dense shrub bearing primrose-yellow flowers with deep yellow centers and grayish-green leaves), 'Red Ace' (low, compact shrub with vermilion flowers and yellow undersides to petals), 'Royal Flush' (similar to 'Red Ace' but with rose-pink flowers), 'Sunset' (small, compact shrub with deep orange to brick-red flowers; best in light shade), 'Tangerine' (wide-spreading dwarf shrub with orange-yellow flowers; best in light shade), and 'Vilmoriniana' (erect shrub with cream-white flowers and silver leaves).

Cultivation

Plant in midfall or early spring in any well-drained soil in a sunny site. Pink- and red-flowered cultivars lose their flower color in sites with hot midday sun and do better in light shade.

Regular pruning is not necessary. Remove weak and old stems occasionally at ground level to keep the shrubs bushy. After flowering, trim off the tips of flowering shoots.

Propagation Take 3 in (7.5 cm) softwood cuttings from lateral shoots in summer. Root in a cold frame. In late spring transplant to a nursery bed, and grow on until midfall of the following year before setting the plants in their permanent positions.

Pests/diseases Spider mites may be troublesome; powdery mildew may attack foliage.

Prunus
ornamental almond, apricot, cherry, peach, and plum

Prunus tenella 'Fire Hill'

❏ Height 2-20 ft (60-600 cm)
❏ Spread equal to height
❏ Flowers late winter to late spring
❏ Ordinary well-drained soil
❏ Sunny site
❏ Hardy zones 2-9

Prunus is an enormous genus containing ornamental trees and shrubs grown for their stunning spring blossoms. Some also have richly colored fall foliage and attractive fruits.

All shrubby species and cultivars described here are easy to grow, given an open, sunny site. They make handsome specimen shrubs; many are also suitable for hedging. (See also pages 48-49.)

Popular species
Prunus × cistena (purple-leaved sand cherry) has small, rich red oval leaves, which set off the white early spring to midspring blossoms. Growing 4-5 ft (1.2-1.5 m) high and wide, it is often used for hedging. Hardy in zones 2-8, it flourishes in midwestern gardens.
Prunus glandulosa (dwarf flowering almond) grows into a neat

bushy shrub 4-5 ft (1.2-1.5 m) high and wide, with erect shoots. It has midgreen leaves and white or pink flowers in midspring. It is hardy in zones 5-8. Popular cultivars include 'Alba Plena' (white double flowers in late spring) and 'Rosea Plena' (syn. 'Sinensis,' bright pink double flowers in midspring).
Prunus incisa (Fuji cherry) can reach 10-15 ft (3-4.5 m) high and wide. The small sharply toothed leaves take on rich fall tints. Pink buds open into white flowers in early spring before the leaves unfurl. It is hardy to zone 6. The cultivar 'Praecox' flowers in late winter.
Prunus mume (Japanese apricot) grows into a round, open shrub, occasionally a small tree, 15-20 ft (4.5-6 m) high and wide. It bears pale pink scented flowers, which cluster thickly along the slender branches in late winter or early spring. The leaves are midgreen. It is hardy in zones 6-9. Popular cultivars include 'Alba Plena' (white semidouble flowers), 'Dawn' (large pink double flowers), 'Peggy Clarke' (deep rose

double blossoms set on red calyxes), 'Rosemary Clarke' (white double, early flowering), and 'W. B. Clarke' (weeping habit and pink double flowers).
Prunus persica (common peach) is a small tree or a vigorous shrub that grows 15-25 ft (4.5-7.5 m) high and wide. It has lance-shaped midgreen leaves and pale pink flowers in midspring. It is hardy from zones 6-9. Ornamental cultivars include 'Alba Plena' (white double flowers), 'Cardinal' (glowing red semidouble flowers), 'Helen Borchers' (large rose-pink semidouble blooms), 'Prince Charming' (rose-red double flowers), 'Royal Red Leaf' (syn. 'Foliis Rubris,' reddish-purple foliage becoming bronze-green; pink single flowers), and several weeping forms — 'Weeping Double Pink' and 'Weeping Double White' are examples.
Prunus spinosa (blackthorn or sloe) is a European native hardy to zone 5. Snow-white blooms smother the spiny branches in early spring before the dark green leaves unfurl. The small plumlike fruits (sloes) are sometimes used

Prunus incisa

Prunus x cistena

in cooking and winemaking. It grows 10-15 ft (3-4.5 m) high and wide. Ornamental garden cultivars include 'Plena' (with white double flowers) and 'Purpurea' (rich purple foliage and white flowers).

Prunus tenella (dwarf Russian almond) syn. *P. nana*, is a low-growing suckering shrub with a height and spread of 2-5 ft (60-150 cm). Hardy in zones 2-6, it has erect willowy stems that bear glossy bright green leaves, which are pale green beneath. Bright pink flowers cover the branches in midspring. The variety 'Fire Hill' has rose-crimson flowers.

Prunus triloba, a species of dense twiggy habit, grows 10-15 ft (3-4.5 m) high and wide. The selection usually grown is 'Multiplex,' which bears rosettelike, clear pink double blossoms in profusion along the slender branches in midspring. These flowers are excellent for cutting. The bright green leaves are coarsely toothed. An excellent shrub for training against a sunny wall, it is hardy to zone 6.

Cultivation

All species and cultivars thrive in ordinary well-drained garden soils. A neutral pH is preferable, but most soils are suitable provided they are neither dry nor waterlogged. The site should be sunny.

Prunus spinosa

123

Prunus persica

Plant in early to midfall or early spring. Most of these shrubs have shallow roots, and should not be planted too deeply, nor should the soil around them be cultivated too often.

For a hedge, use 1½-2 ft (45-60 cm) high plants and set them 2 ft (60 cm) apart. After planting, cut back the upper third of all shoots to promote bushy growth.

Little pruning is needed except to remove weak, damaged, or dead shoots as soon as they are noticed. On *P. glandulosa* and *P. triloba*, especially well-trained types, cut back flowered shoots to within two or three buds of the base immediately after flowering.

Clip hedges at any time, ideally after flowering.

Propagation Take 3-4 in (7.5-10 cm) long heel cuttings in late summer to early fall, and root them in a cold frame. Pot up the rooted cuttings, then transfer them to a nursery bed in spring and grow on for 1 or 2 years before transplanting.

P. tenella can also be increased by removing and replanting rooted suckers, and *P. glandulosa* by layering in early spring. Sever from the parent plant 2 years later.

Pests/diseases Aphids may infest leaves and young shoots; caterpillars sometimes feed on the leaves; and scale insects may be a serious problem. Borers may tunnel into the base of trunks. Leaf spot may disfigure foliage; canker may girdle and kill branches or trunks.

Punica
pomegranate

Punica granatum

❑ Height 3-20 ft (90-600 cm)
❑ Spread similar to height
❑ Flowers early summer to early fall
❑ Ordinary well-drained soil
❑ Sunny, sheltered site
❑ Hardy zones 8-10

Pomegranate, cultivated for centuries in hot climates for its succulent fruits, is worth growing for its crimson trumpet-shaped flowers, borne singly or in clusters from early summer to fall.

Pomegranate is frost sensitive and suitable only for mild southern regions. Even there it prefers a warm, sunny spot close to a south-facing wall. In suitable conditions it will grow to 20 ft (6 m) with an equal or lesser spread. The oblong leaves are pale green to midgreen and yellow in fall.

Popular cultivars
A few garden cultivars have been developed from *Punica granatum*. 'Alba Plena' is compact, 6-10 ft (1.8-3 m) tall, with cream-white double flowers. 'Chico' is also compact, with orange-red double flowers. 'Nana' grows 3 ft (90 cm) high and wide, and bears red flowers.

Cultivation
Plant in late spring in any well-drained soil in a sunny, sheltered site against a south-facing wall.
Propagation Take 3 in (7.5 cm) long softwood cuttings in early summer to midsummer.
Pests/diseases Trouble free.

QUINCE — see *Chaenomeles*
RASPBERRY — see *Rubus*

Rhamnus
buckthorn

Rhamnus frangula

❑ Height 10-12 ft (3-3.6 m)
❑ Spread 8-12 ft (2.4-3.6 m)
❑ Foliage shrub
❑ Any well-drained soil
❑ Sunny or lightly shaded site
❑ Hardy zones 2-7

The alder buckthorn (*Rhamnus frangula*) is a hardy shrub grown for its attractive foliage and its colorful fall berries. The dark green glossy leaves are ovate and toothed; they turn yellow in fall.

Inconspicuous white flowers in spring are followed by abundant clusters of berries that ripen slowly from green to red and finally black. Good cultivars include 'Asplenifolia,' with narrow, threadlike foliage, golden in fall, and 'Columnaris,' a slenderly upright form to 12 ft (3.6 m) high.

Cultivation
Plant in fall or spring in any well-drained soil, in full sun or light shade. Buckthorn tolerates salt sprays and air pollution.

Regular pruning is unnecessary; remove dead or damaged shoots in early spring.
Propagation Increase buckthorn by layering in spring; roots should have formed after 1 or 2 years, when the new plants can be separated from the parent.
Pests/diseases Fungal cankers may cause dieback of branches and shoots.

Rhododendron (Azalea)
azalea

Rhododendron Knap Hill hybrids

❏ Height 3-15 ft (90-450 cm)
❏ Spread 2-15 ft (60-450 cm)
❏ Flowers midspring to midsummer
❏ Moist, rich, acid soil
❏ Sheltered, lightly shaded site
❏ Hardy zones 4-9

Though botanically classified as rhododendrons, azaleas tend to be more delicate in flower and leaf and so are often regarded as a separate group by gardeners.

Azaleas are either deciduous or evergreen. Those described here are deciduous, have an upright habit, and bear clusters of wide trumpet- or funnel-shaped blooms with distinct petals.

Deciduous azaleas are among the most brightly colored spring-flowering shrubs. When the spectacular blooms open, they are often so profuse that they cover the entire bush.

Azaleas vary in their adaptation to summer heat and winter cold. Some azaleas are suitable for northern climates, others for southern ones. These shrubs appeal to every taste, with a wide range of colors, particularly yellows, oranges, and orange-reds — and they are often fragrant. In fall the leaves take on marvelous rich red, orange, and yellow hues before falling to the ground.

Like other rhododendrons, azaleas will grow only in acid soil and generally thrive in sheltered, lightly shaded sites. This makes them an obvious choice for woodland gardens and mixed or shrub borders in partial shade. Azaleas look most effective in a massed planting, in single or mixed but harmonious color combinations.

Popular species
Unless otherwise indicated, the following species flower in mid- to late spring.
Rhododendron albrechtii, 3-15 ft (90-450 cm) high with an equal spread, has clusters of mauve-pink, green-flecked flowers. The rounded leaves are midgreen above and pale green below; they turn yellow in fall. This species is hardy to zone 6 but should be set in a sheltered spot in the North, as it is susceptible to spring frosts.
Rhododendron arborescens grows 4-8 ft (1.2-2.4 m) or more high, again with an equal spread. It has ovate, glossy bright green leaves that are gray and hairy underneath; they are tinted red in fall. Clusters of funnel-shaped, highly fragrant white flowers, sometimes flushed pink, are borne in late spring to midsummer. It is hardy in zones 5-9.
Rhododendron calendulaceum, one of the most vividly colored azaleas, grows 4-10 ft (1.2-3 m) tall and wide. The leaves turn vivid orange and crimson in fall. In late spring it bears huge clusters of yellow, orange, or scarlet flowers. Hardy in zones 6-8, it offers many fine cultivars, such as

Rhododendron luteum

'Chattooga' (ruffled pink blooms with a yellow blotch), 'Cherokee' (apricot with red stamens), 'Frank Lunsford' (fuchsia and white), and 'Soquee River' (large trusses of orange, red, and yellow).

Rhododendron kaempferi, syn. *R. obtusum kaempferi,* is one of the parents of the evergreen Kurume azaleas. The species itself is usually deciduous, up to 10 ft (3 m) high and 5-6 ft (1.5-1.8 m) wide, with ovate dark green leaves, downy in the young stages. It flowers in late spring, with a profusion of small clusters of funnel-shaped flowers ranging from orange to salmon-pink and brick-red. It is hardy in zones 5-8.

Rhododendron luteum, syn. *R. flavum,* bears fragrant yellow flowers in late spring. A suckering shrub with a height of 8-10 ft (2.4-3 m) and a spread of 4-6 ft (1.2-1.8 m), it has light green leaves, which turn rich orange, purple, and crimson in fall. It is hardy in zones 6-7.

Rhododendron occidentale has clusters of fragrant white flowers tinged pink in early to midsummer. It reaches 10 ft (3 m) high and 4-6 ft (1.2-1.8 m) wide and has shiny lance-shaped green leaves. The parent of many azalea hybrids, it is hardy to zone 6.

Rhododendron reticulatum grows 10 ft (3 m) or more high, spreading to 8 ft (2.4 m), and bears strongly veined and rounded to diamond-shaped leaves. These are purplish and hairy when young and turn orange and red in fall. Bright purple flowers, borne singly or in pairs, appear in midspring, before the leaves. It is hardy to zone 6.

Rhododendron schlippenbachii has wide funnel-shaped flowers ranging from white to shades of pink speckled with dull red. It reaches 5-10 ft (1.5-3 m) high and 4-8 ft (1.2-2.4 m) wide and bears rounded midgreen leaves, which assume red and orange tints in fall. Hardy in zones 5-8, it flowers in midspring.

Rhododendron vaseyi, a pink-flowered species, reaches 5-6 ft (1.5-1.8 m) in height with a similar spread. It bears lance-shaped pale green leaves, which turn orange and red in fall. It is hardy in zones 5-8.

Rhododendron viscosum, a bushy shrub known as the swamp honeysuckle, grows to a height of 6-8 ft (1.8-2.4 m) and a spread of 4-6 ft (1.2-1.8 m). The leaves turn orange and red in fall. It is a late-spring-flowering species, with clusters of sweetly scented honeysuckle-like flowers that are white, tinted pink. It is hardy to zone 4.

Azalea hybrids generally flower in late spring and early summer. The popular hybrids fall into six different categories.

Ghent hybrids grow up to 5-6 ft (1.5-1.8 m) high and wide and have long-tubed, usually fragrant flower clusters. They are hardy in zones 6-7. Popular cultivars are 'Corneille' (cream tinged with rose), 'Daviesii' (cream-white blotched yellow; hardy through zone 5), 'Narcissiflora' (double blooms, soft yellow; hardy through zone 8), and 'Unique' (large orange-yellow; hardy to zone 5).

Knap Hill and Exbury hybrids all have large trusses of wide trumpet-shaped flowers in late spring. Hardy in zones 5-7 and into zone 8, they range from 4-7 ft (1.2-2.1 m) high with a spread up to 5 ft (1.5 m). The leaves are often tinted with bronze when young and are attractively colored in fall. Popular hybrids include 'Ballerina' (white with orange markings), 'Balzac' (fragrant orange-red), 'Berryrose' (salmon-pink blotched yellow), 'Firefly' (rose-red flushed orange), 'Gibraltar' (bright orange),

Rhododendron Knap Hill hybrid

Rhododendron Northern Lights hybrid

'Klondyke' (orange-gold), 'Persil' (white blotched orange), 'Pink Ruffles' (carmine-rose blotched orange), 'Silver Slipper' (white flushed pink with a yellow blotch), and 'Strawberry Ice' (translucent pink with yellow blotches).

Mollis hybrids flower in late spring, usually on naked branches. The funnel-shaped flowers have no scent, but they come in brilliant colors. Average height and spread is 4-6 ft (1.2-1.8 m), though the shrubs can grow wider under ideal conditions. Narrow hairy leaves cover the shrubs and turn bright orange and scarlet in fall. Popular named hybrids include 'Dr. M. Oosthoek' (rich orange-scarlet) and 'Snowdrift' (white). They are hardy in zones 5-8.

Northern Lights hybrids are closely related to the Mollis hybrids but are far more cold-tolerant, generally proving hardy through zone 3. Reaching 2-4 ft (60-120 cm) high, they flower in late spring and are the best azaleas to grow in cold-weather regions, such as the upper Midwest and northern New England. This group includes 'Golden Lights' (yellow and fragrant), 'Rosy Lights' (dark pink, fragrant), 'Spicy Lights' (tangerine-orange, fragrant), and 'White Lights' (large and white with yellow center, fragrant).

Occidentale hybrids have fragrant delicately colored blooms in late spring and early summer.

The shrubs reach 6-8 ft (1.8-2.4 m) high and 8-10 ft (2.4-3 m) or more wide. These hybrids offer flowers in colors ranging from white to yellow and red and include the old favorite rose-pink 'Irene Koster.'

Rustica hybrids have fragrant double flowers in late spring and early summer. They reach 4-5 ft (1.2-1.5 m) high and wide and include 'Il Tasso' (rose-red and salmon) and 'Norma' (late-blooming, double rose-red).

Cultivation

Azaleas have the same soil requirements as other rhododendrons — moist, acid soil with a rich organic content. But while evergreen azalea species and hybrids grow best in a sheltered, partially shaded site, the deciduous types also tolerate more open spots and will thrive in sun, provided their roots are kept cool and moist. In northern regions it is best to protect azaleas that flower in early spring from morning sun after night frost or their flower buds may be damaged by sudden thawing. Plant in midfall or in early spring. Azaleas have shallow roots; they should be set in the ground with their root ball just below soil level.

In spring give azaleas a mulch of shredded bark or a similar material and use an acid fertilizer.

Regular pruning is not necessary, though it is important to deadhead. Use your fingers to twist off the faded flower trusses.

Propagation Deciduous azaleas are best increased by layering, which can be done at any time of year. Separate from the parent when rooted, after about 2 years, and plant out.

Pests/diseases Weevils may infest azaleas, hiding among the roots by day and crawling out to devour the leaves at night — they will also feed on the roots, killing whole plants. Stem borers may tunnel into twigs, while rhododendron borers may bore into the trunks. Lace bugs may cause stippling of leaves with whitish spots; azalea leaf miners tunnel into leaves and then roll them together. In neutral or alkaline soils, leaves turn yellow as a result of chlorosis.

Rhus
sumac

Rhus glabra, fall color

❏ Height 9-25 ft (2.7-7.5 m)
❏ Spread equal to or greater than height
❏ Foliage plant
❏ Ordinary garden soil
❏ Sunny site
❏ Hardy zones 2-9

Sumacs are grown for their magnificent foliage, which turns stunning shades of red and orange in fall after a warm summer. These hardy suckering shrubs bear felty spikes of small red or green flowers in summer, followed by colorful plumes of fruits.

Popular species
Rhus glabra (smooth sumac) grows 9-15 ft (2.7-4.5 m) high and wide. Its large, smooth, deeply divided leaves are midgreen with blue-green undersides, turning bright red in early fall to midfall. Conical spikes of light red flowers borne in early summer develop into striking clusters of deep red seeds. It is hardy in zones 2-9.
Rhus typhina (staghorn sumac) is

named for the velvety coating of brown-red hairs on its bare winter branches. It grows 15-25 ft (4.5-7.5 m) high with an equal or greater spread. The midgreen leaves are up to 1½ ft (45 cm) long and turn orange-red, purple, and yellow from early fall onward. Long, conical spikes of red and green flowers appear in summer, followed in fall by clusters of crimson fruits on female plants. This species is particularly good for city gardens, as it tolerates air pollution. It is hardy in zones 3-8. The cultivar 'Laciniata,' a female clone, has deeply cut leaflets.

Cultivation
Plant in midfall or early spring in ordinary garden soil in a sunny spot. For abundant, large foliage, prune to the ground between late winter and midspring.
Propagation Remove and replant suckers in fall.
Pests/diseases Generally trouble free.

Ribes
flowering currant

Ribes sanguineum 'Album'

❏ Height 6-10 ft (1.8-3 m)
❏ Spread 4-7 ft (1.2-2.1 m)
❏ Flowers early spring to early summer
❏ Any well-drained soil
❏ Sunny or lightly shaded site
❏ Hardy zones 5-8

In addition to edible currants and gooseberries, the *Ribes* genus includes several ornamental flowering shrubs. These decorative species have drooping or upright spikes of blooms in early spring to early summer. They come in white, cream, red, and varying shades of pink. Generally hardy, these shrubs are easily grown, reaching 6-10 ft (1.8-3 m) high and slightly less wide.

Popular species
Ribes odoratum has bright yellow clove-scented flowers held in drooping clusters in midspring. The shrub grows 6-8 ft (1.8-2.4 m) high and 4-5 ft (1.2-1.5 m) wide and bears pale green toothed leaves, which turn yellow with an orange flush in fall. It is hardy in zones 5-7.
Ribes sanguineum grows 6-10 ft (1.8-3 m) high and nearly as wide. It bears rounded midgreen leaves with pale undersides. The flowers are held in long, drooping clusters between early spring and midspring and are followed, in fall, by round, blue-black inedible berries. The shrub has a strong, pungent aroma. It is rarely grown in the East but is popular on the West Coast. It is hardy in zones 6-8. Some popular cultivars include

Robinia
rose acacia

Robinia hispida

❑ Height 6-8 ft (1.8-2.4 m)
❑ Spread equal to height
❑ Flowers late spring to early summer
❑ Ordinary well-drained soil
❑ Sheltered, sunny site
❑ Hardy to zone 6

The lovely pink-flowered shrub rose acacia (*Robinia hispida*) thrives in poor soil and spreads vigorously by suckering. It makes a fine cover for eroding banks or exhausted soils, and an unusual and attractive choice for training against a sunny, sheltered wall. Its delicate, deep green leaves are divided into several pairs of leaflets. They provide a perfect foil for the deep rose-pink pealike flowers that open in late spring and early summer. The sparse branches, covered with red bristly hairs, fan out to a height and spread of 6-8 ft (1.8-2.4 m).

Cultivation
Plant between midfall and early spring in ordinary well-drained soil in a sheltered spot. As a wall shrub, tie in the vigorous shoots to a wire or trellis support in summer. Remove winter-killed shoots and unwanted suckers from ground level.

Propagation Remove suckers from below ground between midfall and early spring, and plant in a nursery bed. Plant out in the permanent site 1 or 2 years later.

Pests/diseases Scale insects may infest the stems. Borers may tunnel into trunks, opening the way for wood decay.

Ribes sanguineum 'Pulborough Scarlet'

'Album' (white flowers), 'Brocklebankii' (smaller, slow-growing; deep rose-red flowers and golden foliage), 'Elk River Red' (rich red flowers), 'King Edward VII' (small deep crimson flowers), and 'Pulborough Scarlet' (rich red blooms).

Ribes speciosum, the showiest ornamental currant, is a native of the southern California coast and hardy only to zone 7, and even there needs the shelter of a sunny wall. It carries profuse clusters of three to four bright red blooms in midspring to early summer. The prickly stems are clothed with deeply lobed midgreen leaves. It grows 6-10 ft (1.8-3 m) high and 4-5 ft (1.2-1.5 m) wide.

Cultivation
Plant in fall or spring in any well-drained garden soil in sun or light shade. Prune annually, after flowering, by removing old and crowded stems at ground level, in order to maintain shape and control growth.

Propagation Insert hardwood cuttings 10-12 in (25-30 cm) long in mid- to late fall in a nursery bed. Plant out in the permanent flowering site a year later.

Pests/diseases Leaf spot and anthracnose cause small brown blotches on the foliage, which drops off. Ribes can be hosts for the white pine blister rust, and planting these shrubs may be prohibited where the white pine is an important source of timber.

Ribes speciosum

Romneya
tree poppy

Romneya coulteri

❑ Height 4-8 ft (1.2-2.4 m)
❑ Spread 4-6 ft (1.2-1.8 m)
❑ Flowers midsummer to early fall
❑ Rich, well-drained soil
❑ Sheltered, sunny site
❑ Hardy to zone 7

The handsome tree poppy (*Romneya coulteri*) is a herbaceous subshrub suitable for mixed or shrub borders, where it draws attention with its large poppylike white flowers. They have crinkled petals and gold stamens in a prominent central boss and appear in midsummer to early fall.

Tree poppies need full sun. Fertile soils may encourage their underground runners to spread too aggressively.

Cultivation
Tree poppies dislike root disturbance, so plant young container-grown specimens in mid- to late spring in a sheltered, sunny spot. Well-drained soil with plenty of organic matter produces the best results.

In midfall cut all the stems down to a few inches above ground level. Protect against frost by covering the base of the plants with straw.

Propagation Dig up and replant rooted suckers appearing well away from the crown in mid- to late spring.

Pests/diseases Poor growing conditions may result in yellowing leaves and wilting shoots.

ROSE ACACIA — see *Robinia*

Rubus
flowering raspberry

Rubus odoratus

❑ Height 1-10 ft (30-300 cm)
❑ Spread equal to height
❑ Flowers late spring to late summer
❑ Ordinary well-drained soil
❑ Sunny or partially shaded site
❑ Hardy to zone 3

Most species in the large *Rubus* genus are grown for their edible fruits, such as the raspberry, blackberry, and loganberry. Several other hardy species, most of which have thorny stems, have ornamental value and are grown in the flower garden for their foliage, flowers, fruits, or handsome winter stems.

Popular species
Rubus deliciosus (Rocky Mountain thimbleberry or Boulder raspberry) is a graceful shrub whose arching thornless branches may reach a height and spread of 3-5 ft (90-150 cm). Its leaves are bright green, and the large flowers, 2-3 in (5-7.5 cm) wide, resemble wild roses when they bloom in late spring. Hardy to zone 5, this shrub thrives in dry soils and is a good choice for western gardens. Despite the name, the fruits of this species do not taste good.

Rubus illecebrosus (strawberry-raspberry) is a dwarf creeping species, 1-1½ ft (30-45 cm) high and wide, grown for the beauty of its fruits. They resemble strawberries, borne on upright stems, and are large and red but fairly tasteless. It is hardy to zone 6.

Rubus odoratus grows 6-8 ft (1.8-2.4 m) high and spreads to 4-5 ft (1.2-1.5 m). It is grown for its bright green vinelike leaves on (virtually) thornless stems and its fragrant, bowl-shaped purple-rose blooms, which open in summer. It is hardy to zone 3.

Rubus phoenicolasius (Japanese wineberry) produces long, flexible stems and is best trained against a wall as a climber. Reaching a height of 6-8 ft (1.8-2.4 m) and a width of 8-10 ft (2.4-3 m), it carries small pink flowers in midsummer and midgreen leaves. The stems are covered in brilliant red hairs. In early fall the sweet and edible orange-red fruits ripen. It is hardy to zone 5 or 6.

Rubus × *tridel* 'Benenden' is a fast-growing hybrid growing 6-8 ft (1.8-2.4 m) high and 8-10 ft (2.4-3 m) wide. In late spring, shiny white saucer-shaped flowers with masses of yellow stamens are borne on thornless arching stems. The broad mid-

Rubus deliciosus

Rubus x tridel 'Benenden'

green oval leaves are three lobed. It is hardy to zone 7.

Cultivation

Plant in midfall or early spring in ordinary well-drained soil in sun or partial shade.

After flowering, remove the oldest shoots from ground level to encourage new growth.

Propagation Take semihard-wood cuttings 3-4 in (7.5-10 cm) long in late summer.

Pests/diseases Generally trouble free.

RUSSIAN SAGE —
see *Perovskia*

Salix
willow

Salix hastata 'Wehrhahnii'

❑ Height 4 in-25 ft (10-750 cm)
❑ Spread 1-15 ft (30-450 cm)
❑ Catkins from late winter to spring
❑ Moist, loamy soil
❑ Sunny site
❑ Hardy zones 1-8

The name *Salix*, or willow, is usually associated with the magnificent weeping willows (see page 55) that grow beside water. There are, however, many hardy shrubby species and cultivars suitable for ornamental use. These have colored stems, attractive foliage, and outstanding catkins. Female catkins and the more conspicuous male catkins are borne on separate trees in late winter and spring before the leaves unfold.

Many of the taller species and cultivars are an invaluable source of interest in the winter and early spring, while the neat and low dwarf willows are ideal as ground cover plants or as specimens in rock gardens, raised beds, and containers.

Willows as a group are gratifyingly vigorous, developing into sizable shrubs within a couple of years of transplanting, but they are also relatively short-lived. Their soft, brittle wood makes them especially vulnerable to ice storms and breakage, a weakness that may leave older specimens looking crippled and ungainly. This is not a problem with the species grown for their colored bark, since the old wood is removed on a regular basis.

Popular species

Salix aegyptiaca has yellow male catkins from late winter to early spring before the midgreen downy leaves unfurl. It grows 10-12 ft (3-3.6 m) high and 8 ft (2.4 m) wide and is hardy to zone 6.

Salix arctica comes from the northern tundra and is the cold-

Salix elaeagnos

Salix caprea 'Pendula'

Salix purpurea

Salix lanata

hardiest willow, flourishing even in zone 1. The branches of this prostrate species are held 4 in (10 cm) above the ground, forming a broad mat of glossy, 2 in (5 cm) long leaves. It's useful in a rock garden or as a ground cover in cold-winter regions.

Salix caprea (European pussy willow or goat willow) is a large, bushy 15-25 ft (4.5-7.5 m) high shrub that is 12-15 ft (3.6-4.5 m) wide. It has gray-green leaves, which are woolly below. Male shrubs have yellow catkins in early spring. It is hardy in zones 5-8. 'Pendula' (syn. 'Kilmarnock'), the most common cultivar, has lovely weeping branches. It is often grafted as a standard.

Salix elaeagnos (hoary willow) has long slender branches covered with narrow gray-green leaves; this species is sometimes called the rosemary willow because its foliage resembles that of the herb. Yellow male catkins appear in midspring. It grows 10 ft (3 m) high and spreads to 8 ft (2.4 m). It is hardy to zone 5.

Salix gracilistyla (rose-gold pussy willow) is a compact pussy willow, reaching a height of only 6-10 ft (1.8-3 m). Hardy in zones 5-8, it bears reddish catkins followed by long, narrowly ovate glossy deep green leaves. 'Melanostachys,' a Japanese cultivar, is startling in late winter, when its bare branches are lined with velvety male catkins so dark crimson as to appear black. Later they become studded with red stamens, and later still, these explode into golden pollen.

Salix hastata 'Wehrhahnii' has striking dark purple-brown bark and, in midspring, silvery male catkins, which mature to yellow. The oval leaves are mid- to gray-green. The shrub grows 4-5 ft (1.2-1.5 m) high and has a spread of 5-6 ft (1.5-1.8 m).

Salix lanata (woolly willow) is slow-growing and suitable for a rock garden. It grows 2-4 ft (60-120 cm) high and 1-4 ft (30-120 cm) wide. A gray-white felt covers its rounded midgreen leaves. Stout, upright yellow catkins appear in early spring to midspring. It is hardy in zones 3-6.

Salix purpurea (purple osier) is named after its purplish young stems, which yellow with age. It has dark green glossy leaves and gray male catkins, which turn reddish purple. It is hardy in zones 3-7. 'Nana,' or 'Gracilis,' is 4 ft (1.2 m) high and wide, and 'Pendula,' a weeping shrub often grafted onto an upright willow stem, forms a small weeping tree about 6 ft (1.8 m) high.

Salix repens (creeping willow) is a dwarf shrub suitable for large ground cover or creeping over drystone walls. It grows 3-6 ft (90-180 cm) high and 5-8 ft (1.5-2.4 m) wide and bears oval gray-green leaves covered with silky silver hairs. These turn dark green in summer. Silver-gray male catkins appear in mid- to late spring on bare branches. It is hardy to zone 5.

Cultivation
Plant in midfall or early spring in moist soil in a sunny spot.

Dwarf species need no regular pruning, but willows grown for their colored stems should be cut back in late winter or early spring every second or third year to a point just above ground level.

Propagation Between midfall and midspring, root hardwood cuttings 9-15 in (23-38 cm) long in moist soil in a nursery bed. Plant out the cuttings a year later.

Pests/diseases Caterpillars and various beetle larvae eat the leaves; gall mites distort young shoots; and sawfly larvae produce galls on the leaves. Aphids and scale insects colonizing on stems and young shoots make them black and sticky. Canker and twig blight may cause dieback of branches. Crown gall may cause swellings to form at the base of stems.

Sambucus
elder

Sambucus racemosa 'Plumosa Aurea'

Sorbaria
false spirea, sorbaria

Sorbaria aitchisonii

❏ Height 10-15 ft (3-4.5 m)
❏ Spread 8-15 ft (2.4-4.5 m)
❏ Flowers late spring to summer
❏ Any good soil
❏ Sunny or partially shaded site
❏ Hardy zones 4-9

Elders are hardy, fast-growing shrubs that flourish in moist soils but also tolerate dry soils. They adapt well to both alkaline and acidic conditions. Their vigor and adaptability mean that they may overrun neighbors if not controlled by occasional pruning. But their vigor also makes them excellent for problem areas.

Elders bear sprays of deeply cut leaves in many colors. Small, white star-shaped flower heads bloom in late spring and early summer; black or scarlet berries follow.

Popular species
Sambucus canadensis (American elder) grows 10-12 ft (3-3.6 m) high and 8-10 ft (2.4-3 m) wide. It is hardy in zones 4-9. 'Maxima' produces large midgreen leaves and big, flattened heads of white flowers in early summer, followed by purple-black fruits.
Sambucus nigra (European elder) grows 12-15 ft (3.6-4.5 m) high and wide. Cream-white flowers appear in late spring or early summer, followed by black berries. It is hardy to zone 6. 'Aurea,' with yellow-green young foliage, is particularly outstanding.
Sambucus racemosa, represented by the cultivar 'Plumosa Aurea,' grows 8-10 ft (2.4-3 m) high and wide. It has finely cut golden leaves, spikes of cream flowers in late spring, and scarlet berries in summer. It is hardy in zones 4-7.

Cultivation
Plant in any good garden soil in midfall or early spring in sun or partial shade. The golden-leaved cultivars color earlier in sunny spots, but retain their yellow-green hue longer in cool, moist shade.

For more brilliant color and for large leaves from young growth shoots, cut the stems back to a few inches above their base or near to ground level in early spring.
Propagation In fall, root hardwood cuttings in an outdoor nursery bed. Grow on for a year before planting out.
Pests/diseases Leaf spot and powdery mildew disfigure leaves and cause premature defoliation; borers and canker cause the death of stems.

SEA BUCKTHORN —
see *Hippophae*
SERVICEBERRY —
see *Amelanchier*
SHADBUSH — see *Amelanchier*
SILVERBERRY — see *Elaeagnus*
SLOE, ORNAMENTAL —
see *Prunus*
SMOKE TREE — see *Cotinus*
SNOWBERRY —
see *Symphoricarpos*

❏ Height 6-9 ft (1.8-2.7 m)
❏ Spread 8-9 ft (2.4-2.7 m)
❏ Flowers late summer to early fall
❏ Ordinary well-drained soil
❏ Open, sunny or lightly shaded site
❏ Hardy zones 2-7

These hardy, easily grown shrubs resemble huge clumps of meadowsweet. *Sorbaria sorbifolia*, the Ural false spirea, is the hardiest species, flourishing to zone 2; *S. aitchisonii*, the Kashmir false spirea, is hardy only to zone 6. Both grow 6-9 ft (1.8-2.7 m) high and wide. In spring a fountain of red-tinged shoots form — more gracefully in the Kashmir false spirea. In late summer to early fall the light ferny leaves set off the white fuzzy flowers.

The shrub spreads rapidly by underground suckers and is suited to informal plantings.

Cultivation
Plant in midfall or early spring in ordinary well-drained soil. The site should be open, in sun or partial shade. In early spring prune all stems near to ground level.
Propagation Remove rooted suckers at any time between midfall and early spring, and grow on in a nursery bed for a year before planting out.
Pests/diseases Trouble free.

SPANISH BROOM —
see *Genista* and *Spartium*

Spartium
Spanish broom

Spartium junceum

- ❏ Height 8-10 ft (2.4-3 m)
- ❏ Spread 6-8 ft (1.8-2.4 m)
- ❏ Flowers early to late summer
- ❏ Any well-drained soil
- ❏ Open, sunny site
- ❏ Hardy zones 7-8

One of the best summer-flowering shrubs for hot, dry sites, Spanish broom (*Spartium junceum*) is especially good for seaside gardens. It thrives in sandy or alkaline soils and is effective in preventing soil erosion.

The shrub is almost leafless, as the bright green stems lose their narrow leaves early. Throughout the summer, it puts on a marvelous display of clear golden pealike flowers with a strong fragrance. Reaching 8-10 ft (2.4-3 m) high and slightly less wide, it is easy to grow but can be damaged by severe winter cold.

Cultivation
Plant young pot-grown plants in midfall or midspring in an open, sunny site in any well-drained soil. Prune them in early spring, but avoid cutting into old wood or the shrubs will die.
Propagation Spanish broom is best increased by seed.
Pests/diseases Trouble free.

SPINDLE TREE —
see *Euonymus*

Spiraea
spirea

Spiraea x *bumalda* 'Anthony Waterer'

- ❏ Height 1-8 ft (30-240 cm)
- ❏ Spread 2½-10 ft (75-300 cm)
- ❏ Flowers early spring to late summer
- ❏ Deep, fertile soil
- ❏ Open, sunny site
- ❏ Hardy zones 4-9

Spireas are hardy, easily grown shrubs popular for their wealth of tiny star-shaped flowers borne in wide heads or sprays from early spring to late summer. Many also have handsome fall foliage. Most are of hybrid origin and display a range of growth habits, sizes, and colors that fit into any landscape.

All spireas revel in sunny, open sites, in mixed borders and rock gardens, or as specimen shrubs. Arching cultivars look splendid trailing over low walls, while suckering types need plenty of room to accommodate their thickets of shoots. Compact bushy types are suitable for informal hedges.

Popular species and hybrids
Spiraea × *arguta* (garland spirea or bridal-wreath) bears profuse white flower clusters on its slender arching stems between early spring and midspring. Often likened to a "fountain" of flowers, it will grow 6-8 ft (1.8-2.4 m) high and wide. The lance-shaped leaves are midgreen. It is hardy in zones 4-9.

Spiraea thunbergii

Spiraea nipponica 'Snowmound'

Spiraea prunifolia 'Plena'

Spiraea × billiardii is a thicket-forming hybrid, growing 4-6 ft (1.2-1.8 m) high and wide. It has narrow green leaves on hairy shoots and dense bright rose flower clusters in summer. In 'Triumphans' they are rose-purple. This shrub does not tolerate alkaline soils. It is hardy in zones 4-6.

Spiraea × bumalda is often treated as a variant of *S. japonica*. Up to 2-3 ft (60-90 cm) high and 3-5 ft (90-150 cm) wide, it produces a broad mound of bluish-green leaves with white to pink flowers in summer. It is hardy in zones 4-8. Cultivars are 'Anthony Waterer' (2 ft/60 cm high; crimson) and 'Goldflame' (2½ ft/75 cm high; orange-red leaves turn yellow, then green; rose-red flowers).

Spiraea japonica forms a twiggy mound, 3-5 ft (90-150 cm) high and wide. Its sharply toothed, lance-shaped leaves are midgreen above and pale to blue-green underneath. It flowers a week or two later than *S. × bumalda*, bearing wide flat heads of pink to rose-red flowers. It is hardy in zones 5-9. Some hybrids are 'Albiflora' (syn. 'Alba'; 2 ft/60 cm high; neat and compact; dense white flower heads), 'Bullata' (slow-growing to 1 ft/30 cm high and wide; dark crinkled leaves; crimson flowers), and 'Nana' (syn. 'Apina'; 1½-2 ft/45-60 cm high, 5 ft/1.5 m wide; lilac-pink flowers).

Spiraea nipponica 'Snowmound' bears a profusion of white flowers in late spring or early summer. It is a dense, bushy shrub reaching 7 ft (2.1 m) high and 8 ft (2.4 m) wide. It is hardy in zones 4-8.

Spiraea prunifolia 'Plena' has profuse clusters of double white flowers on arching branches in early spring to midspring. Its fall leaves are fiery oranges and reds. It grows 6 ft (1.8 m) high and 8 ft (2.4 m) wide. It is hardy in zones 5-8.

Spiraea thunbergii has wide clusters of white flowers in early spring to midspring before the pale green lance-shaped leaves unfurl. It is a 5-6 ft (1.5-1.8 m) high shrub with a spread of 6-8 ft (1.8-2.4 m). It is hardy in zones 5-8.

Spiraea × vanhouttei is a vigorous hybrid with arching branches bearing clusters of white flowers in late spring. It reaches 7 ft (2.1 m) high and 10 ft (3 m) wide. It is hardy in zones 4-8.

Cultivation

Plant in midfall or early spring in deep fertile soil in an open, sunny spot. For hedging, set the plants 15-24 in (38-60 cm) apart and cut them back to 6 in (15 cm) off ground level.

Some spireas, such as *S. × billiardii* and *S. japonica*, flower on shoots of the current season and should be cut back in early spring to 4 in (10 cm) above ground level—hard-pruned plants produce the largest flower heads. Deadhead after flowering. Other spireas flower on shoots of the previous year. Prune these right after flowering, thinning old wood as needed. Trim hedges after flowering.

Propagation In midfall, root 8 in (20 cm) hardwood cuttings in a nursery bed; transplant in fall.

Pests/diseases Spireas have problems similar to those of the rose family, such as fire blight, leaf spot, and powdery mildew, but they are very resilient, and the damage is rarely serious.

Spiraea × bumalda 'Goldflame'

Stachyurus
stachyurus

Stachyurus chinensis

❑ Height 8-10 ft (2.4-3 m)
❑ Spread equal to height
❑ Flowers late winter to midspring
❑ Ordinary well-drained soil
❑ Sheltered, sunny or partially shaded spot
❑ Hardy zones 7-9

Stachyurus is grown for its unusual early blooms. These first make their presence known in midfall, when they appear closed in pendent clusters like long, slender catkins. It is not usually until spring that they open their bell-like shapes. The shrub has an open, branching habit and ovate and slender-pointed mid-green leaves.

Popular species
Stachyurus chinensis has translucent yellow bell-shaped flowers in 4 in (10 cm) long racemes in early spring and midspring.
Stachyurus praecox has pale yellow flowers with dull red calyxes. These appear as early as late winter and continue until midspring.

Cultivation
Plant in any well-drained soil, enriched with organic matter, in midfall or early spring. A sunny or partially shaded site sheltered from cold winds is suitable.
Propagation Take heel cuttings in midsummer.
Pests/diseases Trouble free.

STAGHORN SUMAC —
see *Rhus*

Stephanandra
stephanandra

Stephanandra incisa

❑ Height 5-7 ft (1.5-2.1 m)
❑ Spread 4-6 ft (1.2-1.8 m)
❑ Flowers late spring to early summer
❑ Ordinary well-drained soil
❑ Sunny or partially shaded site
❑ Hardy zones 5-8

Some shrubs depend for their charm not on their flowers, leaves, or fruits but simply on their growth habit. The hardy *Stephanandra incisa*, from the mountain slopes of Japan, is such a plant. It is a graceful shrub with rich brown, arching branches. At the tip of each shoot, an open cluster of tiny yellow and white flowers appears in late spring to early summer.

The deeply cut, lobed green leaves, which resemble those of currant bushes, turn bronze and clear yellow in fall.

Cultivation
Plant in midfall or early spring in any well-drained soil in sun or partial shade.

Thin old and decayed shoots in late winter to early spring.
Propagation Remove rooted suckers in midfall or early spring. Plant directly in the permanent positions, or if they are small, grow on for a year in a nursery bed before planting out in permanent sites.
Pests/diseases Trouble free.

SUMAC — see *Rhus*
SWEET PEPPERBUSH —
see *Clethra*

Symphoricarpos
snowberry

Symphoricarpos 'White Hedge'

❑ Height 6 ft (1.8 m)
❑ Spread equal to height
❑ Grown for berries
❑ Ordinary well-drained soil
❑ Shady or sunny site
❑ Hardy zones 4-7

The crowning glory of snowberry (*Symphoricarpos × doorenbosii*) is its white or pale pink berries, which weigh down the branches from midfall into winter.

The hardy shrub forms a dense bush of smooth blue-green leaves from spring to fall, with small pink bell-shaped flowers appearing in clusters all summer long.

Popular cultivars
'Magic Berry' is a compact, spreading shrub with abundant rose-pink berries.
'Mother of Pearl' has white, rose-flushed marblelike berries.
'White Hedge' has white berries held in upright clusters. It makes a fine informal hedge.

Cultivation
Plant in midfall or early spring in any well-drained soil in sun or partial shade. For hedging, set plants 15-18 in (38-45 cm) apart, and cut them back to 12 in (30 cm). In midfall to late winter, thin overgrown shrubs and remove unwanted suckers. Trim hedges in summer.
Propagation Plant rooted suckers from midfall to late winter.
Pests/diseases Leaf spot disfigures leaves, and anthracnose attacks foliage and fruits. Aphids and scale infest twigs and leaves.

Syringa
lilac

Syringa microphylla 'Superba'

- ❏ Height 4-15 ft (1.2-4.5 m)
- ❏ Spread 4-12 ft (1.2-3.6 m)
- ❏ Flowers late spring and early summer
- ❏ Fertile garden soil
- ❏ Sunny or lightly shaded site
- ❏ Hardy zones 2-8

Lilacs are very popular spring-flowering shrubs and small trees. They are fully hardy and easily grown. While the foliage is not striking, the flowering display is glorious. The large upright or gently arching flower panicles may be heavily scented and come in white, cream, yellow, pink, and many shades of blue and purple.

Lilacs make handsome specimens and look equally effective in shrub borders. The bushier species and cultivars may be used for informal hedges or screens. Lilacs are useful in city gardens, as they tolerate pollution.

Popular species and hybrids
Syringa × *chinensis* grows into a dense bushy shrub 8-10 ft (2.4-3 m) high and 6 ft (1.8 m) wide. Its scented purple blooms are held in upright spikes in late spring. It is hardy in zones 4-7.
Syringa meyeri 'Palibin' is a slow-growing cultivar 4-5 ft (1.2-1.5 m) high and 5-7 ft (1.5-2.1 m) wide. The dome-shaped shrub is covered with small sprays of scented lilac blooms in late spring and early summer. It is hardy in zones 4-7.
Syringa microphylla, a small lilac, grows only 4-5 ft (1.2-1.5 m)

Syringa x *chinensis*

high and wide. It has a delicate growth habit — when the panicles of scented rose-lilac flowers appear in late spring, and sometimes again in early fall, the slender twigs bend over with their weight. It is hardy in zones 5-7. The cultivar 'Superba' has rose-pink flowers and is 6-8 ft (1.8-2.4 m) high.
Syringa × *persica* (Persian lilac) is a bushy rounded shrub 6-8 ft (1.8-2.4 m) high and 6-7 ft (1.8-2.1 m) wide. Its upright clusters of fragrant lilac flowers open in late spring. It is hardy in zones 4-8. 'Alba' has white flowers.
Syringa × *prestoniae* is a group of Canadian hybrids noted for their hardiness (zones 2-7) and large, erect or drooping flower panicles in late spring. They grow 10 ft (3 m) high and wide. Popular cultivars are 'Elinor' (purple-red buds opening to pale lavender

Syringa x *persica*

Tamarix
tamarisk

Syringa vulgaris 'Vulcan'

Tamarix parviflora

❏ Height 10-15 ft (3-4.5 m)
❏ Spread equal to height
❏ Flowers late spring and late summer
❏ Ordinary well-drained soil
❏ Sunny, open site
❏ Hardy zones 2-9

Hardy tamarisks epitomize a certain habitat — the seaside garden. Tamarisks thrive when exposed to harsh salt winds and when grown in dry areas.

Popular species
Tamarix parviflora has feathery, pink blooms in late spring. It is 10-15 ft (3-4.5 m) high and wide, with scalelike green leaves. It is hardy in zones 5-9.
Tamarix ramosissima has feathery spikes of tiny rose-pink flowers on thin branches in late summer. It grows 12-15 ft (3.6-4.5 m) high and wide and has narrow pale green leaves. 'Rubra' has deep rose-red flowers. It is hardy in zones 2-8.

Cultivation
Plant in well-drained soil in an open, sunny site in midfall or early spring. Prune *T. parviflora* after flowering and *T. ramosissima* in early spring.
Propagation Take 9-12 in (23-30 cm) hardwood cuttings in midfall.
Pests/diseases Cankers destroy branches or trunks; scale insects infest branches and foliage; and powdery mildew attacks leaves.

TRUMPET VINE — see *Campsis*

flowers), 'Isabella' (pale purple blossoms), and 'Royalty' (violet-purple blooms).
Syringa vulgaris (common lilac) is the parent of many popular hybrids. They have heart-shaped leaves and pyramidal panicles of fragrant single or double flowers in late spring. Typically these shrubs grow 8-12 ft (2.4-3.6 m) high and 5-10 ft (1.5-3 m) wide and are hardy in zones 3-7. Popular cultivars are: 'Charles Joly' (double deep purple-red), 'Firmament' (single pinkish mauve), 'Katherine Havemeyer' (double purple-lavender), 'Madame Lemoine' (double cream-white), 'Maréchal Foch' (single carmine-rose), 'Massena' (single deep purple), 'Maud Notcutt' (single white), 'Mrs. Edward Harding' (semidouble pink and red), 'Président Poincaré' (double claret-mauve), 'Primrose' (single pale yellow), 'Souvenir de Louis Späth' (single wine-red), 'Vestale' (single pure white), and 'Vulcan' (single reddish mauve).

Cultivation
Plant in mid- to late fall or early spring in full sun or very light shade. Lilacs thrive in any good, well-drained soil and are particularly happy in alkaline ones. For hedges and screens, set plants 2-4 ft (60-120 cm) apart.

Remove faded blooms, and from midfall onward, thin out crossing and weak branches. Cut down overgrown bushes in late winter to 2-3 ft (60-90 cm) above ground level. Flowers should appear on new growths after 2 to 3 years.

Remove suckers by cutting off as close as possible to the roots.
Propagation Take 3-4 in (7.5-10 cm) long heel cuttings of half-ripe shoots in mid- to late summer, and root in a propagating box.
Pests/diseases Lilac borers tunnel into branches or trunks; leaf miners tunnel into the foliage. Leaf and twig blights cause dieback, and powdery mildew commonly attacks foliage. Scale insects infest twigs and leaves.

Vaccinium
blueberry

Vaccinium corymbosum

❏ Height 4-12 ft (1.2-3.6 m) or more
❏ Spread 6-10 ft (1.8-3 m)
❏ Flowers midspring
❏ Moist, acid soil
❏ Sunny or partially shaded site
❏ Hardy zones 4-9

Blueberries are grown for their edible fruits, but many species are also useful for the shrub border. Small clusters of bell-shaped flowers appear in spring, but the true beauty is in the foliage, with its rich fall colors, and the striking, shiny berries.

Popular species
Vaccinium ashei (rabbit-eye blueberry) is a southern species that thrives from lower section of zone 7 through zone 9. It is slow-growing but may eventually reach a height of 18 ft (5.4 m); but 4-10 ft (1.2-3 m) tall and wide are more typical. It bears white flowers in spring followed by edible blue berries. In fall the foliage turns yellow, orange, or even scarlet.
Vaccinium corymbosum is the northern equivalent, a 6-12 ft (1.8-3.6 m) shrub that is hardy in zones 4-7. This species bears its pink-flushed white flowers in midspring, which are followed by blue berries. The glossy dark green leaves turn brilliant orange and scarlet in fall.

Cultivation
Plant in midfall or early spring in moist, acid soil in sun or partial shade. Yellowing foliage during the growing season is a common symptom of alkaline soil. Trim established shrubs in midspring.
Propagation Layer long shoots in early fall.
Pests/diseases None serious.

Viburnum
viburnum

Viburnum lantana

❏ Height 3-20 ft (90-600 cm)
❏ Spread 3-15 ft (90-450 cm)
❏ Flowers late winter through fall
❏ Any moist, well-drained soil
❏ Sunny or lightly shaded site
❏ Hardy zones 2-8

The *Viburnum* genus has species and cultivars of wide diversity. These hardy shrubs provide color and interest in the garden all year round — some bear flowers on bare branches in late winter in mild regions, others bloom in spring, others in summer and fall. The flowers are often scented and borne in dense, round clusters or in flat, wide heads. Several species produce striking berries. The leaves, mostly broadly ovate, often have attractive fall colors.

Viburnums are both evergreen and deciduous; those described here are deciduous.

Popular species and hybrids
Viburnum betulifolium is 8-12 ft (2.4-3.6 m) high and wide. It bears clusters of white flowers in late spring; on mature plants profuse red berries follow.
Viburnum × bodnantense bears clusters of scented white flowers, flushed pink, on bare branches in late winter or early spring. It reaches a height and spread of 9-12 ft (2.7-3.6 m). The young leaves are often tinged bronze. It is hardy in zones 5-8. Outstanding cultivars are 'Dawn' (rose-red buds and scented white flowers, flushed pink) and 'Deben' (shell-pink buds and fragrant white blooms, flushed shell-pink).
Vibernum × carlcephalum grows 6-10 ft (1.8-3 m) tall and wide and is hardy in zones 6-8. It bears broad rounded heads of fragrant white blossoms in mid- to late spring. The foliage is light green, tinted reddish-purple in fall.
Viburnum carlesii is a small species, 4-5 ft (1.2-1.5 m) high and wide. The clusters of deeply fragrant waxy white flowers appear in midspring among dull green

Viburnum plicatum tomentosum 'Mariesii'

leaves, which turn red in fall. It is hardy in zones 5-7. 'Aurora' has red buds and pink flowers.

Viburnum dentatum (arrowwood) is an erect shrub growing 10 ft (3 m) or more high and spreading to 8 ft (2.4 m), with many straight stems growing up from the base. The rounded, coarsely toothed leaves are glossy green in summer and red in fall. Clusters of creamy white flowers appear in the late spring; dark blue berries follow in fall. It is hardy in zones 2-8.

Viburnum farreri is 9-12 ft (2.7-3.6 m) high and wide. The richly scented white, pink-tinged flowers are borne in drooping clusters in late winter or early spring, depending on the climate. The leaves are bright green, bronze when young. It is hardy in zones 5-8.

Viburnum lantana (wayfaring tree) is grown for its red berries, which mature to black, and for its dark red fall leaves. White flowers appear in late spring. It grows 10-15 ft (3-4.5 m) high and wide. It is hardy in zones 4-8.

Viburnum opulus (European cranberry bush) is grown for its flat heads of very fragrant white flowers, which appear in mid- to late spring. Translucent red berries

Viburnum x bodnantense

Viburnum x carlcephalum

Vitex
chaste tree

Vitex agnus-castus

❏ Height 10-20 ft (3-6 m)
❏ Spread 10-12 ft (3-3.6 m)
❏ Flowers summer into early fall
❏ Fertile, well-drained soil
❏ Sunny, sheltered site
❏ Hardy zones 6-8

follow. It is a bushy species, 12-15 ft (3.6-4.5 m) high and wide, with dark green maplelike leaves that are richly colored in fall. It is hardy in zones 4-8. Popular cultivars are 'Compactum' (3 ft/90 cm high and wide), 'Roseum' (snowball bush; creamy-white globular flower heads), and 'Xanthocarpum' (yellow fruits).

Viburnum plicatum tomentosum is distinguished by its horizontal branches that bear dull green leaves, which turn wine-red in fall. It grows 8-10 ft (2.4-3 m) high and 10-15 ft (3-4.5 m) wide

and bears white lace-cap flowers in midspring. It is hardy in zones 5-8. Also popular are 'Mariesii' (small profuse flowers) and 'Pink Beauty' (pink flowers).

Viburnum sieboldii grows 15-20 ft (4.5-6 m) tall and up to 15 ft (4.5 m) wide. It is a vigorous shrub, clothed with toothed yellow-green leaves, which take on bronze-red colors in fall. Clusters of cream-white flowers in late spring are followed by striking berries that ripen from green to pink, red, blue, and finally black. It is hardy in zones 4-7.

Cultivation
Viburnums thrive in any good, moist but well-drained soil in full sun; they tolerate light shade. Shelter early-flowering types from cold winds and the early-morning sun. Plant in midfall or early spring; for good fruit production it is advisable to plant two or three shrubs together.

Prune to remove deadwood, and thin overcrowded shrubs right after flowering.
Propagation Root softwood cuttings in summer in a cold frame.
Pests/diseases Aphids and borers may be troublesome; downy mildew and leaf spot may attack foliage.

Vitex agnus-castus, though only moderately hardy, will generally flourish in southern gardens if grown in a sheltered spot. It is valuable for its slender spikes of small, fragrant violet-blue flowers, which appear throughout summer and into early fall. The cultivar 'Alba' has white flowers, while 'Latifolia' is a hardier, more vigorous form.

Though naturally a small tree, this species may be maintained as a bushy shrub, 10-12 ft (3-3.6 m) high and wide, through pruning. It has aromatic, narrow lance-shaped leaflets that are arranged like the fingers of a hand along gray downy shoots.

Cultivation
Plant in midspring in any good, well-drained soil in a sunny, sheltered site.

In early spring, remove dead, frosted, or weak growth, cutting back the previous year's shoots to 3-4 in (7.5-10 cm).
Propagation Take softwood cuttings in early summer to midsummer; root in a propagating box.
Pests/diseases None serious.

Viburnum opulus 'Compactum'

Vitis
grape vine

Vitis coignetiae, fall

❏ Height 20-80 ft (6-24 m)
❏ Foliage climber
❏ Rich, well-drained but moisture-retentive soil
❏ Sunny or lightly shaded site
❏ Hardy zones 5-8

Ornamental grapes are hardy vigorous climbers ideal for growing up walls, pergolas, fences, and tall trees, where they support themselves by twining tendrils. Their large, handsome bold leaves are especially attractive when showing off their brilliant fall colors.

Popular species
Vitis coignetiae (Japanese crimson glory vine) is the most vigorous species — it easily grows 80 ft (24 m) high, and shoots may increase by 50 ft (15 m) in one season. The large, thick, heart-shaped midgreen leaves turn yellow, orange-red, and purple-crimson in fall. Clusters of green flowers appear in summer, followed by inedible black berries.
Vitis vinifera (European wine grape) may also be cultivated as an ornamental vine. It flourishes along the Pacific Coast and locally in the coastal Northeast; check with local nurseries for the names of cultivars adapted to your region. In general, vinifera grapes grow about 20 ft (6 m) high and offer not only handsome fruits but also yellow fall foliage colors.

Cultivation
Plant in fall or spring in humus-rich soil that is well drained but moisture retentive. If the soil is acid, add lime. Any exposure will suit, though a sunny site is preferable for fruiting vines. Thin old shoots and shorten young ones in late summer.
Propagation Layer year-old shoots of *V. coignetiae* in fall. They should have rooted a year later. *V. vinifera* can be increased by taking 4-5 in (10-12 cm) heel cuttings from half-hardened growth in summer.
Pests/diseases Scale insects and aphids may infest the plants; powdery mildew and Japanese beetles often attack the foliage.

Weigela
weigela

Weigela florida 'Variegata'

❏ Height 3-9 ft (90-270 cm)
❏ Spread equal to height
❏ Flowers late spring to early summer
❏ Good, well-drained soil
❏ Sunny or partially shaded site
❏ Hardy zones 4-8

Weigelas are among the most popular of flowering shrubs, with small but abundant clusters of funnel-shaped blooms clothing the arching branches in late spring and early summer. They flourish in the North or upper South, are easy to grow, and thrive in most soils and sites.

Popular species and hybrids
The species have largely been superseded by garden cultivars.
Weigela florida bears clusters of rose-pink flowers with pale insides. It grows 6-9 ft (1.8-2.7 m) high and wide and is of arching habit. The oval, prominently veined and wrinkled leaves are light green. Cultivars include 'Foliis Purpureis,' a dense slow-growing shrub up to 4 ft (1.2 m) high and wide, with dark purple foliage and rose-pink flowers, and 'Variegata,' with green, cream-edged leaves.
Weigela × hybrida is the name for a group of showy free-flowering shrubs. They commonly grow 5-6 ft (1.5-1.8 m) high and 5-8 ft (1.5-2.4 m) wide, with oval, wrinkled midgreen leaves. Readily available hybrids include 'Abel Carrière' (carmine-rose flowers), 'Avalanche' (white flowers), 'Bristol Ruby' (dark buds and ruby-red

Weigela 'Bristol Ruby'

flowers), 'Eva Rathke' (compact shrub; bright crimson flowers), 'Minuet' (2½ ft/75 cm dwarf shrub; ruby-red flowers), and 'Pink Princess' (lavender-pink flowers).

Cultivation
Plant in midfall or early spring in any good, well-drained soil that does not dry out in summer. The site can be sunny or partially shaded. Every year after flowering, remove one or two of the old stems, cutting them back to ground level.

Propagation Take softwood cuttings in summer, and root in a propagating unit.

Pests/diseases Trouble free.

WILLOW — see *Salix*
WINTER HAZEL —
see *Corylopsis*
WINTERSWEET —
see *Chimonanthus*

Weigela florida

Wisteria
wisteria

Wisteria floribunda 'Alba'

Wisteria sinensis, standard

❑ Height 30-70 ft (9-21 m)
❑ Climber, flowers mid- to late spring
❑ Any deep, fertile soil
❑ Sunny site
❑ Hardy zones 5-9

There is no sight more breathtaking than an established wisteria in full bloom. This vigorous hardy climber is capable of reaching a height of 30-70 ft (9-21 m). It is unsuitable for small gardens unless it is trained as a small weeping standard. Wisteria is usually grown on a firm support against a sunny wall or pergola, or up through an old tree.

The flowers that appear in midspring to late spring are one of the joys of the gardener's year. As the elegant pale green leaf sprays unfold, long streamers of pale purple, white, or pink flowers cascade from every twig.

Popular species
Wisteria floribunda grows up to 30 ft (9 m) high and has light green to midgreen leaflets. The scented violet-blue flowers are borne in 1 ft (30 cm) long racemes. It is hardy in zones 5-9. Cultivars include 'Alba' (white), 'Rosea' (pale rose-pink and purple), and 'Violacea Plena' (double violet-blue).

Wisteria sinensis is the most vigorous (70 ft/21 m high) and popular species. It produces dark green to midgreen leaves, with fewer leaflets than *W. floribunda*, as well as 8-12 in (20-30 cm) long drooping racemes of fragrant purple flowers. It is hardy in zones 5-8. Popular cultivars are 'Alba' (white), 'Black Dragon' (double purple-blue), and 'Plena' (double lilac-mauve).

Wisteria venusta reaches 30 ft (9 m) high and has dark green leaves covered with down. The lightly fragrant white flowers are borne in shorter but denser racemes than those of the other species. It is hardy in zones 5-8.

Cultivation
Plant out pot-grown specimens in midfall or early spring. Wisterias will grow in any soil except a poor, thin one, though a moist, rich loamy soil provides the best conditions. Provide support and tie in the shoots until the twining stems have gained a firm hold. Wisterias rarely flower until they are 7 or more years old.

In late winter cut back all new shoots to within two or three buds of the base of the previous year's growth. Where climbers need to be restricted, cut the season's young growths back to five or six buds in summer.

Propagation Most wisterias are grafted by nurseries, but *W. sinensis* can be increased by layering in late spring. The layers should root within a year.

Pests/diseases Aphids may infest young growths; leaf beetles, mealybugs, and plant hoppers may also attack wisteria vines. Leaf spot may disfigure foliage.

WITCH HAZEL — see *Hamamelis*
WOADWAXEN — see *Genista*
WOODBINE — see *Lonicera*

Wisteria sinensis

Floribunda rose The clear yellow, fragrant 'Mountbatten' is an outstanding modern bush rose.

A–Z of Roses

When and where the rose first appeared in the garden is long forgotten, but for thousands of years it has been a symbol of purity and perfection, and it remains the supreme joy of most gardeners. The rose, though, is hardly a singular plant; it is so diverse in habit, bloom, foliage, and performance that it fits into any garden and almost every garden site. Wild roses are native to virtually every part of the Northern Hemisphere; and the modern garden hybrids vary from miniatures only a few inches high to ramblers as much as 60 ft (18 m) tall. The blooms, whatever their size and shape, are perfect in form and may be single, semidouble, or fully double; they range from the delicate five-petaled flowers of some species roses, through the full-blown cabbage roses and quartered gallicas, to the elegant high-pointed hybrid teas.

A single, short flowering season was the rule among roses north of the Deep South until the beginning of the last century. Most of the old-fashioned types, such as alba roses or damask roses, flower according to this schedule, but such is the charm and perfume of their blossoms that they continue to be grown even today. Modern roses, however, are the results of crosses of hardy northerners with everblooming frost-tender southern roses, such as teas or China roses. These hybrids not only thrive even in cold-winter regions, they also flower more or less continuously throughout the growing season, blooming from early summer well into fall.

The choice of roses is so vast that they are organized into groups according to origin, flower type, and habit. The roses described here are arranged as follows: climbing roses, floribunda roses (cluster-flowered bush roses), hybrid tea roses (large-flowered bush roses), miniature roses, modern shrub roses, old garden roses, polyantha roses, rambler roses, and species roses.

Climbing roses

'Mme. Grégoire Staechelin'

'Altissimo'

❏ Height 6-30 ft (1.8-9 m)
❏ Flowers early summer to
   early fall
❏ Rich, well-drained soil
❏ Full sun or partial shade
❏ Hardy zones 4-9

Climbing roses generally derive from one of two sources: they may be either descendants of climbing species or "sports" of bush roses — spontaneous mutations that cause part of a shrub suddenly to adopt a climbing form of growth. The climbers described on the following pages have relatively large flowers carried in small trusses. The blooms are single or double, often fragrant, and come in a range of colors that include scarlet, pink, orange, yellow, and white. Most modern climbing roses are repeat-flowering — blooming at intervals from early summer to early fall.

Climbing roses are scrambling shrubs rather than true climbers, as they have no means of attaching themselves to their supports and need to be tied in. Vigorous tall cultivars are suitable for training on large house walls or for scrambling up trees. Less vigorous types are suitable for more restricted areas — pillars, pergolas, fences, arbors, and screens.

Climbers, like all roses, vary greatly in their winter hardiness — their tolerance to cold. Hardiness varies not only from class to class (floribundas, for example, are typically hardier than hybrid teas), but also within a class, where one climber may be vastly hardier than another. Most of the climbers cited in this book perform well from zone 5 south through the cooler parts of zone 8. For zone 4 and north, plant types described as outstandingly cold hardy, while in the Deep South, gardeners will do best with types described as heat tolerant. Southern gardeners will also experience greater success if they plant shrubs that have been grafted onto rootstocks appropriate to the South, such as *Rosa* × *fortuniana*.

Popular cultivars
'Aloha' has double rose-pink flowers of the hybrid tea type. They are sweetly scented and repeat-flowering. This is a slow grower that reaches only 8 ft (2.4 m) and is best trained up a pillar or low wall. The foliage is resistant to fungal diseases such as black spot, mildew, and rust.
'Altissimo' has large single flowers with blood-red petals and golden stamens. It is repeat-flowering. Growing 12 ft (3.6 m) high, it is suitable for boundary walls, fences, and pillars.
'Bantry Bay' has bright pink semidouble blooms with conspicuous yellow stamens. It is repeat-flowering and lightly scented. Not overvigorous, reaching only 10 ft (3 m) high, it is best trained up a wall, fence, or pillar.
'Casino' bears double yellow blooms fading to soft yellow as they age. It is repeat-flowering, with a sweet scent, and grows 10 ft (3 m) high. Semihardy, it is best grown along a warm, sheltered wall.
'Climbing Cécile Brünner' is a climbing sport of the polyantha rose, with small, double, fragrant shell-pink flowers. It flowers in summer and again in fall with a smaller display. Extremely vigorous, up to 20 ft (6 m) high, it is an excellent choice for training up an old tree.
'Climbing Crimson Glory' has double, deep velvet-crimson,

'Aloha'

'Dublin Bay'

strongly fragrant flowers of the hybrid tea type from midsummer to early fall. It reaches 9-10 ft (2.7-3 m) high — ideal for growing over arches or along a fence.

'Climbing Étoile de Hollande' has double, deep red, loosely formed flowers. These are of the hybrid tea type and are highly fragrant. This repeat-flowering cultivar grows 10-12 ft (3-3.6 m) high.

'Climbing Iceberg,' a climbing sport of the floribunda rose, bears double and slightly fragrant white blooms. It is repeat-flowering. Up to 10 ft (3 m) high, it looks most effective growing against a wall. Mildew can be a problem.

'Climbing Masquerade' bears large trusses of slightly fragrant blooms that open yellow, then turn pink and red. It is repeat-flowering, although a later flush appears only if early flowers are deadheaded. It reaches 8 ft (2.4 m) high and can be grown as a shrub or trained along a fence.

'Climbing Shot Silk' bears salmon-pink blooms flushed yellow. They are of the hybrid tea

'Compassion'

type, double, and heavily fragrant. This repeat-flowering cultivar reaches 10-12 ft (3-3.6 m) high.

'Compassion' has a profusion of large, double apricot-pink blooms among handsome, dark glossy green foliage. It is repeat-flowering and strongly scented. New growth comes freely from the base, but it is not tall enough to cover a house wall. Pillars, pergolas, and arches make more suitable supports.

'Danse du Feu' has spectacular double scarlet-orange blooms but no fragrance. It is repeat-flowering and grows 12 ft (3.6 m) high. It looks effective covering

a screen and grows well on a north-facing wall.

'Dortmund' has large single flowers with crimson-red petals, white eyes, and golden stamens. This repeat-flowering pillar rose, reaching 8-10 ft (2.4-3 m) high, is unusually winter hardy and disease resistant.

'Dublin Bay' bears large, double, deep red flowers that are slightly fragrant. Repeat-flowering and moderately vigorous, it reaches 8 ft (2.4 m) high. It is disease resistant and winter hardy.

'Galway Bay' has large, double, cerise-pink blooms, borne in great profusion. It is repeat-flowering. Plenty of shoots grow from the base, and it reaches 8 ft (2.4 m) high, making a good pillar rose. It is resistant to most rose diseases.

'Gloire de Dijon' has double buff-yellow blossoms that are sweetly scented. It is a repeat-flowering cultivar — one of the earliest to bloom when grown against a warm wall. It reaches 10-15 ft (3-4.5 m) high. Despite its susceptibility to mildew, it remains extremely popular.

'Golden Showers' bears large bright golden-yellow and fragrant flowers. It reaches 8 ft (2.4 m) high and makes a good pillar rose; it is almost thornless.

'Guinée' has dark velvet-red, double, sweetly scented flowers. A strong repeat-flowering climber, it reaches 8-10 ft (2.4-3 m) and looks most effective when trained against a wall or wooden screen.

'Handel' has moderately scented double cream-white flowers, heavily flushed and tipped carmine. This shrub is both winter hardy and disease resistant. A repeat-flowering cultivar, it reaches 10-12 ft (3-3.6 m) high. Train up a wall or pergola.

'Golden Showers'

'Handel'

'Climbing Iceberg'

'Meg'

'Mermaid'

'New Dawn'

'Joseph's Coat' is of moderate vigor; it is sometimes grown as a large shrub but is also ideal as a pillar or arbor rose. This well-branching cultivar, about 6 ft (1.8 m) high, has recurrent flowers that are yellow-orange and red. It is disease resistant.

'Kathleen Harrop' is a sport of 'Zéphirine Drouhin' but less vigorous, growing up to 7 ft (2.1 m) high. It is repeat-flowering, with strongly scented, double blush-pink blossoms.

'Leverkusen' bears large sprays of semidouble pale yellow blooms. Repeat-flowering and slightly fragrant, it is vigorous and grows 10-12 ft (3-3.6 m) high. This useful cultivar is disease resistant and exceptionally winter hardy.

'Maigold' has fragrant, semi-double golden yellow flowers. Normally it flowers once a year, in early summer, though dead-heading may encourage another smaller flush. It reaches 11 ft (3.3 m) high and is suitable for growing against a wall.

'Meg' bears trusses of large, single, sweetly scented apricot-pink flowers. It is rarely repeat-flowering, though occasionally there may be a few late blooms. The average height is 10 ft (3 m) — grow it up a pergola or a pillar, or along a fence.

'Mermaid' bears single, scented cream-yellow flowers. It is a repeat-flowering climber — one of the tallest, reaching 25-30 ft (7.5-9 m) high. Train it against a south-facing or west-facing house wall, where it is less likely to be affected by frost. This disease-resistant cultivar tolerates heat and humidity.

'Mme. Alfred Carrière' has pink-flushed white blooms of the old-fashioned noisette type. They are strongly scented and borne in great profusion. It is a repeat-flowering climber that reaches 15-20 ft (4.5-6 m).

'Mme. Grégoire Staechelin' has large, double pink blooms with ruffled petals and a particularly heady fragrance. The magnificence of the blooms makes up for the fact that it flowers for only a few weeks in early summer. A vigorous climber, 15-20 ft (4.5-6 m) high, it is suitable for training against the north-facing wall of a house. It is prone to mildew.

'New Dawn' bears a profusion of small, semidouble shell-pink blossoms. It is repeat-flowering and fragrant. Up to 9 ft (2.7 m) high, it has a bushy habit that makes it suitable as a pillar rose or for growing through a fence. It is disease resistant and winter hardy.

'Parkdirektor Riggers' produces large clusters of semidouble blood-red flowers. A vigorous repeat-flowering climber, it reaches 12-15 ft (3.6-4.5 m) high. It is prone to mildew and black spot.

'Pink Perpétué' has two-toned deep pink flowers appearing in early summer and midsummer, and again in early fall. The double blooms are slightly fragrant. Though it only reaches 6-8 ft (1.8-2.4 m) high, it spreads well, making it a good choice for a low wall or fence.

'Schoolgirl' has large double apricot-orange blooms, shaded pink. Repeat-flowering and fragrant, it grows 10-12 ft (3-3.6 m) high. It is suitable for training against a wall, though it tends to grow leggy and bare at the base.

'Summer Wine' bears large, single, soft coral-pink blooms with prominent red stamens. It is repeat-flowering and strongly fragrant, with dark green foliage. It grows up to 10 ft (3 m) high.

'Swan Lake' has large, double white blooms tinged pink in the center. They are slightly fragrant. It is repeat-flowering and reaches 7-8 ft (2.1-2.4 m) high — ideal for training up an arch, pillar, or pergola. Black spot and mildew can be troublesome.

'Pink Perpétué'

'Gloire de Dijon'

'Sympathie' has double, bright red velvety blooms of the hybrid tea type. It is repeat-flowering, fragrant, resistant to disease, and winter hardy. It grows 10 ft (3 m) high.

'White Cockade' has double white blooms of the hybrid tea type. Repeat-flowering, it bears a profusion of flowers, continuing well into fall. Reaching 6-8 ft (1.8-2.4 m) high, it is suitable for training along a fence or up a pillar; it can also be grown as a shrub.

'Zéphirine Drouhin' is a climbing bourbon rose with richly fragrant semidouble carmine-pink blooms. It is repeat-flowering, often with a fall display more spectacular than the summer display. It grows 9 ft (2.7 m) high and is both disease resistant and winter hardy.

Cultivation

Plant bare-rooted roses in late fall or early spring to midspring; put in container-grown roses during any part of the growing season. Like all roses, climbers need rich, well-drained soil. Most cultivars thrive in full sun, though one or two will tolerate partial shade. Prepare a planting area of at least 4 ft x 4 ft (1.2 m x 1.2 m) for each climber and dig in plenty of organic matter. After planting keep the ground free of weeds.

In midspring to late spring, mulch both recently planted and established roses; feed them from late spring to midsummer once a month.

As the plants grow, train them up supports. Climbers against walls and fences should be trained into a fan shape: tie in the main shoots as horizontally as possible to encourage flower-bearing lateral shoots to grow. Wind the stems of roses trained up pillars and pergolas around the support in an upward spiral. No climbers are self-supporting, so they need to be tied with wire.

Pruning methods are the same for all climbers. Little pruning is needed in the early years, except to remove damaged and crossing stems. Thereafter, cut back lateral shoots to three or four buds in the fall, and remove the tips of soft, immature growths. Remove old or unwanted growth at the same time and dig in plenty of organic matter. Deadhead all cultivars — if you can reach them.

Propagation Most modern roses are propagated by grafting or budding, processes best left to professional rose growers.

Pests/diseases Black spot, the most common rose disease, may develop on the leaves, eventually causing them to drop off. Mildew sometimes affects leaves, stems, and flower buds. Rust appears as bright orange pustules in spring, then develops into yellow patches on the leaves in summer, gradually turning black in fall. The leaves eventually drop. Spray against aphids in summer — these are usually found in large numbers on the tips of growing shoots.

'Zéphirine Drouhin'

Floribunda roses
(cluster-flowered bush roses)

'Matangi'

'Amber Queen'

❏ Height 1½-7 ft (45-210 cm)
❏ Spread 2-2½ ft (60-75 cm)
❏ Flowers early summer to midfall
❏ Rich, well-drained soil
❏ Full sun
❏ Hardy zones 5-8

Floribunda roses are crosses between the old-fashioned polyantha roses and modern hybrid teas. These bushy offspring vary widely in height, but all bear profuse flowers in clusters. Hardier and more disease resistant on average than hybrid teas, floribundas are also somewhat easier to integrate into a garden because of their compact shrubby habit. Their flowering season extends from early summer to midfall.

Grow floribundas in beds of their own, in mixed borders, or as hedges. Tall cultivars make good specimen shrubs, and dwarf types are suitable for ground cover and edging.

Popular cultivars
Many floribunda cultivars exist, and new ones are constantly being introduced.

'Amber Queen' produces well-formed, fragrant amber-yellow flowers. A fine bedding rose, it is 2-2½ ft (60-75 cm) high.
'Angel Face' bears double, highly fragrant deep mauve blossoms. Disease resistant and winter hardy, this bushy, spreading shrub grows 2-3 ft (60-90 cm) high.
'Anne Cocker' bears vivid vermilion, long-stalked flowers. Good for cutting, exhibiting, and bedding, it grows 3 ft (90 cm) high. It is susceptible to mildew.
'Arthur Bell' bears large and fragrant golden yellow flowers that fade to a cream color. It grows 3½ ft (105 cm) high.
'Betty Prior' bears an abundance of medium to deep pink single blooms with an effect like that of dogwood. Disease resistant and winter hardy, it is 5-7 ft (1.5-2.1 m) tall.
'Chinatown' has large, strongly fragrant yellow flowers flushed pink. It is vigorous, 4-5 ft (1.2-1.5 m) high, and a good specimen shrub.
'City of Leeds' bears slightly fragrant, rich salmon flowers. It grows 2½-3 ft (75-90 cm) tall.
'Elizabeth of Glamis' has large, fragrant, well-formed salmon-pink flowers, which fade slightly with age. Vigorous and upright, it reaches 2½ ft (75 cm) high.
'Europeana' bears cupped dark crimson blossoms that are outstanding for exhibition and cutting. Winter hardy and disease resistant, this shrub reaches 2½-3 ft (75-90 cm) high.
'Eyepaint' bears an abundance

'Sunprite'

'Arthur Bell'

'Redgold'

of small, single scarlet flowers with white centers and gold stamens. Up to 4 ft (1.2 m) high, it is good as a hedge or in a border.

'Fashion' has double, coral hybrid-tea-type blooms. This is a vigorous, disease-resistant, and winter-hardy cultivar, growing 3½-4½ ft (105-135 cm) high.

'Gene Boerner' bears medium pink double flowers of the hybrid tea type. Disease resistant and winter hardy, it forms an upright shrub 4-5 ft (1.2-1.5 m) tall.

'Hannah Gordon' bears hybrid-tea-shaped white flowers, shaded deep pink. A good bedding rose, it grows up to 2½ ft (75 cm) high.

'Iceberg' has small, pure white

early blooms, flushed with pale pink in fall. This free-flowering rose is 5 ft (1.5 m) high, with a vigorous branching habit, so it needs space. Use it as a hedge, at the back of a bed, or as a specimen shrub. Although winter hardy, it is susceptible to black spot.

'Lilli Marlene' has slightly fragrant scarlet-red flowers. Though somewhat susceptible to mildew, this is overall a vigorous bedding

rose, growing 2½ ft (75 cm) high.

'Margaret Merril,' 4 ft (1.2 m) high, has beautifully formed, scented white flowers. It is prone to black spot.

'Masquerade' bears flowers that open yellow, turn pink, then red. Suitable for a hedge, it is disease resistant, winter hardy, and vigorous and grows 4 ft (1.2 m) high.

'Matangi' has orange-red flowers, with gold stamens and petals shaded silvery white toward the center. It is disease resistant. A good bedding rose, it grows up to 2½-3 ft (75-90 cm) high.

'Orangeade' bears large clusters of bright orange flowers. It grows

'Eyepaint'

'Elizabeth of Glamis'

'Orange Sensation'

2½-3 ft (75-90 cm) tall. Susceptible to mildew in cool, wet climates, it needs winter protection in the North.

'Orange Sensation' has clusters of fragrant, bright vermilion-orange flowers. It is of bushy, spreading habit and 2½ ft (75 cm) high. Black spot and mildew can be troublesome.

'Pink Parfait' has salmon-pink and ivory flowers, opening flat to reveal golden stamens. It is prolific and vigorous, growing 3 ft (90 cm) high.

'Queen Elizabeth' may be classified as a grandiflora rose rather than a floribunda because unlike a typical floribunda, it produces hybrid-tea-type flowers borne on long hybrid-tea-type stems. It does, however, bear the flowers in floribunda-type clusters. In any event, this is a very popular rose, bearing well-shaped clear pink blooms with a slight fragrance. It has a very vigorous upright growth and can reach 6-7 ft (1.8-2.1 m) high. Use it at the back of

'Queen Elizabeth'

a large border, as a hedge, or as a specimen shrub. Black spot can be a problem.

'Redgold' produces cup-shaped yellow flowers edged with red — though the red color develops only in sunny sites. This disease-resistant and winter-hardy rose grows 3-3½ ft (90-105 cm) high. The blossoms are long-lasting as cut flowers.

'Rosemary Rose' bears bright carmine blooms, similar in form to those of old-fashioned shrub roses. Of vigorous branching growth, to 2½ ft (75 cm) high, it is good as a bedding rose, but susceptible to mildew.

'Sun Flare' bears numerous fragrant, luminous yellow blossoms and grows 4 ft (1.2 m) high.

'Sunsprite' is a fine yellow rose; the large, fragrant blooms keep their color. Growing up to 2½ ft (75 cm) high, it is bushy.

'Trumpeter' bears a profusion of slightly fragrant, bright orange-scarlet flowers. Reaching 20 in (50 cm) high, this low-growing compact rose is suitable for the front of a border. It is disease resistant and winter hardy.

'White Lightnin' produces small white blossoms in small clusters but blooms repeatedly. The flowers are highly fragrant. This disease-resistant and winter-hardy shrub reaches a height of 4½-5 ft (1.4-1.5 m).

Cultivation

Plant bare-rooted floribundas in late fall or early spring to midspring. Set the shrubs 2-2½ ft (60-75 cm) apart in rich, well-drained soil. All require a sunny site.

Prune in early spring. Cut back newly planted roses to 6 in (15 cm) above ground. On established bushes remove all dead, crossing, and diseased wood, and reduce the remaining stems by up to half.

Mulch in midspring to late spring, and feed two or three times from late spring onward.

After flowering, remove the entire truss of dead flowers, cutting it back to the first true leaf.

Propagation Floribunda roses are budded or grafted professionally; cuttings are rarely successful.

Pests/diseases Floribundas are susceptible to most common rose troubles, including aphids, mildew, black spot, and rust.

'Margaret Merril'

Hybrid tea roses
(large-flowered bush roses)

'Whisky Mac'

'Alec's Red'

❏ Height 2-6 ft (60-180 cm)
❏ Spread 2-2½ ft (60-75 cm)
❏ Flowers early summer to late fall
❏ Rich, well-drained soil
❏ Open site in sun or light shade
❏ Hardy zones 5-9

To most gardeners, hybrid teas represent the ultimate in roses. Born of a cross between the old-fashioned hybrid perpetuals and tea roses, they produce the largest and most perfectly formed flowers, in a color range that includes all but true blue and black. Somewhat less winter hardy than floribundas, hybrid teas often fall prey to fungal diseases, especially black spot, and maintaining a disease-free planting generally requires at least some treatment with fungicides.

The blooms are usually double, though a few single-flowered cultivars are available. Each flower starts off as a well-shaped conical bud and opens into a bowl-shaped bloom with velvety petals arranged around a high central cone. Many have a fragrance, some a strong one, though hybrid teas cannot match the intense perfumes of the old garden roses. Hybrid tea flowers are not produced as profusely as those of floribunda roses — there's usually only one per stem. They appear in flushes rather than continuously, at intervals from early summer until the end of fall. They are excellent for cutting.

Hybrid tea bushes have a vigorous upright habit. Ideal for growing in rose beds, their stiff, twiggy look may be difficult to integrate into mixed bed and borders. The cultivars with a more spreading habit are sometimes budded onto tall stems and grown as standards, while roses with perfectly shaped blooms are popular for exhibiting.

Popular cultivars
Numerous cultivars are available, and new ones are regularly being introduced.

'Alec's Red' is one of the most popular red-flowered hybrid teas. The blooms have a rich fragrance and are suitable not only for beautifying the garden but also for cutting and exhibiting. The growth is vigorous and upright, reaching 3 ft (90 cm) high; this cultivar does not adapt well to hot climates.

'Alexander' has brilliant orange-vermilion blooms with a slight fragrance. It is exceptionally vigorous and disease resistant. Growing 5 ft (1.5 m) high, it is suitable for a large bed or as a hedge.

'Blessings' has profuse, fragrant coral-pink flowers from early summer until midfall. A disease-resistant cultivar, it makes a good bedding rose, with vigorous upright growth and a height of 3 ft (90 cm).

'Brandy' bears 4½ in (11 cm) wide apricot blossoms with a good fruity fragrance. Somewhat susceptible to black spot, this cultivar is resistant to powdery mildew and rust and is winter hardy if given some protection. An upright, vigorous shrub, it reaches a height of 4-5 ft (1.2-1.5 m).

'Chrysler Imperial' was introduced more than 40 years ago, and its intensely perfumed deep red blossoms continue to make it a favorite in the garden. Winter hardy, it is also fairly disease resistant, but it is susceptible to mildew in cool, wet climates. A

'Blessings'

vigorous grower, it reaches a height of 4-5 ft (1.2-1.5 m).

'Double Delight' has unusual ivory flowers edged with cherry-red. Their fragrance is strong, and the form is fine enough for use in exhibitions. The foliage is disease resistant, though some-what prone to mildew in cool, wet climates. Growth is vigorous and upright, with a height of 2½ ft (75 cm); this cultivar is winter hardy in the North.

'Dutch Gold' has large, well-shaped yellow blooms, which keep their color as they age. They are strongly fragrant, freely pro-duced, and excellent for exhibi-tion. This is a vigorous upright bush, reaching 3 ft (90 cm) high.

'Elina,' also known as 'Peau-douce,' has large, pale primrose blossoms. They are well formed, with a pleasant fragrance. It is suitable for use as a bedding rose, for cutting, and for exhibiting. The growth is vigorous and bushy, to 3 ft (90 cm) high.

'Ernest H. Morse' bears rich red, well-shaped, fragrant flow-ers. The blooms appear in great numbers, making this an ideal bedding rose and useful for cut-ting and exhibiting. The growth is vigorous and upright, with a height of 3 ft (90 cm).

'Evening Star' has well-shaped white blooms, borne in great pro-fusion. They have a pleasant scent. Reaching 3½ ft (105 cm) high, it has vigorous and upright growth.

'Fragrant Cloud' bears large shapely flowers that are red in bud, open to coral-salmon, and then fade with age. They have a particularly strong fragrance and

'Fragrant Cloud'

appear in profusion early in the summer. Disease resistant and winter hardy, this vigorous up-right bush grows 3 ft (90 cm) high.

'Irish Gold' bears an abundance of large, well-formed pale yellow blooms that gain pink edges with age. This good bedding rose is dis-ease resistant but not reliably winter hardy in northern zones without protection. The vigorous upright growth reaches 2½ ft (75 cm) high.

'Just Joey' has attractive cop-per-veined red buds, followed by flowers that fade to copper-or-ange. The slightly ruffled petals make it an excellent rose for cut-ting. Free-flowering, it is also a good bedding rose. It grows 2½ ft (75 cm) high.

'Miss All-American Beauty' (also sold as 'Maria Callas') pro-duces a heavy crop of very double and highly fragrant deep pink

blossoms. Up to 4-5 ft (1.2-1.5 m) tall, this cultivar is disease resis-tant and winter hardy.

'Mister Lincoln' is possibly the most popular red hybrid tea of all time. Introduced in 1964, it bears dark red, very fragrant blossoms that expand to a diame-ter of 5-5½ in (12.5-14 cm). Dis-ease resistant and winter hardy, this upright shrub grows to a height of 4½-5½ ft (1.4-1.7 m).

'National Trust' bears a profu-sion of perfectly shaped dark crimson flowers. It is a good bed-ding rose of vigorous upright habit, grows up to 2½ ft (75 cm) high, and is rain resistant.

'Oklahoma' bears an abundance of deep maroon-red, very fragrant flowers throughout the season. It grows 5-6 ft (1.5-1.8 m) high and is disease resistant and winter hardy.

'Ophelia' is an old favorite, with pale pink flowers that are yellow

'Just Joey'

'Irish Gold'

at the base. They are fragrant and good for cutting. Growth is upright, with slightly spindly stems up to 2½ ft (75 cm) high.

'Oregold' produces deep yellow, slightly fragrant blossoms that open into the classic high-centered hybrid tea form, then spread to a cup shape. Moderately vigorous, but somewhat susceptible to both black spot and mildew, this cultivar also needs winter protection in the northern zones. It grows up to 3½-4 ft (105-120 cm) tall.

'Pascali' bears a mass of faintly scented white flowers. They are carried on long, upright stems and are ideal for cutting. The growth is upright and vigorous, 3 ft (90 cm) high. The cultivar is disease resistant and winter hardy.

'Paul Shirville' has elegant blooms with light salmon-pink petals, shaded yellow at the base. Their fragrance is strong and sweet. Of strong upright habit, the shrub grows 3 ft (90 cm) high. It is good as a bedding rose and for cutting.

'Peace' — often regarded as the world's favorite rose — bears pale yellow blooms edged with cerise-pink. They are large but only slightly fragrant. Bushy and vigorous, reaching 4½ ft (1.4 m) high, it should be given plenty of space. It is disease resistant and winter hardy.

'Pink Favorite' bears large, well-formed blooms in shades of rose-pink. Renowned for its excellent resistance to disease, it is usually grown as a bedding plant. It is also suitable for cutting. Growth is upright and vigorous, 3 ft (90 cm) high.

'Precious Platinum' produces handsome, glowing, rich red flowers with a sweet fragrance. They are carried in an abundance of small clusters. The cultivar is usually grown as a bedding rose;

it has good disease resistance and a vigorous branching habit, 3 ft (90 cm) high.

'Prima Ballerina' bears richly scented, deep rose-pink flowers, up to 5 in (13 cm) wide. It is bushy, grows up to 3 ft (90 cm), and is susceptible to mildew.

'Royal William' has classically shaped, velvety, deep crimson flowers that are strongly scented. It has upright growth, to 3 ft (90 cm) high.

'Silver Jubilee' bears an abundance of fragrant coral-pink blossoms. They are perfectly formed and keep their color well. A good bedding rose, it is disease resistant, with vigorous bushy growth, 2½ ft (75 cm) high.

'Sutter's Gold' has well-shaped fragrant yellow flowers, shaded red and orange. They are good for cutting. The growth is upright but spindly, to 3 ft (90 cm) high.

'Tiffany' has won many awards with its medium to deep pink, very fragrant blossoms. Disease resistant and winter hardy, it

'National Trust'

'Peace'

'Pascali'

makes an upright shrub 4-4½ ft (1.2-1.4 m) tall.

'Tropicana' is an upright cultivar with fragrant, brilliant light vermilion blooms. It is free-flowering, with the fall flush often borne in clusters. Disease resistant and winter hardy, it is up to 4 ft (1.2 m) high.

'Whisky Mac' has attractive amber-yellow blooms with a strong fragrance. Despite its susceptibility to disease and its tendency to dieback, it is one of the most popular hybrid teas. Growth is vigorous, reaching 2½ ft (75 cm) high.

Cultivation

Plant bare-rooted hybrid teas in late fall or midspring, and container-grown bushes at any time during the growing season. Set the shrubs 2 ft (60 cm) apart in well-drained soil enriched with well-rotted manure or compost and bonemeal. Choose a sunny or lightly shaded site, sheltered from prevailing winds but well away from high trees or walls.

In spring, prune newly planted bushes, cutting back the stems to 4 in (10 cm) off the ground above outward-facing buds (many roses arrive from the nursery already pruned in this fashion). On established roses, remove dead, diseased, and crossing stems. Prune the remainder by removing about one-third of the stems. Roses grown for exhibition should be pruned hard, leaving only a few stems cut back to four buds.

Disbudding is important if exhibition shrubs are to produce large, perfect flowers. Remove any buds clustering below the main terminal flower bud.

Mulch all roses in mid- to late spring, to retain moisture in the soil around them. Feed with a specially formulated rose fertilizer every 4 weeks from late spring onward. To encourage a long flowering season, deadhead regularly.

Propagation Like floribunda roses, hybrid teas are budded, a propagation method best left to the professionals.

Pests/diseases Hybrid teas suffer from the same troubles as other roses. Look out for black spot — yellow-flowered cultivars tend to be especially susceptible. Mildew and rust can also be problems. In summer, aphids often infest bushes.

'Silver Jubilee'

Miniature roses

'Baby Masquerade'

'Starina'

- ❏ Height 3-18 in (7.5-45 cm) for shrubs; climbing forms to 5 ft (1.5 m)
- ❏ Spread 3-10 in (7.5-25 cm) for shrubs; climbers to 10 ft (3 m)
- ❏ Flowers early summer to fall
- ❏ Rich, well-drained soil
- ❏ Full sun
- ❏ Hardy zones 5-9

True to their name, miniature roses (in the bush forms) reach only 3-18 in (7.5-45 cm) high and resemble tiny floribundas or hybrid teas, with perfectly formed but diminutive leaves and flowers. The climbing miniatures produce longer canes, but their foliage, branches, and flowers are similarly delicate and reduced in scale. Miniatures are the most recently developed class of roses — they've become popular only in the last 40 years or so.

Miniature rose blooms may be scarlet through pink to orange, yellow, or white, and most are double or semidouble. They are borne in clusters, and some are fragrant. The flowering season begins in early summer to midsummer and commonly continues into fall. Many growers cultivate miniatures in pots as well, coaxing them into bloom indoors (often with the help of fluorescent lights) through the winter, too.

In the garden, miniatures can be grown as edging or in a small rose bed of their own; they are also suitable for pockets in a rock garden and for raised beds. They look charming in window boxes and other decorative containers. As a group, the miniatures tend to be somewhat hardier than hybrid teas, and the most compact types may be overwintered successfully in the North with no more protection than a mulch of dried leaves or straw. In milder regions miniatures should overwinter with no protection at all.

Popular cultivars

'**Angel Darling**' produces mauve 10-petaled blossoms on a 1-1½ ft (30-45 cm) bush. It is vigorous and winter hardy, though susceptible to black spot and mildew. It is good for bedding and mixed borders.

'**Angela Rippon**' has profuse and well-shaped, fragrant, double salmon-pink blooms on compact, healthy bushes 1½ ft (45 cm) high.

'**Baby Masquerade**' has fragrant double blooms that open yellow, then turn pink, and finally rosered. They appear in great profusion over a long flowering season. A bushy miniature, this winter-hardy and disease-resistant rose grows 15 in (38 cm) high.

'**Beauty Secret**' produces perfumed, double red blossoms on 10-18 in (25-45 cm) tall bushes. Disease resistant and winter hardy, they are used for beds, borders, edging, and containers.

'**Cinderella**' grows just 8-10 in (20-25 cm) high but is a vigorous bush and both disease resistant and winter hardy. Its spice-scented flowers are ¾ in (2 cm) wide, very double, and light pink fading to white. It is excellent for rock gardens or indoor cultivation.

'**Darling Flame**' has rich orange-vermilion flowers with a yellow reverse. These double blooms have a fruity fragrance. Growth is bushy, reaching 15 in (38 cm).

'**Green Ice**' is a sprawling bush that grows 8 in (20 cm) high but spreads to 16 in (40 cm) and may be trained as a climber or ground cover. The slightly fragrant double flowers open white and then darken to green. This winter-hardy and disease-resistant rose is excellent for hanging baskets.

'**Lavender Jewel**' bears small, dainty soft lavender blooms, produced freely on a vigorous bush reaching 15 in (38 cm) high.

'**Nozomi**' produces 5 ft (1.5 m) long canes and is typically grown as a ground cover or cascading

'Beauty Secret'

'Angel Darling'

down over the edge of a wall. The white apple-blossom-like flowers are borne in early summer to mid-summer and do not repeat.

'Starina' bears well-formed scarlet and golden blooms that appear in great numbers from early summer onward. A vigorous grower, it reaches 10-12 in (25-30 cm) high.

'Sweet Fairy' has delicate lilac-pink double blossoms that are sweetly scented. It grows only 8 in (20 cm) high.

'Yellow Doll' bears lightly fragrant, pale yellow double flowers from early summer on. This disease-resistant and winter-hardy rose normally grows 8-10 in (20-25 cm) high; in its climbing form it may reach 4 ft (1.2 m) high.

Cultivation

Miniature roses are usually shipped as container-grown specimens, since many have been raised from cuttings. In this form they can be planted at any time in the growing season, though early spring or fall is ideal. Set them 6-10 in (15-25 cm) apart in fertile, well-drained soil in a sunny site.

Miniature roses for containers should be planted in 4-5 in (10-13 cm) pots filled with potting soil. Repot annually, in late winter or

early spring. Overwinter on a sunny, south-facing windowsill or under fluorescent lights. To overwinter outdoors, harden off the plants by reducing fertilization in late summer and leaving them exposed to the cool fall nights. Before the first hard frost, plunge the

pots in a deep soil bed. When the cold weather arrives, mulch with dried leaves or straw to protect the roots from frost and keep them moist.

Prune in spring, cutting old stems to a few inches above ground and lightly pruning the newer shoots, removing up to one-third. Prune back hard all recently planted bushes.

Mulch in mid- to late spring, then feed every 4 weeks from late spring on. Water frequently during dry weather.

Propagation In late summer and early fall, root heel cuttings in a cold frame.

Pests/diseases Mildew, black spot, and aphids are problems.

'Lavender Jewel'

Modern shrub roses
(including new "English Roses," hybrid musk and rugosa roses)

Rosa rugosa alba

'Buff Beauty'

- ❏ Height 3-8 ft (90-240 cm)
- ❏ Spread equal to height
- ❏ Flowers late spring to late fall
- ❏ Rich, well-drained soil
- ❏ Full sun
- ❏ Hardy zones 3-9

Modern shrub roses have been developed from the interbreeding of many species and old roses. This diverse parentage has produced a varied group, with members adaptable to many different climates and situations. Shrub roses may form large informal bushes or relatively compact, neat mounds of foliage and flowers. As such, these roses make excellent landscaping shrubs that blend easily with other shrubbery or mixed borders and furnish ideal material for a flowering hedge.

Among the more notable members of this group are the new "English Roses." This group originated in a cross of hybrid teas and floribundas with old garden roses, and it offers the floral charm and perfumes of the antiques combined with the broader color palette and reblooming habit of the modern bush roses. Also in this group are the hybrid musk roses, prized for their delicious fragrance, and the rugosa roses, which are among the cold hardiest and most disease resistant of all roses. Many rugosas are hardy through zone 3, and their foliage is rarely, if ever, troubled by black spot or other fungal diseases.

Unless otherwise stated, the modern shrub roses described here are repeat-flowering, with flushes of blooms appearing between early summer and late fall. They have single, semidouble, or double blooms in a wide range of colors.

Popular cultivars
'**Ballerina,**' a hybrid musk rose, bears an abundance of tiny apple-blossom-pink flowers in early summer and again in early fall. They are carried in clusters on disease-resistant and winter-hardy shrubs that grow 4 ft (1.2 m) high and spread to 3 ft (90 cm).
'**Blanc Double de Coubert**' is a rugosa shrub rose with large, very fragrant, pure white semidouble blooms. Outstandingly disease resistant and winter hardy, it grows 6 ft (1.8 m) high and 5 ft (1.5 m) wide.
'**Bonica**' forms a bushy, spreading shrub that bears large clusters of slightly fragrant, double

pink flowers. Blooming continuously through the summer, it is highly disease resistant and requires almost no pruning. It grows to a height of 3 ft (90 cm).
'**Buff Beauty,**' another hybrid musk rose, produces clusters of large, double, pale orange-apricot blooms that fade to ivory with age. This sweetly scented hybrid musk has a spectacular fall flush of blooms. Mildew can be a problem, but this cultivar is otherwise disease resistant and winter hardy. The loose growth reaches 4 ft (1.2 m) in height and spread.
'**Constance Spry**' bears sprays of double, fragrant, clear rose-pink flowers. The arching stems, spreading 6 ft (1.8 m) wide and reaching 7 ft (2.1 m) high, are best trained up a wall. It is disease resistant and winter hardy.
'**Cornelia,**' a hybrid musk rose,

'Constance Spry'

'Marguerite Hilling'

'Fru Dagmar Hastrup'

'Roseraie de l'Hay'

bears a profusion of double apricot-pink flowers with a pleasant fragrance and good resistance to rain. The best blooms appear in fall. It grows 5 ft (1.5 m) high and 7 ft (2.1 m) wide, and is disease resistant and winter hardy.

'Fru Dagmar Hastrup' bears single shell-pink flowers with a strong fragrance. As a rugosa shrub, it produces a striking display of large red hips in fall. It is of compact habit, 3 ft (90 cm) high and wide. A good hedging shrub, it is disease resistant and winter hardy.

'Gertrude Jekyll,' an "English Rose," is of strong upright habit, to 4 ft (1.2 m) tall and 3 ft (90 cm) wide. It bears large, strongly scented cerise-pink flowers.

'Golden Wings' has large, single, sweetly scented pale yellow blooms, which fade with age. This cultivar is one of the earliest and longest-blooming roses. Disease

resistant and moderately winter hardy, this rose grows to 6 ft (1.8 m) high and 5 ft (1.5 m) wide.

'Heritage' has large and perfectly quartered, heavily fragrant blooms of clear shell-pink. This strong-growing, free-flowering "English Rose" grows 3 ft (90 cm) high and wide.

'Graham Thomas' is an "English rose" that bears large cup-shaped fragrant blossoms of pure

rich yellow. It grows 4 ft (1.2 m) high and wide.

'Marguerite Hilling,' a modern shrub rose, is a sport of 'Nevada.' Its pale pink flowers, flushed darker pink, are semidouble and slightly fragrant; they appear in abundance in early summer and again in early fall. It is disease resistant and winter hardy.

'Mary Rose' is a bushy, wide-branching shrub, usually 3 ft (90 cm) high and wide. This is an "English Rose," whose large pink flower clusters are of typical

'Golden Wings'

'Scabrosa'

'Mary Rose'

'Graham Thomas'

damask-rose shape, full petaled and richly scented.

'Nevada,' a modern shrub rose, produces cream buds opening into large, semidouble white flowers with gold stamens. During early summer and midsummer it flowers abundantly; for the rest of the season it is less prolific. Of arching habit, it grows 7-8 ft (2.1-2.4 m) high and wide. It is prone to black spot, but otherwise disease resistant and winter hardy.

'Penelope' is a hybrid musk rose with fragrant semidouble apricot-pink flowers. These are borne in large clusters in early summer and again in early fall. A good hedging shrub, with a height and spread of 6 ft (1.8 m), it is disease resistant and winter hardy.

Rosa rugosa alba, a variety of the species rose *R. rugosa*, has large, single, pure white flowers with golden centers and a sweet fragrance. Large, round orange-red hips appear in fall. A good hedging or specimen rose, growing 5 ft (1.5 m) high and wide, it

is exceedingly winter hardy and disease resistant.

'Roseraie de l'Hay,' a rugosa shrub, bears large, double, fragrant crimson-purple blooms. It has no fall hips. With a height and spread of 7 ft (2.1 m), it is an excellent disease-resistant shrub for the North.

'Scabrosa,' a rugosa shrub, has large, single magenta-pink flowers. It has a spreading habit and is suitable for use as a hedging or specimen rose. It grows 5 ft (1.5 m) high and spreads up to 6 ft (1.8 m). It shows typical rugosa disease resistance and extreme winter hardiness.

Cultivation

Plant bare-rooted specimens in late fall or early spring to mid-spring, and container-grown ones at any time during the growing season. Like most roses, they require rich, well-drained soil and a sunny site.

In spring, lightly prune the shrubs to shape and remove crossing branches, winter-killed wood, and old weak stems from the base.

Mulch in mid- to late spring, and feed with a rose fertilizer every 4 weeks from late spring to midsummer.

Deadhead to encourage rebloom. Leave the faded flowers of most rugosa cultivars to produce attractive hips.

Propagation Take heel cuttings in early fall, and root in an outdoor nursery bed.

Pests/diseases Black spot, mildew, rust, and aphids are common problems.

'Heritage'

'Gertrude Jekyll'

Old garden roses
(Alba, bourbon, centifolia, China, damask, gallica, hybrid perpetual, moss, and tea roses)

'Fantin-Latour'

'Céleste'

❑ Height 1½-15 ft (45-450 cm)
❑ Spread similar to height
❑ Flowers summer or repeat-flowering
❑ Ordinary well-drained garden soil
❑ Full sun
❑ Hardy zones 3-9

The informal elegance of the old garden roses has made them popular in recent years — the shrubs' loose, open growth habit and overwhelming displays of summer blooms in delicate and dusky colors pose a stark contrast to the perfectly formed blooms and rigid formality of hybrid tea bush roses.

The class of old garden roses is a catchall that includes various races of roses descended from many different wild species. This diversity is the old garden roses' greatest strength, for the class offers not only some of the most cold-hardy rose cultivars, it also includes the roses best adapted to the heat, drought, and humidity of southern summers. The gallicas, for example, are known for their winter hardiness, while the tea roses adapt well to southern conditions.

The flowers of old garden roses are usually double or semidouble. They come in subtle shades of white, cream, and pink, as well as dusky reds and purples. Some are quartered, the flattened center of each flower consisting of densely crowded petals that are loosely arranged in four groups.

Most old garden roses have one main flowering season, in early summer and midsummer, though the bushes may repeat sparingly afterward, and the Chinas and tea roses perform almost as everbloomers in the South. But even among the once-blooming northern roses, the beauty of the individual blooms and their rich fragrance, as well as the handsome foliage, are often ample compensation for the less extended season of flowering.

Old garden roses are some of the best roses for growing in mixed shrub borders, and they make equally effective specimen roses. Train those with a climbing habit up a wall or pillar.

Popular cultivars
Old garden roses are commonly represented by these nine main groups: alba, bourbon, centifolia, China, damask, gallica, hybrid perpetuals, moss, and tea roses.
ALBA ROSES have sweetly scented flowers up to 3 in (7.5 cm) wide. They are borne in profusion in early summer and midsummer. The shrubs are very winter hardy and vigorous, with an upright habit; they thrive in all kinds of conditions. The soft gray-green leaves are composed of five to

'Boule de Neige'

'Mme. Pierre Oger'

'Fantin-Latour'

seven, finely toothed leaflets. Alba roses can be trained as espaliers on a wall or up a trellis.

'Alba Maxima' produces double cream-white flowers with a hint of pink. It is a large shrub, growing up to 8 ft (2.4 m) high, with a spread of 5 ft (1.5 m).

'Céleste' (syn. 'Celestial') bears large and fragrant, soft pink semidouble blooms. It grows 6 ft (1.8 m) high and 4 ft (1.2 m) wide.

'Königin von Dänemark' bears tightly packed, quartered blooms that are strongly fragrant. The pink color deepens toward the center of the flower. The shrub grows 5 ft (1.5 m) high and 4 ft (1.2 m) wide.

'Maiden's Blush' has sweetly scented double blush-pink flowers, with pale pink edges. It grows 5 ft (1.5 m) high and 4 ft (1.2 m) wide.

BOURBON ROSES have densely petaled blooms that are cup-shaped or globular and up to 4 in (10 cm) wide. They are deeply scented and repeat-flowering, starting in early summer and continuing sparingly until the first fall frosts. All are hardy, tolerating summer heat almost as well as winter cold. Bourbons are vigorous shrubs with an open habit and glossy dark green leaves.

'Boule de Neige' has crimson buds that open to form perfect double white flowers. It grows 6 ft (1.8 m) high and 4 ft (1.2 m) wide.

'Louise Odier' produces well-formed rich pink flowers, softly shaded lilac. Of vigorous habit, it

'Centifolia' rose or 'Cabbage' rose

'Mme. Hardy'

grows 4 ft (1.2 m) high and wide.
'Mme. Isaac Pereire' has large,
quartered deep pink blooms with
tightly packed petals. It is one of
the most fragrant of all roses.
Grown and pruned as a bush, it is
6 ft (1.8 m) high and 5 ft (1.5 m)
wide; trained up a wall or pillar it
may reach 15 ft (4.5 m).
'Mme. Pierre Oger' bears large
clusters of pale silver-pink, cup-
shaped flowers. It has a height
and spread of 4 ft (1.2 m).
CENTIFOLIA ROSES, known
also as Provence or cabbage roses, have fragrant double flowers
up to 4 in (10 cm) wide. They are
borne in clusters in early summer
and midsummer. The floppy,
thorny stems, bearing pale green
to midgreen leaves, need support.
'Fantin-Latour' bears well-
formed blush-pink flowers, deepening to shell-pink in the center.
It grows 6 ft (1.8 m) high and 5 ft
(1.5 m) wide.
'Petite de Hollande' has pale
pink blooms, edged a deeper pink
near the edges. It is a compact
shrub 4 ft (1.2 m) wide and 3 ft
(90 cm) wide.
'Robert le Diable' bears multi-
shaded blooms of purple, slate
gray, cerise, and scarlet. It is a
vigorous shrub, growing up to 4 ft
(1.2 m) high and 3 ft (90 cm) wide.
'Rose de Meaux' is a small, neat
shrub of erect and dense habit. It
grows 1½-3 ft (45-90 cm) high
and 1½ ft (45 cm) wide, with a

'Old Blush'

profusion of small pale pink flowers that are very fragrant.
CHINA ROSES, as their name
suggests, came to the Western
world from China in the 18th century. They are not reliably winter
hardy north of southern zone 7
but flourish all through the
Southeast, blooming throughout
the growing season. Neat and
compact, they rarely reach more
than 4 ft (1.2 m) high, with slender hairy stems, midgreen hairy
foliage, and clusters of pompon-
shaped flowers.
'Cramoisi Supérieur' bears
clusters of double crimson flowers on a 3½ ft (105 cm) tall bush.
'Mutabilis' has single flowers

that open flame colored, change
to coppery yellow, and then coppery crimson. It grows up to
3-4 ft (90-120 cm) high and 3 ft
(90 cm) wide.
'Old Blush' bears slightly fragrant, silvery pink flowers with
a crimson flush. It grows 5 ft
(1.5 m) high and 4 ft (1.2 m) wide.
DAMASK ROSES have short-
lived fragrant flowers borne in
loose clusters during early summer and midsummer; a few cultivars rebloom in fall. The shrubs
have a loose, open habit, with
thorny and bristly stems bearing
rounded gray-green leaves. In
late summer the shrubs produce
long, hairy hips.

'Ferdinand Pichard'

'Rosa Mundi'

'Comte du Chambord' is technically a damask perpetual or Portland rose; it bears flat pinkish-lilac and double flowers with a strong fragrance. It blooms in early summer to midsummer and occasionally again in fall. This small shrub is just 3 ft (90 cm) high and wide.

'Ispahan' bears bright pink semidouble flowers that keep their color well and last considerably longer than most damask roses. The shrub reaches 4 ft (1.2 m) high and 3 ft (90 cm) wide.

'La Ville de Bruxelles' has pink double blooms that are quartered and scented. They are borne on a strong upright plant 5 ft (1.5 m) high and 3 ft (90 cm) wide.

'Mme. Hardy' has clusters of pure white flowers with small green "button-eye" centers. They are tinted pink in bud and heavily scented. The shrub grows 5 ft (1.5 m) high and wide.

GALLICA ROSES form one of the larger — and notably winter-hardy — groups of old shrub roses. They flower profusely from early summer to midsummer, with solitary flowers in colors varying from pink to crimson and mauve. They are double, 2-3 in (5-7.5 cm) wide, and richly scented. These roses thrive in poor soil. The shrubs have a compact and

erect habit and dark green leaves.
'Belle de Crécy' grows 4 ft (1.2 m) high and 3 ft (90 cm) wide, with lax stems that usually need support. It bears large flowers of purple-red, maturing to violet.

'Camaieux' has deep crimson-purple flowers, splashed and striped with white. The arching branches reach 3 ft (90 cm) high and 2 ft (60 cm) wide.

'Cardinal de Richelieu' has deep violet blooms. With a height and spread of 4 ft (1.2 m), it makes a good hedging rose.

'Charles de Mills' bears rich maroon flowers with a hint of purple. The petals are closely packed and produce a glorious fragrance. A good hedging rose, it has a height and spread of 4 ft (1.2 m).

'Rosa Mundi' has crimson flowers striped white. It is a long-established showy rose and makes a good low hedge, with a height and spread of 4 ft (1.2 m).

'Tuscany Superb' has double purple blooms that open flat to reveal golden stamens. It is 4 ft (1.2 m) high and 2 ft (60 cm) wide.

HYBRID PERPETUALS were extremely popular in Victorian times. Typically tall shrubs, they make superb shrub roses for a mixed border and look well trained against walls. The rounded, double cabbagelike flowers

are 3-4 in (7.5-10 cm) wide and open out flat. Borne singly or in clusters, they appear between early summer and midfall. The shrubs are vigorous, upright, and usually very winter hardy. They bear dark green leaves.

'Ferdinand Pichard' has globular pink flowers striped with crimson and purple. Bushy in habit, it reaches 4 ft (1.2 m) high, with a spread of 3 ft (90 cm).

'Mrs. John Laing' has double, fragrant soft pink blooms borne on stiff stems. It has an upright habit, growing 5 ft (1.5 m) high and 3 ft (90 cm) wide.

'Paul Neyron' bears huge, fragrant rich pink flowers, which keep their color with age. It has an upright habit, growing 5 ft (1.5 m) high and 3 ft (90 cm) wide.

'Roger Lambelin' has double, rich crimson-purple flowers with white margins to the petals. It grows 4 ft (1.2 m) high and 3 ft (90 cm) wide.

MOSS ROSES all have mosslike growths of balsamic-scented glands on the bristly stems and around the buds. The deeply fragrant flowers are double or semidouble and are borne singly or in small clusters in early summer and midsummer. The size of the shrubs varies, from dwarf cultivars to tall pillar roses. Moss roses are generally winter hardy and flourish with winter protection even in zone 4.

'Général Kléber' bears large, soft mauve-pink blooms that open flat and are quartered. Often considered the most beautiful moss rose, it has a height and spread of about 4 ft (1.2 m).

'Nuits de Young'

'Henri Martin' has semidouble vivid crimson flowers with sparse moss. A graceful shrub, it is 5 ft (1.5 m) high and 4 ft (1.2 m) wide.
'Nuits de Young' has double, deep maroon-purple blooms with prominent golden stamens. It is a wiry bush, growing up to 5 ft (1.5 m) high and 3 ft (90 cm) wide.
'William Lobb' bears large clusters of double purple-magenta blooms, fading to lavender. It is 6 ft (1.8 m) high and wide, and looks best trained up a pillar.
TEA ROSES (*Rosa odorata*) are principal ancestors of the modern hybrid teas. Not generally hardy north of zone 8, they are perhaps the best roses for southeastern gardeners and perform well in the milder parts of the Pacific Coast. The shapely flowers are borne continuously from late spring or early summer to frost on rather spindly stems.
'Duchesse de Brabant' bears cupped, fragrant salmon-pink flowers, 4-5 in (10-13 cm) wide, on a disease-resistant shrub 3-5 ft (90-150 cm) tall.
'Lady Hillingdon' bears apricot-yellow flowers all through the summer. The shrub is 3 ft (90 cm) high with a spread of 2 ft (60 cm). A climbing form is also available.

Cultivation
The popular old garden roses are hardy plants, needing less attention than the modern bush cultivars. They grow in most ordinary well-drained garden soils. Plant bare-rooted shrubs in late fall or early spring to midspring, and container-grown ones at any time of the growing season.

Maintain healthy growth of these long-lived shrubs with an annual mulch of organic matter in spring. Feed with rose fertilizer every 4 weeks from late spring to midsummer.

Deadhead only if the faded blooms are unsightly. It is preferable to leave the petals to drop so the fall hips can develop.

Old roses flower on shoots of the previous year; when light pruning is necessary, it should be done immediately after flowering by cutting away any old deadwood from the base. Lightly tip the branches that have carried flowers in order to encourage side branching.

Propagation Take 10-12 in (25-30 cm) long heel cuttings in early fall, and root in a cold frame or sheltered bed.

Pests/diseases The more popular kinds of old garden roses are less prone to disease and pest attack than the average modern rose, though black spot, mildew, rust, and aphids occasionally affect them. Usually the shrubs are strong enough to recover without chemical treatment.

'William Lobb'

Polyantha roses

'Cécile Brünner'

❏ Height ½-4 ft (15-120 cm)
❏ Spread 1-10 ft (30-300 cm)
❏ Flowers early summer to early fall
❏ Well-drained ordinary soil
❏ Sunny site
❏ Hardy zones 5-9

Polyanthas, a small group of turn-of-the-century roses, have recently returned to popularity. They bear a profusion of small pompon-shaped flowers in large, closely packed clusters in summer and again in early fall.

Compact polyantha roses are ideal in beds of their own or as edging for borders. They will thrive in a half whiskey barrel full of potting soil. Many are not reliably winter hardy in the North, but will overwinter into zone 5 or 6 with protection. They perform well in zones 8 and 9.

Popular cultivars
'Baby Faurax' has an abundance of small lavender-purple flowers. The compact shrub is 1½ ft (45 cm) high and wide.
'Cécile Brünner' has pale pink flowers shaded cream, with the color becoming darker in the center. The blossoms are borne in small clusters. Height and spread are 2½-3 ft (75-90 cm).
'Katharina Zeimet' bears clusters of double white flowers from summer into fall. Up to 20 in (50 cm) tall and wide, with attractive and disease-resistant dark green foliage, this is one of the most winter hardy polyanthas.
'Marie Pavié' makes a mounded shrub to 15 in (38 cm) tall, bearing very fragrant, pink-tinged white flowers.
'Perle d'Or' bears dense clusters of small creamy yellow blooms. A vigorous rose, it grows 4 ft (1.2 m) high and 3 ft (90 cm) wide.
'The Fairy' has globular double pink flowers, appearing later than most polyanthas, in late summer and early fall. It is 2½ ft (75 cm) high and wide.

Cultivation
Polyantha roses grow in ordinary well-drained soils in full sun. Plant bare-rooted shrubs in late fall or early spring to midspring and container-grown ones any time during the growing season.

Mulch in late spring, and feed them monthly from early spring through midsummer. Deadhead

'The Fairy'

regularly. When the fall flush is over, lightly prune the shrubs and cut away old deadwood from the base.
Propagation Take heel cuttings in early fall, and root in a cold frame.
Pests/diseases While mildew and black spot are problems sometimes, aphids are the most serious pest.

Rambler roses

'Paul's Scarlet Climber'

'Emily Gray'

❏ Height 9-25 ft (2.7-7.5 m)
❏ Spread similar to height
❏ Flowers early summer to midsummer
❏ Rich, well-drained soil
❏ Sunny site
❏ Hardiness varies, but often very cold tolerant, to zone 4

Ramblers, like climbers, are ideal roses for training up pillars, pergolas, arches, and trees. They are less suitable for growing up walls — the lack of air circulation encourages mildew, a disease to which many cultivars are prone. Vigorous ramblers are ideal for smothering unsightly garden features, while those of extreme vigor look spectacular scrambling up trees. Several ramblers are also available as weeping standards.

The main disadvantage of rambler roses is the short flowering season, in early summer to midsummer unless otherwise stated.

Popular cultivars
'Albéric Barbier' has yellow buds opening to large clusters of fragrant, cream-white double blooms. Its vigorous stems grow 25 ft (7.5 m) high and can be trained up arches, pillars, trees, or trelliswork. It is disease resistant and winter hardy.
'Albertine' bears a mass of double, glowing copper-pink blooms with a rich scent. The vigorous growth reaches 15 ft (4.5 m) high, ideal for arches or pergolas.
'American Pillar' bears a profusion of deep pink flowers with white eyes. They are borne in clusters. The vigorous growth reaches 20 ft (6 m) high. It is disease resistant and winter hardy.
'Bobbie James' has semidouble, musk-scented white flowers.

'American Pillar'

'Dorothy Perkins'

'Albertine'

These appear in large trusses on vigorous stems up to 25 ft (7.5 m) high. It is ideal for training up a tree.

'Crimson Shower' bears profuse trusses of semidouble crimson flowers from midsummer on. Of moderate vigor, 9-10 ft (2.7-3 m) high, it is suitable for growing up arches or for training as a weeping standard.

'Dorothy Perkins' is an old favorite, though it is prone to mildew. Its masses of double deep pink flowers are borne in large trusses. It grows 10 ft (3 m) high up an arch or along a trellis. It is very vigorous and winter hardy.

'Emily Gray' produces small,

semidouble buff-yellow flowers with a rich fragrance, appearing in early to late summer. The dark green glossy foliage, bronze-tinted when young, is almost evergreen. Scrambling 15 ft (4.5 m) high, it tolerates poor soil and shade.

'Félicité et Perpétué' is an old favorite, with slightly fragrant, double ivory blossoms faintly flecked with red. Borne in large clusters, they stand up well to rain. Suitable for growing up a wall, it can reach 15 ft (4.5 m) high.

'François Juranville' has double pale pink blooms with a sweet fragrance. They form a dense mass in midsummer. A vigorous grower, it reaches 20 ft (6 m) high

and is ideal for covering a trellis or pergola.

'Paul's Scarlet Climber' bears abundant clusters of double, bright scarlet flowers, whose color dulls with age. Train this 10-15 ft (3-4.5 m) high rambler up a pillar, pergola, or arch. It also does well on a north-facing wall.

'The Garland' bears large clusters of small, fragrant semidouble blush-pink flowers, which fade to white. This established vigorous rose is ideal for scrambling up an old tree or tall wall. It reaches 15 ft (4.5 m) high.

Cultivation

Plant bare-rooted ramblers in fall or early spring to midspring; plant container-grown ones at any time of year. They thrive best in rich soil and full sun.

Plant ramblers near their support, setting them 7 ft (2.1 m) apart and tying in stems as they grow.

In mid- to late spring, mulch the roses to keep the soil around them moist; feed them once a month through midsummer.

When flowering is over, cut the stems that carried blooms down to ground level and tie in young shoots as replacements.

Propagation In early fall root heel cuttings in a cold frame.

Pests/diseases Mildew is the main problem; black spot and aphids may also be troublesome.

173

Species roses

Rosa californica 'Plena'

Rosa moyesii

❏ Height 2-15 ft (60-450 cm)
❏ Spread similar to height
❏ Flowers late spring to midsummer
❏ Fertile well-drained soil
❏ Sunny site
❏ Hardy zones 6-8

These are the wild roses, the true species from which all modern roses have been bred. They are easy to grow and shrug off pests and diseases with little trouble.

The simple beauty of their flowers sets them apart from other garden plants. Usually single, they come in traditional pinks, reds, whites, and yellows. Even though species roses cannot compete with the continuous blooming of floribundas and hybrid teas — all of those listed here flower only once a year, in late spring to midsummer — many species have very handsome foliage and spectacular hips in fall.

Species roses look most effective grown in an informal or wild part of the garden or in a large, sunny, open border. They are also striking as specimen roses, planted singly, and beautiful in small groups of one chosen species.

Rosa moyesii, hips

Popular species

Rosa californica 'Plena' has clusters of semidouble, fragrant deep pink flowers in early summer; globular red hips follow. It is a graceful shrub, growing 8 ft (2.4 m) high and 6 ft (1.8 m) wide. It is hardy to zone 6.

Rosa 'Canary Bird' has small, bright yellow flowers in late spring and early summer. The dainty foliage is fresh green and deeply cut. It grows 6 ft (1.8 m) high and wide. It is probably a naturally occurring cross between *Rosa xanthina* and *R. hugonis*. It is hardy to zone 6.

Rosa × dupontii has large, fragrant, single cream-white flowers, borne in clusters in early summer. It is a vigorous but lax shrub or climber with a height and spread of 7 ft (2.1 m).

Rosa eglanteria, syn. *R. rubiginosa*, known as sweetbriar, has clusters of bright pink single flowers in early summer, followed by orange-scarlet hips. The leaves are covered in glands that give off a sweet, pungent fragrance. With a height and spread of 8 ft (2.4 m), it makes a good hedge. It is hardy to zone 6.

Rosa foetida bicolor (Austrian copper) has single copper-orange flowers with golden yellow petal reverses. They appear in early summer on arching branches that grow 6 ft (1.8 m) high with a similar spread. It is prone to black spot. It is hardy to zone 5.

Rosa glauca, syn. *R. rubrifolia*, bears single red-purple flowers in small clusters in early summer, but it is grown as much for its handsome gray-purple foliage and decorative dark red hips as for the flowers. It is excellent as a background plant in a border. The arching branches reach 7 ft (2.1 m) high and spread over 5 ft (1.5 m). It is hardy to zone 2.

Rosa × harisonii bears clear yellow semidouble flowers in late spring. It grows 6 ft (1.8 m) high and 5 ft (1.5 m) wide. It is hardy to zone 5.

Rosa × highdownensis is related to and closely resembles *R. moyesii*. It bears a profusion of single soft crimson flowers with conspicuous yellow stamens in early summer. They are followed by magnificent flask-shaped and glossy red hips. It grows up to 10 ft (3 m) high and wide.

Rosa hugonis has pale yellow flowers borne freely in late spring. The hips in late summer are round and dark red. The arching branches, 9 ft (2.7 m) high and 7 ft (2.1 m) wide, are clothed with dainty fernlike leaves. It is hardy to zone 6.

Rosa 'Canary Bird'

Rosa glauca

Rosa moyesii bears single, vivid blood-red blooms in early summer, followed by flask-shaped red hips. It makes a handsome specimen shrub, with a spread of 8 ft (2.4 m) and a height of 12 ft (3.6 m). 'Geranium' has a more compact habit, suitable for smaller gardens. It is hardy to zone 6.

Rosa × paulii is thorny and bears clusters of fragrant white flowers with crinkly petals in early summer. It is an arching, thicketforming shrub, 4 ft (1.2 m) high with an impressive spread of 15 ft (4.5 m). Excellent as ground cover on banks, it can also be trained up a wall.

Rosa pomifera, syn. *R. villosa*, resembles the wild dog rose (*R. canina*). It grows up to 7 ft (2.1 m) tall and wide; it has downy, aromatic gray-green foliage. The solitary flowers, bright pink and semidouble, appear in early summer; they are followed by large, round, dark red hips covered with bristly hairs. It is hardy to zone 6.

Rosa primula has pale yellow flowers borne singly in late spring. On warm evenings the leaves have a heady fragrance. An upright shrub, it grows 8 ft (2.4 m) high and wide. It is hardy to zone 7.

Rosa virginiana bears single pink flowers throughout summer and showy red hips accompanied by scarlet foliage in the fall. A fine specimen shrub, it grows 7 ft (2.1 m) wide and 5 ft (1.5 m) high. It is hardy to zone 4.

Rosa willmottiae bears solitary, fragrant rose-purple flowers in late spring and early summer. It is an elegantly arching, purplestemmed shrub with a height and spread of 8 ft (2.4 m). It is hardy to zone 6.

Cultivation

Plant bare-rooted shrubs in late fall or early spring to midspring, and container-grown ones at any time of year. They thrive in fertile, well-drained soil. The planting site should be open and sunny.

Mulch these shrubs in late spring, and feed them once each month until midsummer.

Don't deadhead, since this will do away with any display of hips. Remove deadwood as and when it occurs, cutting back to live wood.

Propagation Increase species roses from seed, or root heel cuttings taken in late summer in a cold frame or open bed.

Pests/diseases Species roses are resistant to most rose pests and diseases.

Rosa foetida bicolor

ACKNOWLEDGMENTS

Photo Credits

A-Z Botanical Collection Ltd 24(tr), 46(tr), 139; Richard Balfour 157(r), 158(l), 159(b), 161(br), 166(t), 172(tr), 173(r); Peter Beales 149(c); Gillian Beckett 94(tr), 106(tl), 118(l); Biofotos 28(tl), 28(b), 110(r), 151(tl), 169(r); Pat Brindley 149(tl), 151(b); Brian Carter 71(b), 152(tr), 154(bl); Eric Crichton 15(l), 20(b), 21(c), 22(l), 23(r), 25(tl), 27(tl), 29(tr), 29(b), 32(tr), 32(bc), 34(c), 35, 36(tl), 36(b), 38(r), 39(tl), 39(b), 40, 41(tr), 41(cr), 43, 45(t), 48(t), 48(cr), 52(t), 53(cr), 54(t), 59(tr), 60(cr), 64, 69(t), 71(t), 72(t), 72(cl), 73(tl), 74, 76, 78(tl), 79(tr), 83(tr), 84(t), 84(c), 85(l), 85(r), 86(t), 88(r), 89(r), 90(b), 92(tl), 93, 96(r), 98(tr), 98(b), 99, 100(b), 101, 103(b), 104(r), 105(r), 106(b), 107, 108(c), 109(tl), 111, 112(r), 119(tr), 121(b), 123(tl), 123(b), 126, 129(tl), 129(b), 130, 132(b), 133(l), 138, 143(t), 145, 159(tl), 160(l), 165(br); Anthony DeBlasi 113(tl); Arnaud Descat 53(tr), 144(r), 150(bl), 172(tl); Christine Douglas 47(c), 49(bl), 124(tl); Earth Scenes (Richard Shiell) 110(l), 127(r), (Jack Wilburn) 131(tl); Derek Fell 18(l), 63(l), 70(tl), 100(tl), 116(r), 154(tr), 160(tr), 161(tr); Philip Ferret 166(b), 167(tl), 168(r), 175(b); Garden Picture Library (John Ainsworth)

97(tl), (David Askam) 152 (tl), (Brain Carter) 30(l), 36(tr), 67(b), 114, 127(l), (John Glover) 6-7, 37(b), 165(tr), (Rowan Isaac) front cover (tc), 165 (bl), (Jerry Pavia) 22(r), 165(tl), (David Russell) 24(b), 113(b), 118(tr), (Brigitte Thomas) front cover(tl), (Didier Willery) 66(b), 139(r); Michael Gibson 150(br), 171(b), 175(tl); John Glover front cover(cr), 1, 10(bl), 13(t), 26(l), 27(b), 72(cr), 72(b), 73(c), 80(tl), 86(b), 87(t), 90(tl), 91(b), 112(l), 117(t), 128(tr), 129(tr), back cover; Derek Gould 77(tl), 96(l); Pamela Harper 21(l), 24(tl), 58(b), 66(t), 88(l), 89(b), 92(b), 103(t), 161(tl); Jerry Harpur 148(tl); Neil Holmes 115(tl); Michèle Lamontagne 17(r), 18(r), 50, 55(tl), 57(r), 60(t), 70(r), 75(t), 85(c), 163, 164(bl), 168(l), 169(l), 174(r), 175(tr); Andrew Lawson 27(tc), 58(l), 81(tr); S & O Mathews 31(cr), 135(b); Tania Midgley 14(cr), 19(b), 21(r), 29(tl), 32(tl), 37(tl), 39(tr), 48(cl), 56(tl), 59(tl), 59(c), 82(b), 94(b), 108(tl), 113(tr), 117(b), 121(t), 122, 123(tr), 124(c), 125, 131(cl), 135(tc), 136(tl), 137, 140, 142, 143(b), 164(tl); Natural Image (Robin Fletcher) 33, 54(cr), 55(tr), 57(r), 63(r), (Bob Gibbons) 41(tl), 46(tl), 47(r), 56(c), (Peter Wilson) 31(tr), 55(cr), 62(b); Clive Nichols front cover (br), 2-3, 10(t), 10(br), 11, 12(t),

68(tl), 68(b), 69(b); Muriel Orans 19(tr), 78(tr); Photo/Nats (Gay Bumgarner) 109(b), (Priscilla Connell) 171(t); Photos Horticultural front cover(tr), front cover(cl), front cover(cc), front cover(bl), front cover(bc), 4-5, 8, 13(t), 14(t), 15(r), 16(l), 17(l), 20(tl), 22(c), 23(tl), 25(tr), 26(r), 27(tr), 28(tr), 30(r), 31(tl), 32(bl), 34(t), 38(l), 42(tl), 44(r), 45(br), 47(l), 49(tl), 49(r), 51, 52(b), 53(tl), 62(t), 67(t), 68(tr), 77(tc), 80(tr), 82(t), 83(cr), 84(b), 87(b), 89(tl), 91(t), 92(tr), 94(tl), 95, 98(tl), 100(tr), 102, 104(l), 105(l), 106(tr), 109(tr), 115(b), 116(l), 119(b), 120, 128(tl), 132(tc), 133(r), 134(b), 134(tr), 136(r), 141(tl), 146, 150(bc), 153(t), 154(tl), 155(bl), 156(tl), 158(b), 159(tr), 162(tl), 162(b), 164(tr), 164(br), 167(tr), 167(b), 170, 173(l), 174(l); Harry Smith Collection 16(tr), 19(tl), 25(cl), 37(tr), 42(tr), 44(tl), 45(c), 61, 73(tr), 77(tr), 79(tl), 80(b), 81(tl), 83(tl), 90(tr), 97(r), 108(tr), 115(tr), 119(tl), 124(tr), 131(r), 132(tl), 132(tr), 134(tl), 135(t), 139(l), 144(l), 148(tr), 149(tr), 150(t), 151(tr), 153(b), 154(br), 155(t), 156(l), 157(l), 158(tr), 162(tr), 172(b); Virginia Twinam-Smith 81(c); Fred Whitehead 20(tr); Gerald Wilkinson 42(cr).